The Killing of Constable Keith Blakelock

The Broadwater Farm Riot

Tony Moore

☷ WATERSIDE PRESS

The Killing of Constable Keith Blakelock
The Broadwater Farm Riot
by Tony Moore

ISBN 978-1-909976-20-7 (Paperback)
ISBN 978-1-908162-94-6 (Epub ebook)
ISBN 978-1-908162-95-3 (Adobe ebook)

Copyright © 2015 This work is the copyright of Tony Moore. All intellectual property and associated rights are hereby asserted and reserved by him in full compliance with UK, European and international law. No part of this book may be copied, reproduced, stored in any retrieval system or transmitted in any form or by any means, or in any language, including in hard copy or via the internet, without the prior written permission of the publishers to whom all such rights have been assigned worldwide.

Cover design © 2015 Waterside Press. Design by www.gibgob.com.

Main UK distributor Gardners Books, 1 Whittle Drive, Eastbourne, East Sussex, BN23 6QH. Tel: +44 (0)1323 521777; sales@gardners.com; www.gardners.com

North American distribution Ingram Book Company, One Ingram Blvd, La Vergne, TN 37086, USA. Tel: (+1) 615 793 5000; inquiry@ingramcontent.com

Cataloguing-In-Publication Data A catalogue record for this book can be obtained from the British Library.

Printed by CPI Group, Chippenham, UK.

e-book *The Killing of Constable Keith Blakelock* is available as an ebook and also to subscribers of Myilibrary, Dawsonera, ebrary, and Ebscohost.

Published 2015 by
Waterside Press
Sherfield Gables
Sherfield-on-Loddon
Hook, Hampshire
United Kingdom RG27 0JG

Telephone +44(0)1256 882250
E-mail enquiries@watersidepress.co.uk
Online catalogue WatersidePress.co.uk

Table of Contents

About the author *viii*
Acknowledgements *ix*
Dedication *xi*
Foreword *xiii*
The author of the Foreword *xv*
Map *xvi*

1. **Introduction** 19
    Robert Culley *19*
    Thomas Green *22*
    Keith Blakelock *26*

2. **The Broadwater Farm Estate** 29
    Description of the Estate *29*
    Early media misrepresentation *32*
    Borough policies *33*
    The Youth Association *39*
    Attempts to improve the Estate by the Council *43*
    Conclusion *45*

3. **Relationship Between Haringey Council and the Metropolitan Police** *47*
    Introduction *47*
    Election of a Labour-controlled GLC *48*
    Haringey and the Metropolitan Police *51*
    First attempt to set up formal arrangements *52*
    More ad-hoc meetings *53*
    Key relationships *54*
    Second invitation to work together *55*
    Police policy in relation to the Estate *56*
    More moderate local administration *57*
    Third invitation to work together *58*
    A fourth opportunity for police and council to work together *62*

Force reorganization   *63*
Fifth and final attempt   *64*
Conclusion   *65*

4. Policing the Estate from 1973 to mid-1984 67
Introduction   *67*
Events elsewhere   *68*
Notting Hill Carnival riot   *70*
'Sus'   *70*
Institute of Race Relations   *72*
Disorder in Britain's inner-cities   *73*
Wood Green High Road   *74*
Meanwhile, back at The Farm   *75*
Publication of the Scarman Report   *76*
Foretaste of what was to come   *78*
Symbolic locations   *83*
Back to Haringey   *84*
National Front   *85*
Some encouragement   *86*

5. Policing the Estate from mid-1984 to October 1985 89
Arrival of Chief Superintendent Couch   *89*
Expectations of the Broadwater Farm team   *90*
Guidance for professional behaviour   *94*
Increasing difficulties in policing the Estate   *95*
Appointment of Sergeant Gillian Meynell   *96*
Handsworth, Birmingham   *99*
Effect of Handsworth on Broadwater Farm   *99*
Brixton   *102*
The effect of Brixton on Broadwater Farm   *103*
Drug problem   *103*
Mounting tension   *104*

6. The Death of Cynthia Jarrett and Build Up to the Riot 105
Arrest of Floyd Jarrett   *105*

Search of 25 Thorpe Road   *106*
The search warrant   *108*
Charging and court appearance of Floyd Jarrett   *109*
The coroner's inquest   *109*
The role of the Police Complaints Authority   *110*
Back to 5 October   *113*
Police options following the death   *114*
Option (a)   *114*
Option (b)   *117*
Option (c)   *117*
Other significant events   *118*
Yankee Control   *121*
Plan to deal with disorder at Broadwater Farm   *122*

7. **The Riot** *123*
The riot starts   *123*
The rioting worsens   *125*
Griffin Road   *126*
Senior officer deployment   *128*
Adams Road   *128*
Griffin Road again   *132*
Summary of activity in Adams and Griffin Roads   *136*
Deployment of baton gunners at Griffin Road   *138*
Willan Road and the surrounding area   *139*
Gloucester Road   *141*
Boyall's rescue attempt   *141*
The violence subsides   *142*
The police finally occupy the Estate   *143*

8. **The Killing of Constable Keith Blakelock** *145*
Gloucester Road   *145*
Serial 502   *146*
Directed to Broadwater Farm   *147*
The immediate aftermath   *154*
And later   *155*

Review of Couch's decision to send Serial 502 into Tangmere   *155*
Funeral   *158*
Bravery awards   *159*
Two heroines   *161*
The final word   *164*

9. Analysis of the Response to the Riot 167

Introduction   *167*
Failure to implement the plan for the Broadwater Farm Estate   *170*
Lack of training amongst senior officers   *170*
Failure to appoint an overall ground commander   *172*
Strategy   *174*
Tactics   *177*
Mobilisation   *179*
Confusion   *180*
Police communications   *180*
Baton rounds   *182*
Failure to use the Special Patrol Group   *183*
Lakes of petrol   *184*
The failure to use the Force helicopter   *185*
Degree of organization amongst the rioters   *186*
Conclusion   *187*

10. The First Murder Investigation 191

Introduction   *191*
The first investigation   *191*
One reason for a climate of fear   *195*
An alternative reason for the climate of fear   *196*
Refusing access to a solicitor   *198*
Charges of murder   *201*
The three juveniles   *202*
The adults   *205*
The investigation into other criminal offences   *210*
Postscript   *211*

11. Appeals, Acquittals and Further Investigations 213
Broadwater Farm Defence Campaign   *213*
Discipline proceedings against Melvin   *215*
The move for acquittal gathers pace   *216*
Melvin and Dingle suspended from duty   *220*
Winston Silcott   *222*
The second investigation   *224*
The third investigation   *227*
Conclusions   *233*

12. Morale and Psychological Stress 235
Introduction   *235*
Effect on morale   *236*
Work-related stress   *242*
Officers at Tottenham   *244*
Units responding to the riot   *246*
Fear   *247*
Frustration and a lack of banter   *249*
Nightmares   *251*
Williams 'operational review'   *251*
Lack of counselling   *253*
Metropolitan Police review   *255*
Conclusion   *255*

13. Where Does the Blame Lie? 257
Introduction   *257*
The wider picture   *260*
Social deprivation   *266*
Insensitive policing   *269*
Pressure groups   *272*
Community policing   *272*
Turnover of senior officers   *275*
The dilemma   *275*
Conclusion   *276*

Index   *279*

About the author

After a year in the Metropolitan Police Cadet Force, Tony Moore spent four years in the British Army, seeing service in Germany and Aden. He then spent the next 28 years in the Metropolitan Police, serving successively at Commercial Street, Holborn, Bethnal Green, City Road, New Scotland Yard, Islington, Caledonian Road, Leyton, Kensington, and on reaching the rank of Chief Superintendent, two years as Divisional Commander at Notting Hill.

Twice on the staff of the Police Staff College, Bramshill and an experienced public order commander, he was involved in a number of high profile policing events, including the Iranian Embassy Siege, Notting Hill Carnival, the wedding of Prince Charles to Lady Diana Spencer, football hooliganism, and clashes between demonstrators.

On leaving the police, he lectured at Cranfield University, based within the Defence Academy of the UK at Shrivenham specialising in crisis and disaster management and counter-terrorism.

He holds an MPhil from the University of Southampton, is President Emeritus and a Fellow of the Institute of Civil Protection and Emergency Management, and a member of both the Police History Society and London Historians. Apart from many articles on policing, his publications include *Tolley's Principles and Practice of Disaster Management* (as co-editor) (three editions 2002–2006); *Jane's Facility Managers Handbook* (as co-editor) (2nd edn. 2006), *Disaster and Emergency Management Systems* (British Standards Institution, 2008) and *Policing Notting Hill* (Waterside Press, 2013).

Acknowledgements

The intention of this book is to give an account of the brutal murder of Police Constable Keith Blakelock on 6 October 1985. But it is impossible to describe why this mild-mannered, community officer was killed without describing the circumstances which led up to his death. In order to accurately deal with all the issues that surrounded the event, I am hugely indebted to a number of people over a considerable period of time.

In 1990, whilst undertaking a research degree at the University of Southampton into public order policing I was fortunate to either meet with and discuss or exchange correspondence with a number of the police commanders who were part of the police response to the riot on Broadwater Farm Estate on 6th October. These were George Boyall, David French, Mike Jeffers, Tom Jones, David Polkinghorne, Bill Sinclair and Bob Wells. I also met with Richard Dellow during this period.

More recently, I have had the good fortune to exchange correspondence and, indeed, meet some of the police officers who were either responsible for policing Tottenham Division in the period leading up to the riot or were with a unit that responded to the riot. These included Nigel Bailey, Ian Clarke, David Gladwell, John Harrison, Paul Hogan, Kevin Hussey, Duncan Kennedy, Mark Lawson, Brett Lovegrove, Paul Morley, Walter Poulter, Lorraine Pullen, Steve Riley, Tony Rowe, Richard Slade, and Sheila White. Barry Day was particularly helpful in providing me with information relating to the policing of Tottenham both before and immediately after the riot and Chris Barker kindly helped me with some background information relating to the problems of the control room on that fateful night, and some former officers, who assisted me, wish to remain anonymous. To add to the list I had contact with in 1990, I also met with and discussed the events of 6 October with Doug Hopkins.

As the Divisional Commander at Tottenham in the period leading up to the riot and on the night itself, Colin Couch figures quite prominently in the book. I twice wrote to him, once in 1990 when undertaking my research at the University of Southampton, and, more recently, in 2014, but he chose not to respond on either occasion.

I am grateful for the assistance Clare Stephens and her team at the Castle Museum in Tottenham. The museum holds some of the archive material relating to Haringey Borough Council and copies of local newspapers. They put up with me on two 'whole day' visits, answering my questions and locating material which I found most useful, particularly in terms of the background to the Broadwater Farm Estate itself and the workings of Haringey Borough Council. Similarly, I am indebted to Stefan Dickers and his staff at the library of the Bishopsgate Institute which houses the Bernie Grant Archives. As some of the material is embargoed for many years to come, Bernie's wife, Sharon, who is secretary of the Bernie Grant Trust was most helpful in deciding and sorting out what I could see. My thanks go also to the team of volunteers at the Metropolitan Police Heritage Centre who were able to provide me with background information relating to some of the police officers who were involved; also to Kate Whittingham for providing the map of the Broadwater Farm Estate that appears before *Chapter 1*.

I am particularly indebted to my friend and former academic colleague Keith Weston who, despite a busy schedule, read through the whole manuscript and made a number of useful comments and observations. Once again, Bryan Gibson and his team at Waterside Press have advised and guided me along the way. As always, that advice and guidance was most helpful. Where comment or observations are not original I have taken care to the best of my ability to acknowledge the sources from whence they came. Where I make my own comments or observations I should emphasise they do not necessarily represent the views of the Metropolitan Police, either then or now, or of the police service in general.

My final note of thanks goes to my wife, Hamide, and her family, who have put up with my absence from family gatherings for the greater part of 2014 whilst I have been writing this book. Their support has been most encouraging.

Tony Moore
January 2015

This book is dedicated to the memory of Constable Keith Blakelock, to his family, to the members of Serial 502, and to all those officers of the Metropolitan Police who either served on Tottenham Division in the period leading up to the riot, or who were part of the response to the events on 6th October 1985, or were involved in the subsequent criminal investigations.

Foreword

Only three Metropolitan police officers have been killed during riots in London since the creation of the force nearly 200 years ago. The horrific killing of PC Keith Blakelock during the riot on the Broadwater Farm Estate in 1985 was the last of these. It also coincided with a change in the way that historians perceived both rioters and police officers.

Before the 1980s, police history was largely the territory of former police officers or people with close links to the police. The assumption reflected in many of their publications was that British society was based on consensus and one in which widespread disorder, when it did occur, was essentially the work of conspirators or extremist demagogues giving the criminal classes and the envious idle the opportunity for pillage and rapine. Invariably support was alleged to have been found from outside the area in which the trouble flared. It went without saying in these books—though it had been said regularly from the end of the 19th century—that the British/English/Metropolitan Police were the best in the world; their behaviour was marred only occasionally by the exception of a rotten apple.

Alongside of this consensus view of British society and the hagiographic portrayal of the police there emerged among academic historians, from the late-1950s, what became known as 'history from below.' This was an attempt, commonly rooted in the exploration of criminal justice records, to find the voice of the common people. Rooted in a Marxist or left-radical perspectives, it saw conflict rather than consensus at the heart of society. In this framework largescale conflict became, in many instances, not the work of demagogues but rather the disenfranchised seeking to bring their problems of labour exploitation, unaffordable food, and poor living conditions to the attention of their social superiors and the government. For these historians the police created in the 19th-century appeared primarily as an instrument by which those possessed of power and authority sought to control and supervise the poor.

The Broadwater Farm riot witnessed both of these views voiced in the press. The rioters were described as 'Trotskyites, social extremists, Revolutionary Communists, Marxists and black militants from as far away as Toxteth';

and also as alienated young men drawing their anger and problems to the attention of the authorities and focusing on the police as the physical manifestation of 'an alien power structure.'

Since the events at Broadwater Farm 'history from below' has shifted to include the study of ordinary police officers. In London, for much of the 19th-century and beyond, the police were the largest labour force working for a single employer. They had their own problems of pay and conditions. They had to be tough to deal with the hard men who lived in some of the poorer districts; one or two streets boasted the title of 'Kill-copper Row.' Sometimes the police were very tough and were considered by the locals as more like an army of occupation than protectors of property, life and liberty. Though many of London's constables had Irish origins, Irish districts were seen as dangerous. The arrival of large numbers of Jewish refugees in the early 20th-century gave the police a new problem — the Jews did not fight like the Irish, but some of them were political radicals; above all, however, they spoke a language that was unknown to most other English people.

Districts occupied by poor migrants and policed by men with their own problems and fears has a modern ring to it, and a ring that loudly echoed on Broadwater Farm. In what follows Tony Moore engages with all of the issues to give a rounded, mature assessment of the murder of Keith Blakelock, the events that led to the deployment of his serial during the disorder and the messy, and in many respects still unresolved aftermath.

Clive Emsley
March 2015

The author of the Foreword

Professor Clive Emsley of The Open University is a leading commentator on police and policing, having concentrated on the history of crime and policing in Western Europe, principally England and France. He has been a visiting professor at the universities of Paris VIII (St Denis), Calgary (Canada), Griffith (Australia) and Christchurch (New Zealand). In 2004 he was visiting research fellow at the Australian National University in Canberra. His more recent work includes a study of the spread of British policing methods since the end of the Second World War (with Dr Georgina Sinclair)(forthcoming) and his earlier publications include *The English Police: A Political and Social History* (2nd edn. 1996), *Gendarmes and the State in Nineteenth-Century Europe* (1999) and *The Great British Bobby: A History of British Policing from the 18th Century to the Present* (revised edn. 2010).

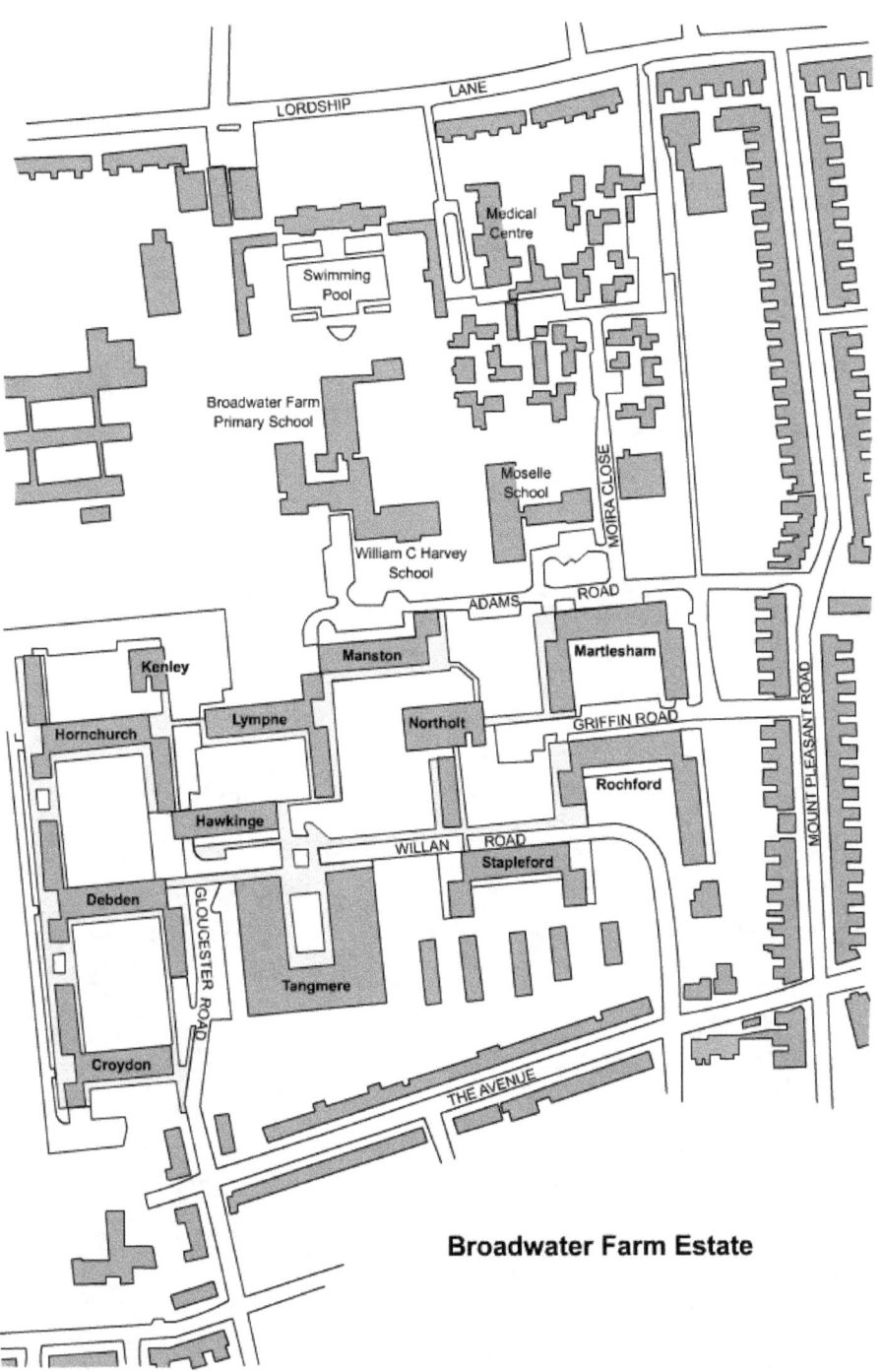

Broadwater Farm Estate

Map drawn by and © Kate Whittingham

CHAPTER ONE

Introduction

Three police officers have been killed in riots in the Metropolitan Police District since its formation in 1829. The first was Police Constable Robert Culley in 1833. The second was Station Sergeant Thomas Green in 1919 and the third was Police Constable Keith Blakelock in 1985.

Robert Culley

Robert Culley was amongst the first group of officers to join the Metropolitan Police stepping out to patrol the streets of London on 21 September 1829. Less than four years later he was dead, murdered. Married, his wife was in the advance stages of pregnancy with their first child. The circumstances surrounding Robert Culley's death are described by Gavin Thurston in his book *The Clerkenwell Riot*. He died from a single stab wound as police officers moved to break up an illegal meeting organized by the National Union of the Working Classes in Coldbath Fields on 13 May 1833. The C Division contingent, of which Culley was a part, were involved in a violent confrontation with demonstrators in Calthorpe Street. Sergeant John Brooks and Constable Henry Redwood were also stabbed but suffered only relatively minor injuries. Following his fatal wound, Culley staggered into the yard of the nearby Calthorpe Arms Public House, where he died.[1] Although the disorder lasted no more than five minutes, there were accusations that the crowd was peaceful and the police had been 'ferocious' and 'brutal' in dispersing it.[2]

The inquest into his death was the responsibility of His Majesty's Coroner for West Middlesex, Thomas Stirling, who was then 88 years of age. It was

---

1. Thurston, Gavin (1967). *The Clerkenwell Riot: The Killing of Constable Culley*. London: George Allen & Unwin, pp. 50–59.
2. Bloom, Clive (2004). *Violent London: 2000 Years of Riots, Rebels and Revolts*. London: Pan, p. 202.

held before 15 jurors in an upstairs room of the Calthorpe Arms. Thurston goes into great detail, describing the evidence given by the various witnesses, but, because that of the police had not been generally accepted, the jury returned a verdict of 'justifiable homicide' on 21 May.[3] Nine days later, following an appeal by the Solicitor-General, the Court of the King's Bench overturned the verdict and substituted one of 'wilful murder by a person or persons unknown'. The revised verdict 'incensed' those who had made up the jury to the extent that they wrote to Parliament claiming that it was with 'great pain and alarm' that they heard 'their conscientious verdict had been quashed'. The letter accused the court of casting a slur 'on their character as jurymen acting under the solemn obligations of an oath and that they prayed the House to take the subject into consideration and pursue such means as might seem requisite to free the petitioners from blame and secure to future jurymen the privileges conferred on them by law.'[4] Parliament responded by setting up a House of Commons Select Committee to inquire into the conduct of the Metropolitan Police in dispersing the meeting. The committee largely exonerated the police of any wrongdoing, pointing out that no 'dangerous wound or permanent injury' was 'inflicted' on the public, 'while on the other hand one of their own number had been killed with a dagger and two others stabbed while in the discharge of their duties.'[5]

A year later, 150 people, including two Members of Parliament, attended a dinner at the Highbury Barn Tavern, where each of the inquest jurors were presented with a cup by the Milton Street Committee[6] on which was inscribed:

> 'This cup was presented on 20th May 1834, by the Milton Street Committee, City of London, to Mr Samuel Stockton, foreman of the memorable Calthorpe Street inquest jury as a perpetual memorial of their glorious verdict of justifiable Homicide on the body of Robert Culley, a policeman, who was slain, while

---

3. Ibid, pp. 68–135.
4. Ibid, pp. 142–143.
5. Report of the Select Committee appointed to inquire into the conduct of the Metropolitan Police on 13th May last, in dispersing a Public Meeting in Coldbath Fields. BPP 1833 (718) XIII.
6. The Milton Street Committee was a group of City men who supported the campaigns for working-class rights.

brutally attacking the people peaceably assembled in Calthorpe Street on the 13th May 1833.'[7]

There was no Criminal Investigation Department at this time and no investigation into Robert Culley's death other than verification by a police surgeon that the knife used to stab both Sergeant Brooks and Constable Redwood was not the knife that caused the fatal wound to Culley. Therefore, no-one was ever prosecuted for Culley's murder. George Fursey stood trial at the Old Bailey, before Mr Justice Gaselee,[8] on 4 July 1833, charged with stabbing John Brooks and Henry Redwood although the latter charge was not proceeded with. The prosecution's case was strong. There was clear evidence of the stabbing and Fursey was arrested on the spot. In addition, 'the defence made no attempt to deny that Fursey stabbed the policeman' but relied on 'abundant evidence of provocation by the police'. The jury returned after just an hour and ten minutes. The foreman read the verdict:

> 'My Lords, we have, as your Lordships are aware, given not only long but close and anxious attention to this case, and have since we retired considered, with all the care which it was possible to bring to bear on it, the evidence of both sides, and we cannot on such evidence consciously pronounce any other verdict than not guilty.'

A few days later, at the Sawyers Arms in George Street, Camberwell, a dinner was given in Fursey's honour.[9]

Robert Culley was buried just four days after his death at St Anne's burial ground in Soho. But there was no respect for the dead. About 200 of his colleagues attending the funeral were booed and jeered outside the church by a mob of some 300 people.[10]

---

7. Thurston, op. cit. 1, p.169.
8. As was the practice in those days, Mr Justice Gaselee sat with Mr Justice Parke, Mr Recorder Law and the Lord Mayor of London. Thurston, op. cit. 1, pp. 154–155.
9. Thurston, op. cit. 1, pp. 153–163.
10. Ibid, p. 105.

Thomas Green

Thomas Green was 51-years-of-age and had only one more year to serve before retiring on pension when he met his death. Married, with two daughters, he had served for eight years with the Royal Horse Artillery before joining the Metropolitan Police in 1895. The circumstances surrounding his death, in particular the investigation into his murder and the political cover-up that followed, were not revealed until retired detective Edward Shortland undertook a five-year investigation in the late 1990s; this was followed by a book by Martin Knight, *We Are Not Manslaughterers*. Green died from a single blow to the head during a riot outside Epsom Police Station on the evening of 17 June 1919. It was inflicted by a Canadian soldier who was lodging at the nearby Woodcote Park Convalescent Hospital which housed some 400 Canadian troops wounded during World War I who were waiting to return to their homeland.[11] When two of their number were arrested after a disturbance at The Rifleman in Epsom High Street, between 300 and 400 troops from the hospital marched on the police station determined to release them. Initially only 12 in number, Inspector Pawley, the officer in charge at Epsom, ordered the police officers to retreat into the station. A number of soldiers were able to enter the cell passageway through a side window but, other than that the police retained control of the station. Along with other officers who lived locally, Station Sergeant Green was summoned from his home, and suggested to Pawley that the only chance they had of regaining a semblance of control was to make a baton charge on the soldiers. This they did but, in what can only be described as a riot, Green was struck over the head shortly after midnight by one of the soldiers with such force that it fractured his skull. He was taken to Epsom Infirmary by a military ambulance from the camp but died at around 7 a.m. that morning without regaining consciousness.[12]

---

11. Although the Armistice had been signed in November 1918, some seven months before the murder, Canadian troops were amongst the last to be sent home because, firstly, there was a need to retain troops in Britain on standby until Germany signed the treaty of Versailles, and, secondly, in any event, there was a shortage of transport ships in which they could be sent.
12. Knight, Martin (2010). *We Are Not Manslaughterers: The Epsom Riot and the Murder of Station Sergeant Thomas Green*. Northern England: Tonto Books, pp. 41–59; see also 'Epsom Military Riot' in the *Epsom Advertiser*, 27 June 1919.

The investigation into Thomas Green's murder was undertaken by one of Scotland Yard's most highly regarded officers, Detective Inspector John Ferrier,[13] but Shortland found that it was

> 'full of anomalies and lost opportunities. There were delays in the questioning of vital witnesses; there was no search for the potential murder weapon; and the main suspect was never put on an identify parade.'[14]

A key decision made very early on in the investigation was that time would not be expended in 'trying to discover who had wielded the fatal blow'. Eight Canadian soldiers, James Connors, Robert McAllan, Allen McMaster, Alphonse Masse, Gervase Porier, Herbert Tait, Frankie Wilkie and David Verex, were eventually charged with 'being concerned together in the manslaughter of Thomas Green'.[15] Two, Porier and Tait, were discharged at the committal proceedings at Bow Street Magistrates' Court.

The inquest[16] into Green's death which was held between the committal proceedings and the actual trial, found that it 'was caused by a blow or blows on the head received while on duty' and it decided the six soldiers already committed for trial, and bugler Robert Todd[17] 'participated in that riot with others of the Canadian forces unknown, all of whom they found guilty of manslaughter.' The inquest jury added a rider commending two people; Inspector Pawley for acting with 'great valour' and Detective Inspector Ferrier for his 'management of the inquiries.'[18]

Thus seven Canadian soldiers stood trial at the Surrey Assizes at Guildford on 22 July 1919 before Mr Justice Darling. In addition to being indicted for the manslaughter of Station Sergeant Green, all were charged with riotous assembly. Two were found not guilty of both charges; the remaining five

---

13. Knight, op. cit. 11, p. 76.
14. Kelbie, Paul (1999). 'Lloyd George accused over police death: Derby Day murder was "hushed up" to save embarrassing the Prince of Wales.' *The Sunday Telegraph*, 12 December 1999, p. 19.
15. Knight, op. cit. 11, pp. 87–88.
16. The chairman of the jury was James Chuter Ede who was elected to the House of Commons in 1923 and went on to be the Home Secretary in the 1945–1951 Labour Government.
17. Todd was added to the indictment on the basis that he had sounded the 'fall-in' on his bugle at the Convalescent Hospital prior to the march on the police station. See Knight, op. cit. 11, pp. 46–47 and 140.
18. Ibid, pp. 140; *Epsom Advertiser* 4 July 1919.

were found not guilty of manslaughter but guilty of riot. Each was sentenced to 12 months imprisonment.[19] Here the story, not for the first time, gets a little messy. According to Metropolitan Police Orders, Mr Justice Darling commended Inspector Pawley and 24 other officers for bravery in connection with the defence of Epsom Police Station during the riot. He also commended Inspector Ferrier and four junior detectives for the investigation; these officers were also commended by the Director of Public Prosecutions.[20] Knight, however, suggested that Mr Justice Darling deliberately ignored the request by prosecuting counsel, Sir Ernest Wild, KC, to commend Ferrier as an indication of the shoddiness of the investigation.[21]

Thomas Green was buried in the grounds of the Wesleyan Chapel in Epsom on 23 June 1919. Led by the band of V Division, and with between 700 and 800 policemen present, the procession left the Greens' house and wound its way through the streets where people stood up to four and more deep. His wife, with whom he would have celebrated their silver wedding anniversary in 1920, was too ill to attend. Some months previously she had suffered a stroke which paralysed one side of her body and she was not responding to treatment.[22] Therefore, his two daughters, clearly distraught, were the chief mourners.[23] Shops closed as a mark of respect. Most of the houses on the funeral route drew their curtains.

A fund was launched by Lord Roseberry, who lived locally, and the Epsom Member of Parliament, Sir Rowland Blades. Seven months later, £310 (which approximates to £18,000 to £20,000 today) was presented to Inspector Pawley to give to Green's widow, who was again too ill to attend. Each of the 24 officers involved in defending the station was presented with a gold watch or medallion, inscribed with the words 'In token of public appreciation of the gallant fight by Epsom police, 17th June 1919'. Inspector Pawley was presented with a silver cigarette case.[24]

A year later, a carefully worded memorial stone was unveiled at the head

---

19. Ibid, pp. 159–160; *Epsom Advertiser* 4 July 1919.
20. Metropolitan Police Orders, dated 30 September 1919.
21. Ibid, p. 163.
22. Ibid, p. 16.
23. Ibid, pp. 115–123; see also 'Epsom's Gallant Sergeant—Public Funeral: Impressive Scenes' in the *Epsom Advertiser,* 27 June 1919.
24. Ibid, pp. 168–169.

of Green's grave:

> IN MEMORY OF
> STATION SERGEANT THOMAS GREEN
> WHO FOUND DEATH IN THE PATH OF DUTY
> HE WAS KILLED IN DEFENDING
> EPSOM POLICE STATION
> AGAINST A RIOTOUS MOB
> JUNE 17th 1919
> THIS MEMORIAL WAS ERECTED BY
> THE OFFICERS AND MEN OF THE
> METROPOLITAN POLICE FORCE

His ailing widow, Lilian, who was to die at the age of 52 years just over a year later, had dragged herself from her hospital bed to see her husband's grave for the first time. Shortly after their mother's death in November 1921, Thomas Green's two daughters, Lily and Nellie, boarded a ship for a new life — in Canada![25]

The riot had occurred 'at a politically sensitive time, when many people in Canada were asking why more than 22,000 Canadians had been killed and thousands more gassed during the First World War.' As a result, it had been arranged that the Prince of Wales would make a tour of the Commonwealth, commencing in Canada, in August 1919. The fact that a Canadian soldier might be arrested for murder and hanged as the prince was visiting Canada would have been a public relations disaster and the Prince's personal safety might have been put at risk. It would have been equally disastrous to have cancelled the tour. As a result, Shortland believed that there was a cover-up that could only have been carried out with 'the complicity' of those at the very top of government which included, in this case, Prime Minister David Lloyd George, Home Secretary Winston Churchill, and the Commissioner of the Metropolitan Police, Sir Nevil McCready. Consequently, Shortland believed the whole incident was played down,[26] which resulted in less serious charges being laid against the Canadian soldiers, acquittal on the manslaughter

---
25. Ibid, pp. 172–174.
26. Kelbie, op. cit. 13; Knight , op. cit. 11, pp. 208–218.

charges and only a short sentence for rioting. McMasters, Yerex, Masse and Connors were released from Wandsworth Prison on 14 November 1919, having served only 16 weeks of their one-year sentence. For reasons that are not apparent, Wilkie was not released until December.[27]

At least one of the officers who faced the rioting Canadian soldiers was unhappy either about the events of that night or what followed because he took the unusual step of writing, from his home address, directly to the commissioner asking to see him. Knight suggested that for him to go straight to the commissioner, particularly in those days, rather than going through the chain of command meant that it was 'incredibly sensitive'. McCready refused to see him and wrote on the file in his own handwriting, 'The Epsom Riot case is closed, but any further correspondence should be drawn to my personal attention.' Knight suggested that it was because the commissioner 'must have considered it to be sensitive or potentially political.'[28]

Ten years after the riot at Epsom, in July 1929, MacMaster walked into the Winnipeg Police Headquarters in Manitoba, Canada, and confessed to the murder of Thomas Green. Having taken a written statement from him in which he admitted striking Green over the head with an iron bar, Chief Constable Chris Newton sent a telegram to the Metropolitan Police requesting instructions. He supported this with a follow-up letter which accompanied a copy of the statement. In reply he received a telegram which merely said: 'MacMaster sentenced in connection with this affair and he is not wanted. Letter following.'

Any letter that followed has not been found. The Metropolitan Police apparently told no-one about the confession. As Knight suggested, 'like many facets of this case, the confession was hurriedly and quietly buried.'[29]

Keith Blakelock

Keith Blakelock was a married man with three children when he was brutally stabbed and beaten to death on the Broadwater Farm Estate on 6 October 1985. He had joined the Metropolitan Police relatively late in life in 1980 at

---

27. Knight, op. cit. II, p. 166.
28. Ibid, pp. 164–166.
29. Ibid, pp. 176–181.

the age of 35 years. His maturity led to him being appointed a Home Beat Officer at Muswell Hill in North London.

Chapter 2 describes the Broadwater Farm Estate and the policy Haringey Borough Council had of dumping homeless and single-parent families on it. It also describes how some of the residents of the Estate, most notably Mrs Dolly Kiffin, were determined to improve life on The Farm, as it was known to many. *Chapter 3* describes the relationship between the two main protagonists, Haringey Council and the Metropolitan Police, and the desire of local politician Bernie Grant, in particular, to exercise some control locally over the police and an equally determined Commander Jim Dickinson who saw his responsibilities for policing as lying with the commissioner and, ultimately, the Home Secretary. *Chapters 4* and *5* describe the policing of the estate from the time it was completed in 1973 and how it became more and more difficult to police in a conventional manner.

Chapter 6 describes the death of Cynthia Jarrett, seen by many as the trigger for the riot that followed, although it was suggested that serious disorder was inevitable anyway, and what happened in the 24 hours immediately following that incident. *Chapter 7* describes the riot itself and *Chapter 8* deals with the killing of Constable Keith Blakelock in some detail.

Chapter 9 analyses the response of the Metropolitan Police to the riot. *Chapter 10* looks at the first investigation into the killing of Constable Blakelock. Following the conviction of three adults as a result of this investigation, *Chapter 11* describes the acquittal on appeal of those who were convicted, the subsequent prosecution of the senior investigating officer and one of his assistants, and two further investigations undertaken in an attempt to discover the identify of those who killed Blakelock.

Chapter 12 looks at the effect the events leading up to the riot and the riot itself had on the morale of the Metropolitan Police, particularly those officers at Tottenham who were responsible for policing the Broadwater Farm Estate, and those who responded to the riot. *Chapter 13* is an attempt to discover where the blame for the riot lay and, in doing so, examines briefly the relationship between the Metropolitan Police and those who came from the Caribbean from 1948 onwards.

What follows then, is the story of the third police officer to be murdered, the killing of Constable Keith Blakelock.

CHAPTER TWO

The Broadwater Farm Estate

Description of the Estate

The London Borough of Haringey came into being in 1965 as a result of the merging of the boroughs of Hornsey, Tottenham and Wood Green. Facing an acute housing shortage, it decided to build high-density housing on the Broadwater Farm site, 21 acres of open land which, at the time, was being used as allotments. Building commenced in 1967 but was held up for a period following a gas explosion in May 1968 in a 22 storey block of flats known as Ronan Point in Limehouse which caused all the floors in one corner to collapse. Four people had been killed and 17 injured.[1] Built on the 'Larsen-Neilson method of system building',[2] the blocks on the Broadwater Farm site were completed one-by-one and, as each was finished, the flats were allocated. The estate was finally completed in 1973 by which time it consisted primarily of 12 residential blocks of varying heights, containing 1,063 separate properties either in the form of flats or maisonettes. Included in the estate were a small group of two-storey houses on higher ground close to The Avenue.[3]

The blocks were named after Battle of Britain airfields. Two of the blocks, Kenley and Northolt, were 18 storeys high but the remainder consisted of only four to six storeys. Tangmere, built in the form of a ziggurat,[4] was different to the remainder in that it consisted of flats, with balconies, surrounding a shopping precinct that was originally intended to be 24 separate units, but

---

1. Wearne, Phillip (1999). *Collapse: Why Buildings Fall Down*. London: Channel 4 Television, tie-in edition.
2. The Larsen-Nielsen method of building consisted of a prefabricated construction technique known as large panel system building in which the structure was assembled from pre-cast concrete panels, slotted together and fastened by bolts to form load-bearing walls, floors and roof slabs.
3. Broadwater Farm (BWF) Tenants' Information Sheet, undated, stored in the archives at the Castle Museum.
4. A ziggurat is built similar to a step pyramid with successively receding floors or levels from the ground upwards or, in this case, as it was built on stilts, from the first floor level upwards.

would include a public house, supermarket, newsagent, etc.[5] Each building had been built on stilt blocks which had to be sunk deep into the marshy ground; the Moselle river, which would occasionally flood following heavy rainfall, ran through the site. Accommodation only existed on the first floor and above of each block. Therefore, the blocks were inter-connected by a series of walkways at first floor level. It was intended that the ground underneath the first floor platforms would be used as car parks for the residents; the council insisted that there should be a car park space for each of the 1,063 properties. But a lack of security meant that few residents actually parked their cars in the allocated spaces.[6] Provisions were made for two areas to be laid out as children's playgrounds which were intended only for children up to 12-years-old.[7]

Along the southern border of the estate ran The Avenue, a narrow road with terraced houses on both sides. With the exception of this small number of houses, the surrounding area was not considered to be part of the estate; indeed they had been built much earlier. Between the terraced houses on the south side there were two vehicular entrances to the estate from The Avenue, via Gloucester Road and Willan Road. Mount Pleasant Road ran along the eastern side of the estate. Again terraced houses spread along both sides of the road. Access into the estate could be gained from Mount Pleasant Road by using Griffin Road or Adams Road, the latter forming part of the northern boundary of the estate.

To the north, between the estate and Lordship Lane, a number of schools and a medical centre had been built. There was also a somewhat older outdoor swimming pool — the Lido. To the west was Lordship Lane Recreation Ground, a large expanse of open ground used, as its name implies, for recreational purposes, although many of the facilities were in a poor state of repair. Nevertheless, according to the Tenants' Information Sheet, there was easy access from the estate which could be used by everyone over 12-years-of-age.[8]

---

5. BWF Tenants' Information Sheet, op. cit. 3.
6. Williams, David A (1986). Internal Police Report on the Disorders of the 6th October 1985 at the Broadwater Farm Estate, Tottenham. London: Metropolitan Police, p.67, para. 2.18.
7. BFW Tenants' Information Sheet, op. cit. 3.
8. Gifford, Lord (1986). The Broadwater Farm Inquiry: Report of the Independent Inquiry into Disturbances of October 1985 at the Broadwater Farm Estate, Tottenham. London: Broadwater Farm Inquiry, p. 17, para. 2.15.

People living in the nearby houses had opposed the building of the estate. One of the occupants told the Gifford Inquiry that it was 'like a wart on one's hand, a monstrosity, out of character for the area.'[9] Another described it as 'monolithic' and compared it with 'Windscale',[10] a nuclear power plant in Cumbria at which Britain's worst nuclear accident had occurred in 1957. The Williams Report described it as 'rising self-consciously from amidst a maze of two storey Victorian terraced housing'. Because of the starkness of its architecture, it was set 'aside from its neighbours' and, as a result, there was 'no sense of it "belonging" to its surroundings.'[11] A black writer described a visit to relatives living there one rainy evening shortly after it was completed:

> '…the grey walls and black cavernous car parks presented the grimmest sight imaginable. Most of the flats [were] built on concrete stilts above wastes of carless car park, with empty overhead walkways at sky-scraping level. Hidden, steep flights of stairs suddenly [appeared] behind concrete pillars, seen through low, narrow doorways.'

Even at that early stage, he 'noticed that several flats were boarded-up' leading him to believe that they were much older than they, in fact, were.[12]

Problems soon emerged. There was a lack of amenities and the estate was inaccessible to many people. There were no nearby bus routes which made it difficult to travel anywhere without a car. Despite initial plans, no community facilities were provided, although a small building, which was not part of the original design, was constructed under one of the walkways on Willan Road. This became the Community and Tenants Social Club. John Murray, a member of the Council's Building Design Services described to the Gifford inquiry how, when they were submitted, tenders were invariably regarded as being too high and therefore things, such as community centres and pubs, were thought to be 'froth or the icing on the cake' and were cut out. Consequently, few of the planned shops in Tangmere Block

---

9. Williams, David A, op. cit. 6, p.66, para. 2.1.2.
10. Power, Anne (1999). *Estates on the Edge: The Social Consequences of Mass Housing in Northern Europe.* Basingstoke: Macmillan, p. 195.
11. Kerridge, Roy (1985). 'The Man on the Tottenham Omnibus'. In *Police*, Vol. XVIII, No. 4, December, p. 30.
12. BWF Tenants' Information Sheet, op. cit. 3.

materialised. But, a member of the Gifford Inquiry Panel pointed out that history had shown that rather than the icing they were the fruit of the cake itself when you had a community of over 3,000 people. Murray agreed.[13]

Early media misrepresentation

There was 'a spiral of deterioration' almost from the start[14] which was 'exacerbated in the mind of the public by sensational reporting in the local press'.[15] As early as May 1973, the *Hornsey Journal* disclosed a 'report' written by a junior school teacher under the headline 'Marriages on Rocks among the Concrete' and went on to describe how '"Problem" families — many of them single parent families — were seen to be placed together' and 'the sight of unmarried West Indian mothers walking about the estate aggravated racial tension.'[16] Although many of the tenants told the newspaper they disagreed 'vehemently' with the report, Gifford described it as 'a first example of the racists labelling which was to become more frequent.'[17]

Three years later, a survey undertaken by two local reporters at the *Tottenham Weekly Herald*, under the headline 'Families who live in the Shadow of Violence', claimed that fear haunted 'the gloomy passages, lifts and entrances of Broadwater Farm Estate'. But again, led by the president of the Tenants Association, residents claimed it was a 'total misrepresentation of the facts.'[18]

Two years later, under the headline 'Expert Raps Terror Flats', the *Weekly Herald* reported that 'an explosive survey carried out by a sociologist appointed by Tottenham Liberals claimed that 'the 1,063 tenants on Broadwater Farm Estate' were 'living in a "sub-culture of violence".' As a result, the sociologist claimed there was 'complete social disorganization.'[19] The following week the newspaper carried a number of letters from residents who disagreed with the report with one of them writing:

---

13. Gifford, op. cit. 8, p. 16, para. 2.10.
14. Ibid, pp. 17–18, para. 2.16.
15. Ibid, p. 19, para. 2.20.
16. *Hornsey Journal*, 11 May 1973.
17. Gifford, op. cit. 8, p. 19, para. 2.20.
18. *Weekly Herald* (Tottenham and Wood Green), 30 April 1976.
19. *Weekly Herald* (Tottenham and Wood Green), 6 October 1978.

'I can speak from personal experience. I am a woman. I do not suffer from tension or depression and have many friends like myself and am extremely lucky to live on Broadwater Farm.'[20]

Borough policies

The acute housing shortage in the area meant there was initially some success in letting the properties on Broadwater Farm.[21] Most of the early inhabitants came from slum clearance schemes and were delighted to be rehoused in these brand new flats. An early resident was Dolly Kiffin, who was subsequently to play a leading role on the estate. Born in Jamaica in 1936, her father was half-Scottish and half-Jamaican whilst her mother was Jamaican. In 1950 she was sent to England to stay with her brother, then working as a mechanic in South-West London. She married at 18 and had four children but the marriage did not work out and she finally moved away with the children to Tottenham, where she rented accommodation in Abbotsfield Avenue. She had another child by a man who went back to Jamaica soon afterwards but in 1972 she married Josiah Kiffin. They applied to Haringey Council for accommodation and were offered a flat in the then newly completed Tangmere Block on the Estate.[22]

The flats themselves were spacious and comfortable but structural problems soon became apparent. Rain penetrated many of the flat roofs, which meant that, initially, the top floor flats in some blocks could not be let until repair work had been carried out. In Tangmere Block, rain leaked through the balconies causing considerable irritation to the residents below. In some flats cockroaches appeared, entering through the small gaps between the industrialised building slabs. The council's response was 'shoddy' from the start.[23] In addition to these 'real grievances', Gifford pointed out there were a number of other 'contributory factors' that quickly went towards creating a 'terrible image' of the estate. They consisted largely of the unjust labelling of the people as well as the buildings in what was described as a 'social

---

20. Ibid, 13 October 1978.
21. Williams, David A, op. cit. 6, p.67, para. 2.2.1.
22. Williams, Paul (1994). Keeper of the Dream: The Story of Dolly Kiffin of Broadwater Farm. London: International Community Talk, pp. 2–8.
23. Gifford, op. cit. 8, p.18, para. 2.17; see also Williams, op. cit. 4, p. 67, para. 2.1.7.

ostracism'. This meant residents 'had severe problems with hire purchase or TV hire facilities, or obtaining goods from catalogues'; also, 'deposits were required for the installation of gas and electricity.'[24]

As more desirable accommodation became available in the area, the enthusiasm with which the first families took up residence soon evaporated and, as early as 1974, a large number of flats on the estate were left unoccupied. It quickly became known as the 'Nightmare Estate', deemed by the Department of the Environment as 'difficult to let' and demolition was being considered even at that early stage.[25] By 1975 three quarters of all vacancies on the estate were being allocated to homeless families compared with one quarter for the remainder of the borough. The downward spiral in the fortunes of the estate continued. By 1976 the council recognised that radical changes were required and the policy of allocating accommodation on The Farm to homeless families was halted pending the outcome of a full investigation which, it was hoped, would lead to the production of a remedial plan.

The comprehensive report by Barry Simmons, then the Borough Housing Officer, pointed out that the rate of refusals for accommodation on the estate was 53 per cent compared with a 35 per cent level over the borough as a whole.[26] Worse still, those who already lived on the estate who wanted a transfer away from it were double the borough average of 20 per cent.[27] The report also pointed out that 'the proportion of unskilled and semi-skilled residents on the Estate was 44% of the total number living on the estate, compared with 30% in the remainder of the Borough'. Finally, the report pointed out that the number of referrals to social services was six times higher than the number of referrals for the South Tottenham area as a whole.[28]

Because many of those high-up on the housing waiting lists refused accommodation on the estate, preferring to wait for something more attractive, the borough offered the accommodation to people lower on the waiting list. Inevitably, this meant homeless families and single-parent families, who had

---

24. Williams, David A, op. cit. 6, p. 67, para. 2.2.2. quoting a Confidential Report by Tricia Zipfel to Robin Sharp of the Department of Environment.
25. Gifford, op. cit. 8, p. 20, para. 2.23.
26. Williams, David A, op. cit. 6, p.68, para. 2.2.3.
27. Gifford, op. cit. 8, p. 21, para. 2.24.
28. Williams, David A, op. cit. 6, p. 68, para. 2.2.3.

little choice but to accept,[29] as Simmons described:

> 'Since very few tenants wished to transfer to Broadwater, and many housing applicants refused accommodation there, dwellings tended to be left to those whose need was most urgent, and the estate has received up until now an unusually large share of homeless and single parent families. In all, 75% of acceptances on voids on Broadwater in 1975 were by homeless families, compared to 24% of voids elsewhere in Haringey.'[30]

One of the two tower blocks was kept for the exclusive use of the elderly, but the other contained a mixture of the elderly and young, single-parent families.[31]

Simmons' report also issued a warning suggesting that 'a policy which has the effect of dispersing ethnic minority away from unpopular estates can be justified if it accords with that minority's issues and takes account of individual preferences.' But the Williams report suggested that, in practice:

> 'The position was made worse by a doctrine of colour blindness in relation to housing allocation. The doctrine postulated the view that persons should be offered housing accommodation according to their needs and their relative position on the housing waiting list. No account was taken of a person's colour or nationality. As the proportion of black residents on the estate rose to levels far in excess of the proportion for the rest of the borough, the council realised its mistake. They had failed to appreciate or if they had appreciated it, then they had chosen to ignore that "applicants with little or no choice included a disproportionate number of ethnic minorities who were more likely to have been living in conditions of housing stress or to be homeless".'[32]

Simons made a number of recommendations, including the introduction of a Special Allocations Scheme designed to exclude certain categories of

---

29. Ibid, para. 2.2.4.
30. Gifford, op. cit. 8, p. 21, para. 2.24.
31. Williams, David A, op. cit. 6, p. 68, para. 2.2.4.
32. Ibid, para. 2.2.5 quoting from Housing Department, Department of Environment (1981). An Investigation of Difficult to Let Housing, Vol. 2, Case Studies of Post War Estates. Directorate Occasional Paper 4/80. London: Her Majesty's Stationary Office.

people, including homeless and single-parent families and the unemployed. At the same time efforts were made to encourage securely employed people who were not on the housing list to transfer onto the estate. Whilst not a complete success, some improvement—particularly in the physical appearance of the place—became evident and the morale of the tenants rose.[33]

The improvement was short-lived. Two years later the start of a nationwide period of economic restraint meant that, by September 1979, many of the recommendations made in the Simons Report had floundered, and the council reverted to its previous policy of 'normal' allocations. Thus, when Haringey Council responded to a new initiative by the Department of the Environment to improve difficult-to-let housing estates, under a scheme known as 'Priority Estates', by proposing Broadwater Farm as the participant estate, it was rejected by the department because 'of the extreme severity of the social, management and security problems.' These included broken security doors on the tower blocks, flooded decks, and walkways that appeared 'desolate and abandoned,' added to which, it was suggested 'the estate was not regularly policed.' The Department therefore felt that 'conditions appeared unsalvageable' and there was little reason to believe that 'the estate could be made to work as a demonstration project for the national rescue of unpopular estates.'[34]

By 1980, the estate had 'declined once more into the abyss'[35] with 70 per cent of the new lettings being made to homeless families, although this did decline to 48 per cent two years later. Gifford pointed out, 'they went to Broadwater Farm because they had no choice' because, prior to 'November 1981, a homeless family was only given one offer.'[36] Joanne George, a homeless parent who went on to become Chair of the Tenants Association and later a social services community worker on the estate described her arrival in 1980:

> 'The estate was dirty, there was lots of vandalism, lots of grass, the flat I was allocated was in a really bad state of repair. There was no kitchen sink, there was no kitchen cupboard [and] there was a hole in the floor. It was just horrendous.'

---

33. Dillon, Dennis, and Fanning, Bryan (2012). *Lessons for the Big Society: Planning, Regeneration, and the Politics of Community Participation*. Aldershot: Ashgate, p. 37.
34. Power, op. cit. 10, pp. 197–198.
35. Williams, David A, op. cit. 6, p. 69, para. 2.2.8; see also Gifford, op. cit. 8, pp. 21–22, para.2.25.
36. Gifford, op. cit. 8, pp. 21–22, para. 2.25.

When she complained about the graffiti and stains on the passages, she was told there was no money for redecoration.[37] The council had singularly failed to make provisions for the needs of homeless families as Dolly Kiffin described, 'they hadn't got any carpet, furniture, anything,' and there was 'a problem with social security to give them these things.' Pointing out that they struggled, and the struggle got 'harder and harder', she claimed 'you could see the frustration in the young people there.'[38]

Before long a high proportion of all residents were young, black and unemployed. A good number were also 'single parents'. The Gifford Report was critical of Haringey Council for not monitoring the lettings of its housing stock to ethnic minorities on the grounds that it deprived it 'of the information which would be essential to consider whether there were any discriminatory practices in decisions' being made about the estate by its officers. A representative of the West Indian Standing Conference, William Trant, told the inquiry that there was nothing wrong in placing a large concentration of black people in a particular area because it provided 'strength and support', but it ought not to be the case 'where the less desirable estates [were] allocated to Black people.'[39] Worse still, the Broadwater Farm Estate had by then 'acquired a reputation for deprivation, violence, drugs and crime' against a backdrop of 'ill-lit walkways, peeling paint, broken glass and vandalised lifts'.[40]

In his evidence to the Gifford Inquiry, Russell Simper, a caretaker at the time, described an increasingly serious problem on the estate by 1981, 'The youths used to hang about, people used to break the windows, doors were hanging off, the wood frames were rotten and it generally started to become a run-down place.' By this time, many of the tenants were 'disheartened' and 'wanted to move'.[41]

It was not surprising that youths were hanging about because, as already indicated, the council had provided no facilities other than a small clubroom built for the Tenants Association which saw itself as a social club and became more like a pub, rather than a community centre. Whilst a number of the

---

37. Ibid, p. 19, para. 2.19.
38. Ibid, p. 22, para. 2.26.
39. Ibid, para. 2.27.
40. Williams, Paul, op. cit. 22, p. 10.
41. Gifford, op. cit. 8, p.18, para. 2.18; see also *Weekly Herald*, 24 September 1981.

older people living on the estate used it regularly, the evidence given to the Gifford Inquiry suggested black people were not welcome. Additionally, financial irregularities in the running of the club led to an investigation and the sacking of staff in 1981.[42]

In an effort to bring facilities nearer to the tenants in the borough, the council set up a number of sub-committees and a Mid-Tottenham Housing Office, which covered the area of the Broadwater Farm Estate, was established in early 1981. By this time, many tenants had had enough and 'turned out in force at the Mid-Tottenham Area Housing Committee' meeting in September to attack 'their council landlords for appalling living conditions.' Under the headline 'Smarten up notorious Farm estate' the local newspaper suggested that 'angry' tenants 'lashed out at horrifying conditions in their home surroundings' describing how graffiti covered the estate, lifts were constantly out of order, there was a 'stink of urine', leaking roofs and outstanding building repairs. The following month, Haringey's Council Housing Committee agreed to allocate £150,000 to cover a series of measures on the beleaguered estate, which would include:

- Re-opening the local estate office with a team of housing officers to deal with local problems;
- Setting up a pilot exercise in two blocks aimed at improving security and making environmental improvements;
- Dealing with water penetration in one of the blocks;
- Employing extra cleaners, caretakers and improving street cleaning;
- A crash programme of repairs to communal areas of the estate.[43]

By this time, crime both on the estate and that suspected to have been committed elsewhere by estate residents was a 'source of serious concern' to the divisional commander at Tottenham Police Station. Amongst many of the people living on the estate there was a feeling of anxiety; crime rates were high and there was concern about the number of people getting assaulted. Indeed it was reported that in the two months between 23 July and 23 September 1981, there had been 36 successful break-ins and ten attempted

---
42. Ibid, p. 23, para. 2.29.
43. *Weekly Herald* (Tottenham and Wood Green), 8 October 1981.

break-ins on the estate. Therefore, the Tenants Association, dominated by white residents, called a meeting to discuss the matter. Only about 20 people attended, most of them white. As the local councillor, Bernie Grant, who was born in Guyana and had come to Britain at the age of 19, took the chair. It was suggested that a police office be opened on the estate but it was clear that Grant had reservations because the meeting was not representative of those living on the estate and he wanted to hear the views of black people before he would agreeing to such a move.[44]

Summing up the situation at the end of 1981, the Gifford report said:

> 'The estate ... offered nothing to young Black people except a home. They were effectively excluded from the social club. They had no other facilities on the estate. The young men, many of them unemployed, had nothing to do. The old people were afraid of them, the police suspected them. The young women with children were isolated and lonely. The teenagers had the use of a flat in Hawkinge block which operated on three evenings a week, but nothing more. The physical appearance of the estate was run down and ill maintained.'[45]

The Youth Association

The response by a section of the black population to the proposal put forward by the Tenants Association that a police office be opened, was both 'swift and predictable'. In the climate that then existed,[46] they saw it as a wholly inappropriate response to the problems of the area and it would only serve to reinforce a police presence that was already regarded as heavy-handed and insensitive. Neither the Tenants Association nor the police were able to alter, what the Williams Report described as this 'entrenched animosity and fear felt by the young blacks towards this new threat'.[47] Dolly Kiffin, who had recently returned from one of her regular trips to Jamaica, called a meeting at her flat which was attended by between 20 to 30 youths, all black, and the

---

44. Ibid; see also Chapter 3.
45. Gifford, op. cit. 8, para. 2.30.
46. For details of the climate that exited, see *Chapter 5*.
47. *Weekly Herald* (Tottenham and Wood Green), 8 and 29 October 1981;

then Director of the Mid-Tottenham Housing Office, Barry Simons. Kiffin was under no illusion about the problems young people created on the estate:

> 'They would hang around in gangs where boredom led to trouble. There was glue-sniffing, theft, vandalism, drug-taking and loud music blaring into the night.'[48]

At the meeting, the youths attacked the attitude of the council in relation to the lack of amenities, particularly for black people. Kiffin enlisted the help of an ex-Army tank driver, Clasford Sterling, who was then working for London Transport and who had a 'natural rapport with young people'. A second meeting was called at which the Broadwater Farm Youth Association was formed. Two trustees, of which Dolly Kiffin was one, and a management committee was formed. Clasford Sterling was elected vice-president. With the help of Barry Simons, it was agreed that a disused chip shop on the Tangmere precinct would become the premises for the Youth Association. Once it was regarded as a 'going concern', they received an initial grant of £300 from the council.[49] In deference to the black view, no police office was provided.[50]

The newly-formed association then sent a strong message to the council, claiming that, despite the existence of over 1,000 flats on the estate, there was no proper youth centre or adventure playground and shops had been closed for years. Additionally, 'young women [were] locked up in their blocks with nowhere to put their kids, and the community centre [had] been turned into a pub'. As a result, there was nothing to do on the estate, particularly as many of the residents were unemployed. So, they outlined a series of demands:

- Empty shops should be made available for day-time letting;
- The community school should be used for recreation, educational and cultural events in the evenings;
- The fish bar should be opened to cater for the employed during the daytime;
- Drying rooms for arts and crafts should be made available; and

---

48. Williams, David A, op. cit. 6, p. 70, para. 3.1.1.
49. Williams, Paul, op. cit. 22, p. 17.
50. Ibid, pp. 18–22.

- An employment cooperative should be set up on The Farm.[51]

Towards the end of August 1982, the newly-formed Broadwater Farm Youth Association, with the help of Haringey Council, organized the first Lordship Lane Festival. The event included live music, children's shows, a five-a-side football competition, African and West Indian art, craft and cookery, theatre and poetry. Attended by approximately 1,500 people, it was regarded as a great success. In the evening, approximately 200 people attended a disco at the social club. Dolly Kiffin expressed her delight, pointing out that there had 'not been a single bit of trouble'.[52] However, the Haringey Independent Police Committee, about which more will be said in the following chapters, took advantage of what was essentially a fun day by having a stall sited on the recreation ground, handing out leaflets appealing for members and voluntary workers and advertising a training a day on 11 September.[53]

An early visitor to the Youth Association once installed in the disused fish and chip shop was Sir George Young, then a Minister at the Department of the Environment. He suggested they applied for an Urban Aid grant, and, in December 1982, with council assistance, an application was submitted.[54] In the meantime Haringey Council was finally persuaded to give an annual grant of £2,000 towards the running costs of the association but this in no way covered the salaries of people like Clasford Sterling and others who were working full-time for the Youth Association so it embarked on a number of fund raising initiatives.[55]

The application for Urban Aid was successful and, in February 1983, the Youth Association was awarded a total of £42,000 per annum to pay the running costs of the centre. Half went towards paying the wages of four staff, including Sterling. Dolly Kiffin did not accept a salary but her husband was appointed caretaker for the centre. The remainder of the money was used to convert two empty shops into premises for the Youth Association. The money, however, was given to the Haringey Council because the Youth Association was not a limited company. Dolly Kiffin was determined that

---

51. *Weekly Herald* (Tottenham and Wood Green), 12 November 1981.
52. Williams, Paul, op. cit. 22, pp. 18–23.
53. Tottenham Police Report, dated 31 August 1982.
54. *Weekly Herald* (Tottenham and Wood Green), 2 September 1982.
55. Williams, Paul, op. cit. 22, p. 23.

people on the estate should be consulted and be involved. After some haggling, she persuaded the council to allow unemployed people living on the estate to carry out the work which she would supervise. An architect was hired — Haverstock Associates — and a building contractor was found who was prepared to employ a quota of youth from the estate. Interim payments were made to the builder by the council after they had been assured by Kiffin that the work had finished. The work was finally completed in 1984 and the official opening ceremony in October was performed by Leader of the Greater London Council, Ken Livingstone, with Sir George Young, representatives from the council, the local police and numerous VIPs in attendance. Meanwhile, in the summer of 1984, Dolly Kiffin and Clasford Sterling had attended a garden party at Buckingham Palace.[56]

The Gifford Report spoke enthusiastically about the achievements of the Youth Association and many people living on the estate at the time of the riot 'paid tribute' to its work. Meals were provided on a regular basis and the occasional outing was arranged for pensioners, the majority of whom were white.[57] At the time of the riot, 60–70 pensioners were receiving meals in their homes' and others came to the Youth Association for lunch. In the meantime, in 1982, Dolly Kiffin and others from the Youth Association were instrumental in opening a day nursery on the ground floor of an under-used hostel, owned by the Borough of Haringey's Social Services Department, to cater for 25 children from the estate. Later, in 1984, funded by the Greater London Council, the upper floor of the hostel became a centre for women offering a range of activities. Joanne George, by now heavily involved, and who had helped set up the nursery, told the Gifford inquiry that because of poverty, unemployment, the bad housing conditions and the fact that they had nowhere to go meant that many of the women on the estate felt isolated and wanted 'something better' both for themselves and their children. She suggested that 'becoming involved changed the lives of many young people.' Also, a play centre for children between five and eleven was opened in the Kenley Block in 1984. The centre was open both in term-time and school holidays. In term-time, the children would be picked up from school and taken to the centre to await collection by their parents at around 5.30 p.m. At

---

56. Williams, David A, op. cit. 6, p.69, para. 2.2.9.
57. Gifford, op. cit. 8, pp. 26–29, paras. 2.38–2.46.

the time of the riot, approximately 40 children were attending the play-centre during term-time. This number rose to about 100 during school holidays. A number of co-operative enterprises, such as a community launderette, a food and vegetable co-operative, a hairdressing salon, together with photographic and sewing workshops were set up.[58]

Attempts to improve the Estate by the Council

Meanwhile, the Mid-Tottenham Housing Office had combined management and repair teams in 1981 so that it could respond rapidly to complaints from tenants on the estate. In 1982, Haringey Council formed a Community Affairs Department and the Housing Department moved into local offices that were more accessible for tenants. In 1983, a neighbourhood office, was opened in Tangmere Block to provide a service that would deal quickly and efficiently with all the physical problems of the estate. It was their responsibility to carry out day-to-day repairs to the structure of the estate and ensure that graffiti and refuse was removed with the minimum of delay. The problems of tenants were also channelled through this office as were the allocation of housing units to new tenants and housing benefit claims. There can be no doubt that the presence of the Neighbourhood Office had a profound effect on the morale of the estate's residents. The number of empty units was reduced from 60 to 13 and the 'refusal rate' came down from 70 per cent to 46 per cent.[59]

In 1984, the council set up a sub-committee, chaired by Councillor Bernie Grant, called the Broadwater Farm Panel, which brought together the Tenants Association, the Youth Association and other agencies to make decisions about the estate. The internal police report issued after the riot claimed that 'it was a matter of regret that, although invited, the police did not become members of this panel.'[60] From its inception the panel was given decision-making powers and a budget to fund short-term projects dealing with cleaning, maintenance and so forth. Its main influence was twofold. Firstly, its decisions were binding on the council; secondly, it brought together all

---

58. Ibid, p. 28, para. 2.43.
59. Williams, David A, op. cit. 6, p. 76, para. 3.3.1.
60. Ibid. The reasons for the police's lack of participation are described in *Chapter 3*.

interested parties, with the exception of the police, in a powerful debating forum. Nevertheless, there remained a number of difficulties, not the least of which was getting council officers who were used to the rigid departmental structure to become accountable to the panel.[61] Despite this, a major project did follow. As a result of the panel's recommendations, a £1 million scheme was put into effect resulting in the replacement of all communal glass with diamond glazed vandal proof glass, the fitting of strengthened front doors to all flats, an installation of entry phones to the tower blocks and a general improvement in the standard of lighting throughout the estate, the repainting of corridor walls and the covering of floor surfaces with rubberised material to dull sound and facilitate cleaning.[62] These improvements coincided with a further application under the Priority Estates Project to the Department of the Environment which was, on this occasion, successful. As a result the Project 'became enmeshed in the fortune of the estate' playing 'the role of honest broker, running Block consultations over improvements, supporting key tenants' leaders and the local office, working with the Broadwater Farm panel, the energetic and go-ahead Director of Housing and other services.'[63]

In 1985, two significant events occurred. One affected the estate directly, the other indirectly. The first occurred in February 1985 when, following a direct approach by her staff to Dolly Kiffin, Her Royal Highness The Princess of Wales visited the Youth Association. Inside the premises, the Princess was treated to a disco dancing display and shown a photographic workshop and the pensioners dining club. Dolly Kiffin gave her a brief synopsis of the Youth Association's history and introduced her to a group of pensioners, one of whom presented her with a crocheted table mat and doily that had been completed in the Association's knitting workshop. A number of council officials including the Mayor, Councillor Viv Fenwick, Labour Leader George Meehan, Chief Executive Roy Limb and Community Relations Officer Jeff Crawford, were in attendance.[64]

The other significant event was Dolly Kiffin's absence from the estate for the two months preceding the riot about which more will said in *Chapter*

---

61. Gifford, op. cit. 8, pp. 29–31, paras 2.48–2.52.
62. Williams, David A, op. cit. 6, p. 77, para. 3.3.3; Gifford, op. cit. 8, pp. 31–32, para. 2.53; Power, op.cit. 10, pp. 200–201.
63. Power, op. cit. 10, p.199.
64. *Weekly Herald* (Tottenham and Wood Green), 7 February 1985.

5. At Kiffin's suggestion, the Borough Council made an 'official' twinning link with the district where she had been brought up in Jamaica, Clarendon. Kiffin visited there in January to make arrangements for a group from the council and representatives from the Youth Association to visit there in the summer for the ceremony. The party, which included the Chief Executive of the Council, Roy Limb and his wife, and Bernie Grant left on 13 July and, although the main party returned at the end of August, Dolly Kiffin did not return to the Estate until 23 September.[65]

Conclusion

Much had been done to turn the estate around. This was primarily due to the political will and administrative leadership that existed within the council, by this time led by Bernie Grant. But the cost was expensive and was unlikely to last if there was a change of leadership. Rent arrears were 'absurdly high' which, given that 80 per cent of the residents were in receipt of housing benefits which covered the full cost, should not have been the case. Therefore the continuation of expensive repairs and the failure to collect rents left the estate vulnerable to a change of administration.[66]

---

65. Gifford, op. cit. 8, p. 57, para. 3.54; Williams, David A, op. cit. 6, p.88, para. 3.7.11.
66. Power, op. cit. 10, p. 202.

CHAPTER THREE

Relationship Between Haringey Council and the Metropolitan Police

Introduction

In 1978, a report sponsored by the Greater London Council (GLC), then under Conservative control, recommended that the sections of the Metropolitan Police that operated 'on a national basis should be detached from those which provide police service for London' and 'closer links should be established through a police committee which would approve the police force budget and have a voice in the appointment of the Commissioner, but not have operational control of the force.'[1]

Sir David McNee, who was then commissioner, claimed that the chairman of the GLC, Sir Horace Cutler, wanted to include the GLC in 'a triumvirate' with the Home Office and the commissioner to oversee 'policing policy'. McNee was against such a policy but had proposed to Home Secretary William Whitelaw that there ought to be formal arrangements for regular consultation between the Home Secretary, the commissioner and the London boroughs. Although Whitelaw apparently agreed, he did nothing about it at the time.[2]

Haringey Borough Council was created in 1965 by the amalgamation of the three former municipal boroughs of Hornsey, Wood Green and Tottenham. It shares borders with six other boroughs, those of Enfield, Waltham Forest, Hackney, Islington, Camden and Barnet. Between 1971 and 1985, the year of the riot, it was Labour controlled. By the beginning of the 1980s, certain 'extremist groups' within Haringey Council were suggesting that it should withdraw 'co-operation from the police, including refusing to take part in identity parades, recruitment campaigns and liaison schemes'. This led to

---

1. Marshall Inquiry Report, para. 13.1 quoted in McNee, Sir David (1983). *McNee's Law*. London: Collins, p.228.
2. McNee, op. cit. 1, p. 229.

a particularly hard-hitting speech by Councillor Jenny Riley, who represented Wood Green, at a law and order debate organized by the GLC. She suggested 'the aim of the extremists was not to create an improved society from the basis of common denominators accepted by the vast majority of [the] population' but 'to intimate, misrepresent and undermine with devious cunning, in order to promote as much social strife as they possibly could.' She continued:

> The bulwark which stands between them and their treacherous aim, here in London, is the Metropolitan police force; therefore they are against the police. Their intent is scurrilous and they are inspired by sedition. They magnify or exaggerate every difficulty that may exist, from time to time, between the police and sections of the community.'[3]

Nevertheless, the Labour Party manifesto issued for the GLC elections of 1981 stated that a Labour controlled GLC would 'invite London boroughs to join in establishing a police committee to monitor the work of the police force as a prelude to their gaining power to control the police'. Later in the manifesto, it went further:

> 'A Labour GLC will campaign for a Police Authority consisting solely of elected members of the GLC and London boroughs to have control of the Metropolitan and City Police. This authority to have the power to appoint all officers to the rank of Chief Superintendent and above, to scrutinize the day to day affairs of the force and to allocate the resources to the various police functions.'[4]

Election of a Labour-controlled GLC

Four weeks after the infamous Brixton riot in April 1981,[5] the county-council elections on 7 May delivered a Labour-controlled GLC led by a young firebrand, Ken Livingstone, who lost no time in setting up a police committee,

---

3. *Weekly Herald* (Tottenham and Wood Green), 31 July 1980.
4. McNee, op. cit. 1, pp. 229–230.
5. See Scarman, The Rt Hon The Lord (1981). The Brixton Disorders 10–12 April 1981. London: Her Majesty's Stationary Office.

putting at its head a young lawyer, Paul Boateng. Only the second black person to be elected to a county council, Boateng's father was from Ghana although his mother was English. Despite coming originally from Africa, Boateng had, from the start of his career as a lawyer, identified with those from the Caribbean.[6] The GLC also made money available for support staff, headed by a former secretary-general of Amnesty International, Martin Ennals, 'to advise and research on policing London.'[7]

The new committee 'had no statutory function' and there were suggestions that it was purely 'political' but Boateng denied that he was pursuing 'a "police-bashing exercise".'[8] Nevertheless, he quickly set about encouraging all London boroughs, particularly those under Labour control to set up police monitoring committees. Reports and publicity emanating from the new GLC Police Committee, or its administration and research unit, ironically named the Police Support Unit (PSU), were almost wholly critical of the police. Indeed, just five months before the Broadwater Farm riot, the PSU issued a film, *Policing London*, which was critical of the way the Metropolitan Police dealt with the black community and distributed it to about 100 London schools.[9]

The Haringey Independent Police Committee was set up in April 1982 with Martha Osamor in the chair and John Kendall as secretary. In announcing the formation of the committee, Kendall said 'This is a campaigning committee — a true police committee has control over the police and that's what we are campaigning for.' The new committee applied to the GLC Police Committee for a grant of £15,000 to enable it to employ a researcher, at the same time claiming that relations between Y District of the Metropolitan Police and the people of Haringey had 'given rise to considerable concern over the past years' and a number of examples were cited. However, having been approved by the chair, Paul Boateng, it was turned down by the full committee by one vote.[10] Nevertheless, from 1984, by which time it had

---

6. Brain, Timothy (2010). *A History of Policing in England and Wales from 1974: A Turbulent Journey*. Oxford: Oxford University Press, p.71: Phillips, Mike and Trevor Phillips (1998). *Windrush: The Irresistible Rise of Multi-Racial Britain*. London: HarperCollins, p.371.
7. Kettle, Martin, and Lucy Hodges (1982). *Uprising! The Police, the People and the Riots in Britain's Cities*. London: Pan Books, p.221.
8. Brain, op. cit. 6, p.71.
9. Coolican, Don (1985). Hate on the Rates. *Daily Express*, 10 October.
10. Weekly Herald (Tottenham and Wood Green), dated 8 April 1982.

become a sub-committee of the Haringey Community Relations Council, it was serviced by a police research unit consisting of three members.[11]

In August 1982, an instruction was issued from Scotland Yard which effectively banned the passing of information to the GLC Police Committee Support Unit and directed any requests for information to be referred to the Community Relations (A7) Branch.[12] The head of Y District, Commander Dickinson, quickly followed by issuing a memorandum prohibiting the passing of any information to people representing the Haringey Independent Police Committee.[13]

The following month, September, the newly-formed committee, 'condemned' the police for the way the Broadwater Farm Estate was policed and said it would: (a) develop a policy for investigating and dealing with racists who attacked and harassed black families on council estates'; (b) 'set up an inquiry into the policing of council estates' generally; and (c) set up 'an information service to inform residents of their rights.'[14] Two months later, the local newspaper reported that 'antagonism towards the local police' had 'intensified' as a result of which the committee had set up a 24-hour telephone line to which people could complain about the police and youths living in Haringey were issued with telephone contact cards 'for use when arrested'.[15]

Following a commitment in the Haringey Labour Party manifesto for the local elections earlier in the year, the Independent Police Committee was taken over by Haringey Council as a sub-committee of the Community Affairs Group at the end of 1982. Consisting of five Labour and two Conservative councillors, its aims were ambitious to say the least:

- Campaign for a change in the law to make the police accountable to the community;
- Study issues of policing, law and order in Haringey, London and the country;

---

11. Gifford, Lord (1986). The Broadwater Farm Inquiry: Report of the Independent Inquiry into Disturbances of October 1985 at the Broadwater Farm Estate, Tottenham. London: Broadwater Farm Inquiry, p.53, para. 3.44.
12. Metropolitan Police General Memorandum 7/82, dated 12 August 1982.
13. Y District Instruction, dated 22 August 1982.
14. *Weekly Herald* (Tottenham and Wood Green), 30 September 1982.
15. Ibid, 12 November 1982.

- Monitor racial attacks and harassment within Haringey and police relations with minority communities;
- Monitor the treatment of suspects;
- Keep an eye on police policies and operations and get feedback from the community;
- Discuss complaints against police actions, and where appropriate, ask the police to account for their actions;
- Promote greater understanding of policing issues, including the social and economic causes of crime, the need for more effective policing of racial attacks and the legal rights of both the public and the police;
- Work with the Greater London Council, other London boroughs and community groups and make recommendations and representations to the police and government.

Chair of the Community Affairs Committee, Philip Jones, was quick to point out that they were 'talking about accountability, not just liaison.'[16]

Haringey and the Metropolitan Police

There were no formal arrangements under which senior officers from Y District met with the senior management team of Haringey Council and vice-versa. However, as the Council's Chief Executive Officer, Roy Limb, explained to the Gifford Inquiry, meetings took place between the two when necessary.[17] Thus when the relationship between the police and some frequenters of the estate began to deteriorate in 1982, as described in *Chapter 4*, it was agreed at a meeting between senior officers on Y District and councillors in mid-August that the police would regularly meet with residents of the estate.

---

16. Smith, Jane, and Peter Guner (1982). 'Police and the Community'. *Weekly Herald* (Tottenham and Wood Green), 2 December, pp. 16–17.
17. Gifford, op. cit. 11, p.53, para. 3.43.

First attempt to set up formal arrangements

The first meeting took place six days later at council premises in Willan Road. In the absence of Bernie Grant, the local councillor, the meeting was chaired by Councillor Ernie Large. Also in attendance from the council were Chief Executive Roy Limb and a member of the Borough's education department. Dolly Kiffin was present along with 50 predominantly black members of the community. The police delegation was led by the officer in command of Tottenham Division, Chief Superintendent Bert Steele. Also in attendance were the Deputy Community Liaison Officer, Inspector Russ Horne, the sergeant in charge of Probationary Training on the division, two home beat officers and three probationary constables, one of whom was a woman. There was no agenda and much of the formal part of the meeting consisted of black youths quoting individual examples of 'bad treatment and demeanour' by police officers in their contact with the youths. In responding, the police 'were frequently noisily interrupted by other members of the audience'. However, once the formal part of the meeting had closed, smaller informal groups formed and the discussion between individual police officers and the youths became more 'amiable.'[18]

The second meeting at the beginning of September was conducted in 'a much better atmosphere', partly because Dolly Kiffin and youth worker Stafford Scott exercised some control over the 'more excitable and disruptive elements.' It was agreed that young probationers participating in the Street Duties Course at Tottenham would visit the Youth Association. In return, the youths requested a visit to the Metropolitan Police Training Centre at Hendon to observe the training in 'racial awareness' given to recruits and it was agreed that 12 would make the visit.[19] A coach was laid on by the police but, unfortunately, on the appointed day, only three youths turned up and the visit was cancelled.[20]

A third meeting took place at the end of September but the police were not represented. Three incidents that month led Dolly Kiffin to withdraw from formal police contacts. The first was the arrest of one of her sons; the

---

18. Tottenham Police Report, 26 August 1982.
19. Ibid, 8 September 1982.
20. Ibid, 4 November 1982.

second related to a short but relatively brief incursion onto the estate one evening by officers on foot from the Y District Immediate Response Unit,[21] and the third to the arrest of a youth for burglary who was to become very prominent in the events that were to unfold. As a result of these incidents Dolly Kiffin told council officials that she did not want the police to attend the meeting and, unfortunately, the council agreed.[22] No further meetings were arranged and the first attempt at creating some kind of formal arrangements to meet and discuss problems over the policing of the estate collapsed, not because of the police but because council officials had bowed to pressure exerted by a self-appointed, but influential member of the community.

More ad-hoc meetings

Nevertheless, senior officers, led by Commander Dickinson, did meet with representatives from Haringey Council, led by the council leader, Angela Greatley, at the Civic Centre in Wood Green at the beginning of November. Dickinson was accompanied by Chief Superintendent Steele and the new Community Liaison Officer, Chief Inspector Paul Gormley. Greatley was accompanied by the deputy leader, Bernie Grant, Councillor Ernie Large and Chief Executive Roy Limb. Policing of the estate had recently increased and Councillor Greatley expressed the council's concern over what it saw as a deterioration in police/community relations. In response Commander Dickinson outlined the alternatives:

- No policing, in which case it became a 'no-go area' which would be unacceptable to the Metropolitan Police;
- Home beat officers patrolling normally; this had been working fairly successfully until recent events when the police had been subjected to incidents of violence and it had therefore become unacceptable on personal safety grounds;
- Heavier foot patrols. In pointing out that it was only a small majority of those on the estate who did not want it, he claimed it had been welcomed by the majority.

---

21. An immediate response unit normally consisted of an inspector and/or sergeant and ten constables.
22. Tottenham Police Report, 27 and 29 September 1982.

The police did make three requests of the council. The first was that representatives should be identified from within the community who could have some influence on the people resident on the estate. Secondly, that the meetings between councillors, police and residents that had been organized so successfully in August and September should be resumed. Thirdly, that a meeting should be set up between the leader of the council and the police commander to discuss the setting up of a police committee in accordance with the Home Office guidelines[23] following Lord Scarman's recommendation in his report on the 1981 Brixton riot that there should be consultative arrangements between the police and London boroughs.[24] The police received no response to these three requests.

Key relationships

The relationship between Haringey Council and the Metropolitan Police mainly revolved around two people, Bernie Grant and Commander Jim Dickinson. Originally from Guyana, Bernie Grant had taken a mining engineering degree course at Heriot-Watt University in Edinburgh. For a brief period in the mid-1960s, he was a member of the Socialist Labour League but quickly became a trade union official. In 1978, he was elected as a Labour councillor to Haringey Council. In 1985, he led the fight against 'rate capping' in Haringey. As a result, there was a split in the local Labour Party and Grant became the leader of the council in March 1985.[25]

Commander Dickinson was an officer 'steeped in the finest traditions of the Metropolitan Police.' He had been appointed as Commander Y District in February 1981. Many of those who served with him regarded him as 'a policeman's policeman'.[26] Indeed, he was given an exceptional send-off when the local representatives of the Police Federation arranged a farewell dinner

---

23. Ibid, 4 November 1982.
24. Scarman, op. cit. 5, p. 96, para. 5.70.
25. Grant, Eric A (2006). *Dawn to Dusk: A Biography of Bernie Grant, MP.* London: Huric Books, p.66.
26. The reports suggested he 'was totally unsuited to the cut and thrust of debate and was frequently unable to see the long term implications of many of his decisions especially when these touched upon relations with the local authority.' Williams, David A (1986). Internal Police Report on the disorders of the 6th October 1985 at the Broadwater Farm Estate, Tottenham. London: Metropolitan Police, p. 78.

for him when he retired in June 1985.[27] He was awarded the Queen's Police Medal for services to policing in June 1984.[28] The Williams Report suggested, however, that the job required something a little different to a 'policeman's policeman', particularly after the publication of the Scarman Report into the Brixton riot of 1981.[29]

Dickinson was no stranger to the political arena having served on the neighbouring Labour-controlled London Borough of Hackney, or G District as it was known in the Metropolitan Police. But, he was always suspicious and authoritarian in his contacts with politicians. He was, the report suggested, 'unsuited to the cut and thrust of debate' which was then part of a senior officer's role, and was, on occasions, not able 'to see the long term implications of many of his decisions especially where these touched upon relations with the local authority'.[30]

Nevertheless, by the end of his first year in charge of Y District, Commander Dickinson had become aware of the gradually worsening state of police/community relations on the Broadwater Farm Estate and resolved to assume complete operational control of policing initiatives on the estate.[31]

Second invitation to work together

Despite a call from within the council for a policy of non-cooperation with the police, the police were invited to attend meetings of the sub-committee on policing. Dickinson refused. Claiming that it appeared the council wanted a 'master servant' relationship, he pointed out that his responsibility remained with the commissioner who, in turn, was accountable to the Home Secretary. However, he was 'happy to talk to councillors on a one-to-one basis'.[32]

Consequently, he wrote back to the sub-committee saying: 'My constitutional position, as police commander responsible to the Commissioner and then the Home Secretary, debars me from involvement in the schemes outlined in the letter.' This was not entirely accurate as Gifford was quick

---

27. Harrison, John, MBE (2014). In correspondence with the author, dated 21 July.
28. Supplement to the *London Gazette*, 16 June 1984, p. B26.
29. Scarman, op. cit. 5.
30. Williams, David A, op. cit. 26, p. 78, para. 3.4.1.
31. Ibid, para. 3.4.2.
32. *Weekly Herald* (Tottenham and Wood Green), 2 December 1982.

to point out. The law did not allow Dickinson to be 'answerable to the local authority', but it did not prevent 'cooperation and consultation' with the council through appropriate channels. Local senior officers in other parts of London were cooperating with the council police committees and in at least one case attended meetings as observers. He claimed that the attitude of Commander Dickinson in refusing to speak or write to the council's police sub-committee was petty-minded and unhelpful for community relations.[33]

Police policy in relation to the Estate

Sir Kenneth Newman became the Commissioner of the Metropolitan Police in early autumn 1982. Within months of taking over, he submitted a preliminary assessment of the problems and priorities of the Metropolitan Police to the Home Secretary in which he clearly said, 'the focus of responsibility in police operations is the chief superintendent' to the extent that 'it would make sense to ensure that they could deploy all the resources in their command areas, with certain agreed or accepted constraints, to achieve the best results.'[34] It does seem that, perhaps for reasons outlined in *Chapters 4 and 5*, there was a constraint in respect of symbolic locations because there is ample evidence to suggest that, in such cases, the control of police operations was exercised by the commander of the district rather than the divisional chief superintendent.[35]

There was also a lack of continuity in the role of the divisional commander at Tottenham. In the three-and-a-half years between April 1982 and October 1985 when the riot occurred, it had four chief superintendents. In April 1982, Peter Taylor was replaced by Herbert Steele who was, in turn, replaced by David J Williams in March 1983. Williams left in May 1984 on his

---

33. Gifford, op. cit. 11, p.53, para. 3.45.
34. Newman, Sir Kenneth (1983). Preliminary Assessment of Problems and Priorities: Report of The Commissioner of Police of the Metropolis to the Home Secretary. Typescript Newman, p.10, para. 27.
35. For All Saints Road, Notting Hill, see Moore, Tony (2013). *Policing Notting Hill: Fifty Years of Turbulence*. Waterside Press, pp. 261–287; re Sandringham Road, Hackney, see Keith, Michael (1993). *Race, Riots and Policing: Lore and Disorder in a Multi-racist Society*. London: UCL, pp. 33–43 and 134–146; for Railton Road, Brixton, see Marnoch, Commander Alec (1992). Brixton SW9: Post-Conflict Policing. In *Community Disorders and Policing: Conflict Management in Action*, edited by Tony F Marshall. London: Whiting & Birch, pp. 93–100.

appointment as Assistant Chief Constable of Hertfordshire Constabulary. He was succeeded by Colin Macdonald who spent only a month in post before being replaced by Colin Couch in July 1984. Commander Dickinson made in abundantly clear to all four chief superintendents that, whilst he was prepared to accept advice from them and his community liaison officer, policing policy for the Broadwater Farm Estate was under his direct supervision and there were almost daily consultations. All were of the same mind, however, that community policing was the way forward.[36] But, at the same time, there was an understanding at senior level that the policy of 'turning the other cheek' was inevitably going to lead to a certain amount of impatience amongst junior ranks and there would be a risk of misunderstanding of the motives of police amongst the local populace.[37] Regrettably, this does not appear to have been addressed with any success.

More moderate local administration

In May 1983, the local council elections resulted in a more moderate administration in Haringey.[38] A meeting with police was requested by the administration and took place shortly afterwards at the Civic Centre, chaired by the new leader of the council, Councillor Meehan, three other councillors were present, including the chairman of the Haringey Police Sub-Committee. Led by Dolly Kiffin, five representatives from the Broadwater Farm Youth Association also attended. The police were led by Commander Dickinson, accompanied by the Tottenham divisional commander and his deputy, Chief Superintendent D J Williams and Superintendent D A Williams, the CLO, Chief Inspector John Gormley, Inspector Dudley Gritty and Sergeant Peter Palmer, who were in charge of the team of officers designated to patrol the estate, and four officers from that team. Two months later a further, broader based meeting was held. Of the meeting, Commander Dickinson wrote:

---

36. Williams, David A, op. cit. 26, p.72, para. 3.2.1.
37. Ibid, p. 72, para. 3.2.2.
38. *Hornsey Journal*, 13 May 1983.

'…a tenuous understanding developed from the other side of police problems and responsibilities…Tolerance reigned and I feel the meeting did serve the purpose of bringing a greater understanding between police and residents.'[39]

Despite the more moderate administration, Chief Superintendent David J Williams felt the borough failed 'to participate in meaningful discussions with a view to setting up a consultative body as recommended by the Home Office guidelines' although it continued to support its own police sub-committee, consisting of seven councillors, 'to discuss questions of police accountability', which in no way met the guidelines.[40]

Third invitation to work together

By the time the third invitation to work together came, Chief Superintendent Couch was firmly in the chair. He was described in the internal report following the riot as 'an intellectual' who was a 'firm believer in consensus policing'. However, at the same time, it was said that, under certain circumstances, he recognised that there was a 'need for hard-nosed tactical policing'.[41]

Following his arrival, there was every reason to believe that things were improving. In October 1984, police were invited by the London Borough of Haringey to be represented when the Leader of the Greater London Council, Ken Livingstone, visited the estate to formally open the Broadwater Farm Youth Association. In February 1985, they were again represented on the occasion of a visit by Her Royal Highness The Princess of Wales.

More importantly, perhaps, the council had set up a sub-committee, known as the Broadwater Farm Panel in 1984 'to bring together the council, the Tenants Association, the Youth Association, and other agencies' to discuss and make decisions on issues which were of concern to the Estate'[42] The panel was anxious to include the police in what was developing into a very useful forum for the discussion by different agencies of problems relating

---

39. Minute by Commander Y District to Commander A7, dated 12 July 1983 on the Broadwater Farm Estate File, No. OG 48/83/7, quoted in Williams, David A, op. cit. 15, p.75, para.3.2.12.
40. Williams, David J (1984). Policing Symbolic Locations: a case for differential policing. Bramshill Papers, Ref. 367/3, p. 4, para. 2.1.
41. Williams, David A, op. cit. 26, p.79.
42. Gifford, op. cit. 11, p.30, para. 2.49.

to the estate. An invitation to participate, underwritten by the then Deputy Leader of the Council, Bernie Grant, was initially accepted by Commander Dickinson, on the recommendation of his community liaison officer and Chief Superintendent Couch. However, when Councillor Grant wrote to Chief Superintendent Couch on 23 January 1985,[43] the invitation contained what was to prove a major stumbling block to police participation. That was the demand that a written report 'setting out the current arrangements for policing the Estate' should be submitted prior to the meeting. According to the Williams Report, when the question of attendance at the Broadwater Farm Panel was first muted, there was also a suggestion that the names of the police representatives should be vetted by the London Borough of Haringey but there was no mention of this being the case in the letter to Couch. Commander Dickinson took the view that both requirements were part of a plan to make police more accountable to local government authorities, particularly those controlled by the Labour Party, rather than the Home Secretary. He was also concerned to keep the Metropolitan Police away from the vagaries of local party politics. Privately, he admitted that his uncompromising attitude was unlikely to achieve a state of harmony in which discussions could progress; in public, he defended his position by pointing to the similarly unyielding stance of Bernie Grant and others on the extreme left-wing of the Labour Party who were in the majority on the Council.[44]

Chief Superintendent Couch replied to the letter on 5 February:

> 'I and my officers attend numerous meetings to respond to community issues and demands, and never has a request been made for a "written report" in the council style. If we did, I and my staff would be permanently preparing reports instead of combatting the increasing crime rate, racial harassment and the problems of minority groups. In your position as ward councillor, I am always willing to inform you of current trends and issues affecting local policing, but I am not prepared to report in advance to the council-sponsored "panel" which makes recommendations to the appropriate committee of the council.'

---

43. Letter from Councillor Bernie Grant to Chief Superintendent Colin Couch, dated 23 January 1985.
44. Williams, David A, op. cit. 26, p.77, para. 3.3.4.

He concluded that, together with Chief Inspector Stacey, he would be happy to meet with Grant in his office at Tottenham Police Station to discuss the matter further.[45] Gifford suggested that this response bore the imprint of Commander Dickinson.[46] Grant eventually responded two months later, accepting Couch's invitation but he wanted to bring a number of people with him, including 'a representative from each of the Broadwater Farm Tenants and Youth Associations and also 'Neale Coleman, the Broadwater Farm Neighbourhood Officer, and an officer from the police sub-committee research unit.'[47]

Chief Superintendent Couch replied on 9 May, expressing 'reservations' about the number of people Grant intended to bring with him, pointing out that from the police he intended there should only be two of them. He proposed:

> 'If you feel that such numbers are required to meet police, then I doubt if we are starting off on the right foot. I would like to know what you require of the police before I meet what appears to me to be a vetting group.'

However, he reiterated that he 'would be delighted' for one of his chief inspectors to be a member of the panel.[48] It appears that the matter ended there, with no further written communications between the two.

The negative result of this exchange of correspondence was that police officers never attended the Broadwater Farm Panel before the 6 October disturbances. The Gifford Report described it as a valuable lost opportunity, laying the blame firmly at the door of the police.[49] The internal inquiry report, produced by the Metropolitan Police, was a little more measured suggesting that 'the stiff and unbending attitudes adopted by the London Borough of Haringey were reciprocated in full' by the senior management of the local police. But, it expressed surprise that, having initially agreed to join the panel and make oral contributions to the discussions, the provision

---

45. Letter from Chief Superintendent Couch to Councillor Bernie Grant, dated 5 February.
46. Gifford, op. cit. 11, p. 54, para. 3.47.
47. Letter from Councillor Bernie Grant to Chief Superintendent Couch, dated 10 April 1985.
48. Letter from Chief Superintendent Colin Couch to Councillor Bernie Grant, dated 9 May 1985.
49. Gifford, op. cit. 11, p.55, para. 3.48.

of a written report was allowed to become an obstacle to police participation. The report continued:

> 'If the Metropolitan Police genuinely wanted a community which was receptive to its presence and supportive of its methods it could not in all conscience allow matters of minor dogma to stand resolutely in the way. As to the question of the submission of police officers to a process of vetting, this was purely a matter upon which negotiations could proceed albeit that the subject matter was a great deal more contentious.'[50]

The report summed up the situation thus:

> 'Predictably, both sides blamed each other that the invitation to join the Broadwater Panel had not been taken up. The decision was seen by at least one community worker as evidence of the lack of sincerity and commitment by the police to the ethos of good community relations. Once again the police were being viewed as the weak link, unprepared to join, for whatever reason, with other agencies in creating a harmonious society.'[51]

The tragic result was that, in the lead up to the events of 6 October, the police never had a chance to discuss any of the policing problems which began to emerge in the summer of 1985 in the open forum that the panel would have provided. In evidence to the Gifford Inquiry, Councillor Grant viewed this as a tragedy in itself, suggesting:

> '…that if the police had come onto the Broadwater Farm Panel from as early as January 1985 when we had invited them to, then I believe that we would have not had those disturbances on 6 October on Broadwater Farm. Because if the police had any problem with regard to the estate, they would have been able to put it down in front of the panel, we would have discussed it properly, it would have been reported on. The Youth Association was represented there, and the Tenants Association, and the matter could have been resolved."[52]

---

50. Williams, David A. op. cit. 26, pp. 77–78, para. 3.3.5.
51. Ibid, p.78, para. 3.3.6.
52. Gifford, op. cit. 11, p. 55, para. 3.48.

Whether this would have been the case is a matter of conjecture. It may well be that the circumstances surrounding the death of Cynthia Jarrett and her son's association with the Youth Association would still have taken matters to another level.

A fourth opportunity for police and council to work together

The next chapter in this history of failed opportunities between the police and the council concerned the Haringey Community and Police Consultative Group. The proposal made by Lord Scarman for a statutory consultative scheme had been incorporated into the Police and Criminal Evidence Act 1984, section 106 which provided:

> 'Arrangements shall be made in each police area for obtaining the views of people in that area about matters concerning the policing of the area and for obtaining their co-operation with the police in preventing crime in the area.'

In London it was the duty of the commissioner to make the arrangements in accordance with guidance issued by the Home Secretary, although he was required to consult with the council of each London borough as to the arrangements that would be appropriate for the borough.[53]

It will be recalled that Commander Dickinson had first requested discussions about the setting up of a police consultative group at a meeting in November 1982 but had received no response. Therefore, on 27 February 1985, he wrote formally to Chief Executive Officer Roy Limb asking for discussions 'with the leader and yourself'. This it will be recalled was whilst Grant and Couch were in correspondence about police participation in the Broadwater Farm Panel. On 2 April 1985, Councillor Narenda Makanji, chair of the Haringey Police Sub-committee, replied to Commander Dickinson. He observed that membership of the existing sub-committee broadly coincided with the recommendations contained in the Home Office guidance and suggested that 'the terms of reference of the council's police sub-committee provide an appropriate basis for this area's consultation arrangements'.

---

53. Home Office Circular No. 54/1982. 'Local consultation arrangements between the community and the police', June 1982.

Accordingly he invited the Metropolitan Police Y District to enter into an arrangement for consultation on the basis of these existing terms of reference. The Gifford Report suggested that 'in writing this letter, the council was itself indulging in obstructive tactics' and 'it must have been quite apparent to them that Commander Dickinson could not possibly agree to enter into consultative arrangements on the basis of the police sub-committee's terms of reference, when the Home Office guidance stressed the importance of arrangements being independent of local authority structures.' Dickinson reply was described as 'swift and inevitable', concluding that he was 'not able to discuss consultative arrangements on this basis further.'[54]

Force reorganization

In early 1985, Sir Kenneth Newman commenced a re-organization of the Metropolitan Police which was still in progress when the Broadwater Farm riot occurred. Instead of the 24 districts, each under the direction of a commander, there would be eight areas, each under the command of a deputy assistant commissioner. One of the ideas behind these changes was to increase the responsibility of divisional commanders, i.e. chief superintendents, for local policy-making.

Commander Dickinson retired from the Metropolitan Police in June 1985. His replacement was Chief Superintendent Ted Hodge who was appointed acting commander pending the abolition of districts. Hodge was a career detective who had been transferred to Y District as the district chief superintendent in March 1984. When, in June 1985, he assumed control of the district, albeit for only three months, he determined that the policy laid down by Dickinson should remain.[55]

By mid-September, re-organization of the force had been partially implemented. The district structure remained but chief superintendents were beginning to assume the greater responsibility that the re-organization intended. This placed Hodge in a difficult position. On the one hand, as acting commander, he was expected to guide the policing practices that were being implemented on the district and be answerable for them. On

---

54. Gifford, op. cit. 11, pp. 55–56, paras. 3.50–3.51.
55. Williams, David A, op. cit. 26, p. 84, paras. 3.6.1–3.62.

the other hand, he was a career CID officer, unfamiliar with the concepts of public order policing, equal in rank to the divisional commanders and aware of the extended autonomy that was now theirs.[56]

One immediate practical effect of the re-organization was the passing of the file relating to Broadwater Farm by Commander Dickinson to Chief Superintendent Couch in June 1985. It was, if you like, a symbolic handing over of the responsibility for policing The Farm from the commander to the local chief superintendent. Although nothing was said, it was implicit that henceforth the chief superintendent at Tottenham was responsible for policing The Farm. However, as will be seen in *Chapter 5*, Hodge continued to influence the policy for policing the estate.

Fifth and final attempt

Despite the negative outcome of the fourth attempt, immediately on taking up his new appointment as the new area deputy assistant commissioner, towards the end of May, Mike Richards invited the council to attend an exploratory meeting at the beginning of June, at which, the setting up of a consultative committee in accordance with Section 106 of the Police and Criminal Evidence Act 1984, and the Home Office guidelines would be discussed. Home Office guidance suggested that 'if a group is to have the confidence of the local community as the focus for local consultations on policing matters, it is essential that its memberships should be as representative as possible of that community.' According to Richards, a good section of community representatives had been invited and would be present. However, it seems that this was not the case. Those invited were predominantly neighbourhood watch schemes, tenants' organizations, and established organizations such as the Church, London Transport and the Probation Service. Indeed, of the 21 organizations present, only six appeared to be black or minority ethnic organizations despite the fact that about 44 per cent of the borough's population was from the ethnic minorities and there were approximately 230 black or ethnic minority organizations listed with

---

56. Ibid, pp. 84–85, para. 3.6.3.

Haringey Council. The council considered that it had not been properly consulted and declined to attend this meeting.[57]

The Haringey Community and Police Consultative Group which was subsequently formed met for the first time less than four weeks after the riot, on 31 October. In evidence to the Gifford Inquiry, the chair of the group, Eric Clark admitted that it was not representative of the Haringey community, in that there were far too few from black organizations. Indeed, one of the organizations represented described the mood at the first few meetings as 'populist' with 'anger' being 'directed primarily against Haringey Council'. Gifford pointed out that the council had 'a serious responsibility to bear for [this] situation' because 'it deprived itself of the opportunity to insist on a truly representative membership list' when 'it indulged in obstructive tactics' right at the outset.[58]

Conclusion

There is no doubt that for much of the four years leading up to the riot, local policing policy was heavily influenced by the attitudes of Haringey Borough Council and more latterly, a long-time resident of Broadwater Farm, Mrs Dolly Kiffin, who was the driving force in setting up the Youth Association and about which more will be said in the following two chapters. Suffice to say at this stage, that 'whilst she did not regard the police particularly highly, she nevertheless, recognised that relations between them and the young blacks could only be improved if lines of communication were kept open.' Senior officers, in particular, 'recognised that she had a difficult role in maintaining her credibility and influence "with an often fickle youth"' and 'at the same time acting as a moderating factor when tensions began to rise. The Williams Report claimed that it was 'for this reason as much as any other [that] she was given a degree of freedom which, from time-to-time, caused friction within the service between senior officers and those on the streets.'[59]

---

57. Ibid, p. 85, para. 3.6.4.
58. Gifford, op. cit. 11, pp. 208–213, paras. 8.40–8.51.
59. Williams, David A, op. cit. 26, p. 72, para. 7.1.9.

CHAPTER FOUR

Policing the Estate from 1973 to mid-1984

Introduction

From the time the Broadwater Farm Estate was complete to the riot was 12 years. In policing terms, the first seven years were relatively uneventful. Tony Rowe, who served at Tottenham as chief inspector (operations) from 1977 to 1979 described it as a busy station that 'involved the whole range of urban policing challenges'.[1] Ian Clarke, who arrived at Tottenham as an inspector in 1980 described it as a very busy station but pointed out that it had 'a number of mixed communities, Jewish, Greek, Turkish Cypriot, African-Caribbean and native British, any of which at times could become confrontational.[2] White Hart Lane, the home of Tottenham Hotspur Football Club was less than a mile from the estate. The club, which played in the First Division of the Football League (now the Premiership) regularly attracted crowds of around 45,000 to home matches and, in the period immediately leading up to the riot, were relatively successful, winning the FA Cup in 1980–1981 and again in 1981–1982, and the UEFA Cup in 1983–1984. Disorder between rival fans both before and after games frequently kept the police busy on match days.

Once complete, the estate produced similar policing challenges to those experienced in many other housing estates around the country—with a slight difference. Not only did its layout make it 'easily defensible' when police attempted 'to take positive action', but 'the design, particularly the walkways and ground level parking areas' gave greater opportunity to those who wanted to commit crime.[3] Paul Ritchie, who arrived at Tottenham as a probationary constable direct from training school, described initially how

---
1. Rowe, Tony (2014). In correspondence with the author, dated 6 August 2014.
2. Clarke, Ian (2014). In correspondence with the author, dated 16 October 2014.
3. Williams, David J (1984). Policing Symbolic Locations: A Case for Differential Policing. Bramshill Papers (typescript), p. 6, para. 2.6.

police constables patrolled 'the estate as part of their normal police duties, serving the community as a whole, arresting those elements committing crimes against the community.' He claimed 'policing was done in a calm, helpful and polite manner', although when necessary the 'lawful use of force' was utilised but always with the principle of 'no more force than is necessary' in mind. Finally, he stressed that they 'were all community policemen' whether they 'were walking the beat or driving a patrol car.'[4]

Events elsewhere

A significant report produced internally by Commander Kenneth Newman, then head of the Metropolitan Police's Race Relations Branch, coincided with the completion of the Estate in 1973. Entitled 'The Policing of Racially Sensitive Areas' it outlined 'the causes and implications of the potentially dangerous tension' that existed between police and black youths 'in some racially sensitive divisions.'[5] The paper commenced by analysing 'the nature and causes of tension' of which there were eight, before identifying six areas of possible conflict, three of which were relevant to the Broadwater Farm Estate:

- It took little to attract a crowd when making an arrest in an immigrant area, which could be 'quick to perceive the police action as discriminatory and quick to exchange curiosity for anger.' He suggested there needed to be 'more guidelines for making arrests in immigrant areas, not for the point of view of going soft... but simply to make police action more effective.'
- There had been too many occasions when the police had been confronted with 'upwards of 200 hostile black youths', with its ensuing potential for serious public disorder, following an incident in the vicinity of a black youth club. Police action on such occasions needed to be quick, effective and adequately supervised.

4. Ritchie, P.J.N (1986). 'Your View—Broadwater Farm: Roots of Riot.' In *Police*, Vol. XVIII, No. 6, February, p. 18.
5. Newman, K.L, Commander (1973). 'The Policing of Racially Sensitive Divisions.' London: Metropolitan Police, typescript, p.1.

- Pointing out that West Indians were 'ultra-sensitive about police officers entering their homes', Newman suggested that their hands were strengthened if they were in possession of a search warrant.[6]

He also suggested that community relations programmes tended to be regarded as 'peripheral to the main operational activities of the force' but they were 'an integral part of law enforcement' because:
- They increased communication and decreased hostility between operational officers and immigrants;
- The officers involved in community relations sought to enlist the understanding and support of West Indian leaders;
- Community relations personnel could mitigate hostility and reduce operational difficulties by preventing the spread of unjustified rumour and suspicion; The relations they had with the community often enabled community relations officers to collect, evaluate and disseminate information essential to operational decision-making in immigrant areas.[7]

The flaw with this argument was that the West Indian leaders with whom the community relations personnel were in touch rarely represented the vociferous minority who were likely to and did cause a breakdown in law and order.

At the conclusion of his paper, Newman recommended the setting up of a working party to consider what command and control policies and procedures should be put in place to reduce the number of confrontations between police officers and black youths and to consider how community relation activities could be integrated more effectively with operational needs.[8] Insofar as the author is aware this was never done.

---

6. Ibid, pp. 8–11, paras 17–18; a more detailed outline of the paper can be found in Moore, Tony (2013). *Policing Notting Hill: Fifty Years of Turbulence*. Hook, Hampshire: Waterside Press, pp. 153–159.
7. Ibid, pp. 12–13, paras 19–23.
8. Ibid, pp. 13–14, paras 25–26.

Notting Hill Carnival riot

Three years after the completion of the estate, the Metropolitan Police received its first serious warning that everything was not right in its policing of ethnic communities, particularly those of African-Caribbean origin.[9] At the end of August 1976, serious rioting, which went on for some four hours, occurred at the annual Notting Hill Carnival in West London. It has variously been described as 'a full scale battle... by black youth against the police'[10] and 'one of the worst outbreaks of public disorder in London since the second world war.'[11] Over 1,000 crimes, in some of which considerable violence was used, were committed over the two days of the carnival and a total of 413 police officers were injured. The police made only 84 arrests, of which only 20 were for what could genuinely classified as crimes.[12] Although there is no record of anyone from the Broadwater Farm Estate being involved in the disorder, it was, nevertheless, the first example of how the black youth could take on the police in London and, if not win, impose humiliation on the ability of the Metropolitan Police to deal with serious public disorder.

'Sus'

Meanwhile, another problem between the police and the ethnic communities was growing in significance. Throughout the 1970s, black youths in particular 'were regarded with suspicion' in London[13] and consequently they were frequently stopped and searched under Section 66 of the Metropolitan

---

9. It has been suggested that the Metropolitan Police received a first serious warning as a result of the Race Riots in Notting Hill in 1958. But on this occasion, the disorder was primarily between the indigenous population and those of African-Caribbean descent with the police trying to keep the opposing factions apart.
10. Howe, D (1977). *The Road Make to Walk on Carnival Day*. London: Race Today Collective, p.11.
11. Annual Report of the Commissioner of Police of the Metropolis for the Year 1976. London: HMSO, p. 10.
12. For a full description of the riot and its immediate aftermath, see Moore, op. cit. 6, pp. 163–190.
13. Benyon, John (1986). 'A Tale of Failure: Race and Policing.' Policy Papers in *Ethnic Relations* No. 3. Warwick: Centre for Research in Ethnic Relations, University of Warwick, p.33; see also Gordon, Paul (1983). *White Law: Racism in the Police, Courts and Prisons*. London: Pluto, pp. 32–35 and Phillips, Mike and Trevor Phillips (1998). *Windrush: The Irresistible Rise of Multi-Racial Britain*. London: HarperCollins, pp. 302–310.

Police Act, 1839, and/or arrested for being a suspected person, commonly known as 'sus', under Section 4 of the Vagrancy Act 1824.[14] A report published by the Runnymede Trust in 1978 claimed that of the 2,112 people who had been charged with 'sus' in 1976, 42 per cent were black.[15] Another report, this time instigated by the Home Office Research Branch reported in 1979 that a black person was 15 times more likely to be arrested for this offence than a white person.[16]

Chief Constable John Alderson described 'the notorious "sus" law' as 'a national scandal, due first of all to its abuse by some police officers against young male residents of the poor inner-city areas (particularly black citizens), and secondly because the idea was offensive to [the] modern notions of justice.'[17] Ramdin described how it was used:

> 'Two or three youths are walking down the street or standing at a bus stop. The police swoop and arrest them. The charges are loitering with intent to steal or attempting to steal from a person or persons unknown. There is, in most cases, some resistance which leads to an additional charge of assault on police.'[18]

From an early stage, it appeared some of the black youths from the Broadwater Farm Estate suffered from the ready use of the 'sus' law. Rose described how, in 1976, five black youths went to Bow Street Magistrates' Court to support a friend appearing on a theft charge. At the lunch adjournment they 'walked into Covent Garden — followed by four detectives who had been involved in the case' and all were promptly arrested for 'sus' and were convicted. On another occasion, another youth from The Farm had gone to Oxford Street with friends, and was arrested for 'sus'.[19] As a consequence, the 'sus' law created much resentment amongst the black community.

---

14. The 1824 Vagrancy Act had been introduced to deal with the many 'idle and disorderly persons' in London as a result of the wholesale demobilisation of soldiers who had fought in the war against Napoleon from 1803 - 1815.
15. Demuth, Clare (1978). '"Sus": A Report on the Vagrancy Act'. London: Runnymede Trust.
16. Stevens, Phillip and Carole Willis (1979). 'Race, Crime and Arrests'. Home Office Research Study No. 58. London: Her Majesty's Stations Office, pp. 31–33.
17. Alderson, John (1984). *Law and Disorder*. London: Hamish Hamilton, p.36.
18. Ramdin, Ron (1987). *The Making of the Black Working Class in Britain*. Aldershot: Wildwood House, p. 479.
19. Rose, David (1992). *A Climate of Fear: The Murder of PC Blakelock and the Case of the Tottenham Three*. London: Bloomsbury, pp. 25–26.

Following a report by the Home Affairs Select Committee, section 4 of the Vagrancy Act was finally repealed by virtue of the Criminal Attempts Act 1981. But the damage had been done!

Institute of Race Relations

Sir David McNee had been Commissioner of the Metropolitan Police for two years when, in 1979, he pointed out that 'policing a multi-racial society' was 'putting the fabric of our policing philosophy under greater stress than at any time since the years immediately after the Metropolitan Police was established in 1829.'[20] He pointed out 'it was fertile ground for extremists' who sought 'to make political capital out of racial issues' before going on to suggest that 'the extremists', both left and right fed 'off each other' and kept 'London's multi-racial melting pot at boiling point'.[21]

The 1970s saw the growth of right-wing neo fascist groups in Britain, the largest of which was the National Front. It called for a total ban on non-white immigration into Britain, blamed ethnic minorities for increasing crime and advocated repatriation of all 'coloured' immigrants, particularly those from Africa, Asia and the Caribbean. A National Front candidate stood for the Tottenham seat in the parliamentary elections of February 1974, October 1974 and May 1979, polling 4.1 per cent, 8.3 per cent and 2.9 per cent of the votes respectively. Whilst those on the left were quick to oppose the neo-fascists, they were also quick to attack the police at every opportunity. A prime example of this was contained in the evidence submitted to the Royal Commission on Criminal Procedure by the Institute of Race Relations in 1979. Whilst there is much to commend it, the report contained a catalogue of clashes and contacts between the police and ethnic minorities, especially those from an African-Caribbean background, both in London and elsewhere, covering the period from 1970 to 1979.[22] The institute did the same again in 1987, only this time covering the period from 1980 to 1987 and, in

---

20. *The Guardian*, 25 September 1979.
21. McNee, Sir David (1983). *McNee's Law*. London: Collins, p. 133.
22. Institute of Race Relations (1979). Police Against Black People. Evidence submitted to the Royal Commission on Criminal Procedure: Race & Class, Pamphlet No. 6. London: Institute of Race Relations.

the main, confining itself to the Metropolitan Police District.[23] For part of this period, the author was the divisional commander of a racially sensitive area in London and has personal knowledge of at least three of the cases mentioned in the report and, as a result of research, detailed knowledge of another two, all five of which are inaccurate and misleading when placed alongside the facts.[24] Clearly, all the institute did was trawl publications, a number of which were anti-police anyway, and regurgitate what had appeared in the initial media report without checking any of the facts. Whilst there was an element of truth, if not the whole truth in some of the reports, the general impression to anyone reading it was that such incidents were far more common than they in fact were.

This was by no means the first occasion this had happened. In 1973, Commissioner Sir Robert Mark felt bound to criticise the Runnymede Trust, whose objectives, he pointed out, included 'the promotion of good race relations' for insisting on publishing a report about 'police relations with the immigrant community in Ealing' even after a number of inaccuracies had been brought to its attention. The report, he said, illustrated 'the continual dangers facing those engaged in the race relations industry of jumping to conclusions before considering all the evidence.'[25]

Disorder in Britain's inner-cities

The first outbreak of disorder in Britain's inner cities, on 2 April 1980, took everyone by surprise. It happened in the St Paul's area of Bristol and resulted from a raid on an 'iconic location', known as the Black and White Café, the arrest of the owner and the seizure of a large quantity of alcohol. The disorder that followed forced the Avon and Somerset Police to retreat from the area and it was seven hours before control was re-established. By this time, a number of buildings had been destroyed or severely damaged. According

---

23. Institute of Race Relations (1987). Policing Against Black People. London: Institute of Race Relations.
24. For part of this period, the author of this book was the Divisional Commander of a racially sensitive area in London and has personal knowledge of at least three of the cases mentioned in the report and, as a result of research, detailed knowledge of another two; none were based on fact.
25. Mark, Sir Robert (1978). *In the Office of Constable*. London: Collins, pp. 141–142.

to Brain, the riot was totally 'unexpected' and 'at the national level' it was hoped that it would prove to be 'a one-off misadventure.'[26]

But worse was to come. Just over 12 months later, from 10–12 April 1981, rioting occurred in Brixton. Described as 'scenes of violence and disorder … the like of which had not previously been seen this century in Britain … a few hundred young people—most, but not all of them, black—attacked the police on the streets with stones, bricks, iron bars and petrol bombs', the last of these for the first time on the streets of the mainland.[27] Destruction was extensive and 279 police officers were injured. The Home Secretary, Willie Whitelaw, moved quickly and appointed Lord Scarman to conduct a formal inquiry under Section 32 of the Police Act 1964.

But, before the inquiry had reported, there were further outbreaks of disorder, firstly in Southall, in West London, on 3 July, where Asian youths clashed with skinheads, before both groups turned on the police. The following night, rioting broke out in Toxteth, a district of Liverpool inhabited by many people of African-Caribbean origin. Next to suffer an outbreak of disorder was Moss Side in Manchester, where 'a rampaging mob' of about 1,000 'black and white youths' clashed with police. Disorder, 'with varying degrees of petrol-bomb and missile throwing, looting, arson, and assaults on police', followed in Brixton (again) and other parts of London, the West Midlands, most notably in Handsworth, and in towns and cities stretching from Crewe in the north of England to Gloucester and Cirencester in the south.[28]

Wood Green High Road

Wood Green High Road in the London Borough of Haringey was no exception. Approximately 500 youths left a 'trail of havoc' in which nearly 60 shops were damaged or looted during rioting which lasted for three hours. For a time, police with shields faced 'a barrage of bricks, bottles and stones' and eight officers were taken to North Middlesex Hospital. Forty-three people,

---

26. See Brain, Timothy (2010). *A History of Policing in England and Wales from 1974: A Turbulent Journey.* Oxford: Oxford University Press, pp. 53–56.
27. Scarman, Rt. Hon, The Lord (1981). 'The Brixton Disorders 10–12 April 1981: Report of an Inquiry (Cmnd. 8427). London: Her Majesty's Stationary Office, p.1, para. 1.2.
28. Brain, op. cit. 26, quoting on p. 69 from *The Times*, 13 July 1981.

mostly aged between 18 and 20 years, were arrested.[29] Whilst there is no record of youths from the Broadwater Farm Estate taking part, given the close proximity of it to the scene of the rioting, it is difficult not to believe that some were involved.

Meanwhile, back at The Farm

It was against this background that events over the next five years began to unfold. By 1980, the Broadwater Farm Estate was referred to as a 'known base for serious crime'. Around the time of the Bristol riot, 'six stolen cars fitted with false number plates' were recovered from basement car parks and, in May, deploying 40 officers, plus dogs, and with a helicopter hovering overhead, the police mounted an operation to arrest a man who was wanted for a series of armed robberies in North London. The man was eventually seen in the basement of Stapleford Block but made good his escape by running up a staircase to Rochford Block and vanishing 'in the maze of flats'.[30]

According to one officer who was serving at Tottenham at the time, the deterioration began with 'the rise of certain vociferous political elements, with an anti-police stance... who took up the cause of a minority of law breakers on the estate.'[31] On Y District crime levels rose. In March 1981, the newly appointed Commander of Y District, Jim Dickinson, 'felt there was a particularly high incidence of street crime and burglaries in Tottenham' and immediately initiated Operation All Sorts, which in three weeks led to 132 arrests and the solving of some 300 crimes, mostly burglaries, robberies, theft and criminal damage.[32] Following the Brixton riot in April, the *Weekly Herald*, Tottenham's local newspaper, posed the question 'Could Brixton happen here?' to which Jeff Crawford, Haringey's community relations officer, responded. It was unlikely, he said, providing the police did not 'try the same kind of provocation they used in Brixton'. Claiming that 'Haringey was slightly better off than Brixton regarding housing and social facilities', he pointed out that the borough had 'a strong, articulate black community and

---

29. *Weekly Herald* (Tottenham and Wood Green), 9 July 1981.
30. Ibid, 15 May 1980.
31. Ritchie, op. cit. 4, p. 18.
32. *Weekly Herald* (Tottenham and Wood Green), 2 April 1981.

a police-CRC liaison committee [that met] regularly'. However, he pointed out that in Brixton people felt 'they were being cornered like caged animals by the police—and so they hit back'. He continued, 'there's going to be no regret and no apology from us' for 'we have been disrespected, humiliated and insulted by the police for too long.'[33]

Less than a week later, 500 youths, most of them black, went on the rampage on Easter Monday at the end of the four-day fair at Finsbury Park, which was part of Y District and only a mile or so from Broadwater Farm. The youths attacked buses and local shops; electrical equipment worth £1,000 was looted from a shop owned by Chris Kavallares, who was vice-chair of the Haringey Community Relations Council. Up until then, as few as 20 officers had policed the fair but more, who had been on stand-by at Stroud Green School because of skirmishes in previous years, were quickly deployed as the trouble flared. Ninety-five people were arrested, mainly under the Public Order Act. Eight police officers were injured, including Commander Dickinson, who suffered a broken nose and badly scarred cheek, and his deputy, Chief Superintendent Patrick Carson, who suffered two broken ribs. The two officers had been on foot together in Seven Sisters Road when they were attacked from behind by youths as they walked towards a group of officers. Jeff Crawford, 'Haringey's outspoken Senior Community Relations Officer', claimed that the trouble was 'caused by a handful of "louts and troublemakers".'[34] But, in what unfortunately became an all too familiar response, at a stormy meeting of the Haringey Community Relations Council the following week, Bernie Grant accused Crawford of blaming the youths when it was the fault of the police. He then went on to claim the numbers of police on standby nearby had been 'provocative' and suggested the police had deliberately engineered the confrontation.[35]

Publication of the Scarman Report

In his report on the Brixton riots of 1981, Scarman made two observations which were particularly applicable to the policing of the Broadwater Farm

---

33. Ibid, 16 April 1981.
34. Ibid, 23 April 1981.
35. Ibid, 30 April 1981.

Estate. The first related to training and supervision. He felt 'the training of police officers [to] prepare them for policing a multi-racial society', was 'inadequate' and suggested officers should be given 'a greater understanding of the cultural background of ethnic minority groups.'[36] He emphasised the need for 'close supervision' in conducting stop-and-search operations[37] but he was not convinced the importance of the role of inspectors and sergeants was 'sufficiently recognised either in the manning of forces or in the degree of management training given to officers in these ranks.' At the same time he said, senior officers must support and give recognition to the sergeants and inspectors under their command because they were the ones who could eliminate 'abrasive, biased, and racially prejudiced conduct by policemen on the streets.'[38]

The second related to home beat officers. He heard evidence that most police officers regarded them as being 'outside the mainstream of operational policing'; in fact, they were known as 'hobby bobbies' by many front-line officers. In his evidence to the Scarman Inquiry, Assistant Commissioner Wilfred Gibson had warned him there was a 'danger' that home beat officers would become 'social workers'.[39] At Brixton for instance, police commanders failed to see a role for them, either in assisting in quelling the disorder,[40] or, more importantly, perhaps, in assisting senior officers 'with their knowledge of local people'. But Scarman felt that 'they could have provided a useful point of contact with the community and of information and advice to senior officers.'[41] He went on to suggest that there was a need to 'improve the supervision' of home beat officers and ensure their 'involvement in the mainstream of operational policing.' Equally, he suggested, there was 'a need to provide opportunities for other operational officers to develop their relationship with the community in non-conflict situations.'[42]

The publication of the Scarman Report coincided with a statement by the chairman of the London Branch of the Police Federation, John Newman,

---

36. Scarman, op. cit. 27, p. 79, para. 5.16.
37. Ibid, p. 79, para. 5.16.
38. Ibid, pp. 85–86, para. 5.37.
39. Ibid, p. 85, para. 5.36.
40. Ibid, p. 90, para. 5.49.
41. Ibid, p. 89, para.5.48.
42. Ibid, pp. 89–90, para. 5.49.

who claimed that the police were now treating 'ethnic minorities in a different manner' than they did 'the white population in London.' He went on, 'to arrest coloured people in areas of high ethnic minority groupings leads to trouble, so we don't and the crime figures soar.'[43]

Foretaste of what was to come

Immediately following the publication of the report, there was an increase in tension between the estate's black and white residents. It emanated from the take-over by Dolly Kiffin of the old chip shop in Tangmere Block and the formation of the Broadwater Farm Youth Association described in chapter two. Almost immediately, Kiffin arranged monthly discos at the social club in Willan Road to raise funds for the Youth Association. Up until that time, the club had mainly been frequented by white people. Some objected, threats were made, and, at the end of February, a white man gate-crashed the first disco and was arrested in possession of an offensive weapon. The threats continued and there were a number of minor incidents over the next few months, primarily, but not solely involving white-on-black. It culminated in June with the election of a new management committee, dominated by black people, which caused further aggravation and some hostility when the outgoing committee refused to liaise with the new committee.[44]

Throughout 1982, the police continued in their attempts to combat crime but they did so 'against a rising level of abuse and assault by a number of youths who frequented the estate.'[45] By July, a pattern of physical obstruction towards police officers carrying out their duties had evolved[46] that was a foretaste of what was to come over the next three years. Late one evening in mid-July, a major confrontation was narrowly averted when a stolen motor vehicle being pursued by police crashed in Adams Road and the occupants decamped. Amongst the officers responding to the incident was Sergeant Roy Colbourne. Whilst having what was described as a 'friendly conversation' with a group of about 30 black youths drinking outside the social

---

43. *Daily Telegraph*, 25 October 1981.
44. Tottenham Police Reports, dated 1 March 1982 and 8 June 1982.
45. Ritchie, op. cit. 4, p. 18.
46. Williams, David A (1986). Internal Police Report on the disorders of the 6th October 1985 at the Broadwater Farm Estate, Tottenham. London: Metropolitan Police, p.70.

club in Willan Road, a bottle was thrown which hit him on the head. He was taken to hospital where four stitches were inserted in a cut. Police units withdrew to a rendezvous point at the junction of The Avenue and Mount Pleasant Road and were joined by the Y District late senior duty officer, Superintendent Max Telling. By this time, the social club had closed but it was believed that a number of black youths had gathered on the walkways of the estate. Telephone calls were made in an attempt to lure police into the estate. Finally, a genuine call was received from an occupant of Northolt Block after his windows had been broken by youths throwing bottles through them, at least one of which contained petrol. The police responded, arranged for the occupant to be taken to hospital for treatment to injuries he had suffered to his face, and promptly withdrew again. Some three hours after the original incident, the community liaison officer for Y District, Chief Inspector Tony Rowe, visited the estate, accompanied by Clasford Sterling, who had recently been elected as chairman of the social club. Rowe was also hit on the head by a bottle thrown from amongst a group of black youths; as a result he, too, was taken to hospital and had three stitches inserted in a cut on his head. The confrontation only ceased when Dolly Kiffin and Haringey councillor Ernie Large were informed by police and managed to persuade the youths to go to their homes.[47] Kiffin, described it as a 'small incident that got out of hand' and went on to say that a meeting should be arranged between the police and the youths on the estate to 'build some sort of understanding.'[48]

A second home beat officer, Andy Hollands, was appointed to Broadwater Farm Estate but within a month he had been assaulted. Following the incident in July, the acting community liaison officer, Inspector Horne, attempted to meet with Dolly Kiffin to discuss 'deteriorating community relations' but it was not until 12 August that he went with Hollands to the premises of the Youth Association. Whilst the meeting was in progress, a black youth struck Hollands on the back of the head with a bottle which broke before the assailant ran off. He was never identified.[49]

Three days later, shortly after 2 a.m., a police area car responding to an alleged disturbance on the estate had a number of bottles thrown at it from

---

47. Tottenham Police Report, dated 19 July 1982.
48. *Weekly Herald* (Tottenham and Wood Green), 22 July 1982.
49. Tottenham Police Report, dated 13 August 1982.

the walkway across Willan Road from Stapleford Block. Other units were called in, including three immediate response units (IRUs), and Inspector David Stubbs organized a search of the estate by sending one unit, Y30, in via the walkway in Willan Road; another, N30, via Adams Road; and the third, K30, via Gloucester Road. Each was accompanied by local officers except Y30 which contained local officers. The units met on the shopping deck of Tangmere Block having found nothing.[50]

Nevertheless, there were some 'successes'. The holding of the first Lordship Lane Festival in August has already been described in *Chapter 2*. An even more significant event took place in September when a team from Tottenham Police took on a team composed of black youths from the estate at football. The result was a 5–1 win for the Broadwater Farm team.[51]

But an uglier side of the estate was emphasised by an incident that initially did not involve the police at all. In late-September 1982, three African-Caribbean men had given a young 19-year-old girl a lift from a 'blues' party to her home in South Tottenham. During the journey certain sexual advancements were made but she was able to leave the car when she arrived home. A week later, on 3 October, whilst she was sitting at home watching television, her front door was smashed in, she was dragged to a car and then driven to the car park below one of the blocks of flats on the Broadwater Farm Estate. There she was 'forced to strip naked in the back of the vehicle' and was raped by each of the three men in turn, in addition to being 'forced to take part in various other sex acts.' She was then 'thrown naked from the car and the men drove off laughing, tossing her clothes out of a window'. The men were eventually traced and after a two-week trial at the Old Bailey, which ended in August 1983, despite pleading not guilty on the basis that the girl had 'willingly and "enthusiastically" taken part in a sex session', they were each found guilty. Sentencing two of them to seven years imprisonment each and the third man to four years imprisonment, Judge Jack Abdela QC said, 'You abducted that girl and then terrorised and humiliated her and subjected her to revolting indignities in a ruthless and callous way.'[52]

With relations already on a downward spiral, at the beginning of November

---

50. Ibid, dated 15 August 1982.
51. Ibid, dated 27 September 1982.
52. *Weekly Herald* (Tottenham and Wood Green), 11 August 1983.

1982 a black youth was arrested on the estate for allegedly breaking into The Farm's social club in Willan Road. This led to a protest by some of the leading members of the Youth Association outside Tottenham Police Station during which police were deployed using protective equipment. Four people were arrested, including the caretaker of the social club, a daughter of Dolly Kiffin, Diane Anderson, and the chair of the Tenants Association, Clasford Sterling,[53] who had his nose broken. The youth who had been arrested originally was later released without being charged. A year later, both Diane Anderson and Clasford Sterling were acquitted; however, the remaining two were convicted, one for causing criminal damage; the other for obstructing a police officer in the execution of his duty.[54] Privately, it was admitted by the police that whilst a minor offence had been committed, it would have been 'more profitable' to have dealt with it in a way which was less harmful to the long-term image of the Metropolitan Police Service. As it was, it merely served to fuel the anxiety of the young blacks living on the estate.[55]

The fallout from this incident was considerable. Bernie Grant, now the deputy leader of Haringey Council, wanted to 'ban future co-operation between the police and the council', and Dolly Kiffin said, 'as far as I am concerned, police relations are completely finished on The Farm', alleging that the police were 'deliberately stirring up trouble'.[56] On the evening following this incident, whilst investigating racist daubing on the walls of Manston Block, Police Constable Barry Stratton, who had been a home beat officer on the estate for eleven years, was viciously attacked by a youth with a billiard cue. He was taken to North Middlesex Hospital for stitches to be inserted in a large cut before being placed on the sick list. Immediately after that attack, police were called to the estate because 'a gang of youths with bottles were hanging around' and, on the same day, two steel beer barrels, which could easily have killed the occupants, were dropped from one of the walkways onto a police car. But an indication that not all people in the area were anti-police came from the large numbers well-wishers, including tenants, school children and teachers, who sent cards and good wishes for

---

53. Ibid, 4 November 1982.
54. Ibid, 10 November 1983.
55. Williams, David A, op. cit. 46, p. 71, para. 3.1.5.
56. *Weekly Herald* (Tottenham and Wood Green), 4 November 1982.

Police Constable Stratton's speedy recovery to Tottenham Police Station.[57] However, he was traumatised by the incident and never returned to patrol the Broadwater Farm Estate.

There were two other incidents in November which suggested that some youths on the estate were totally out of control. Neither involved the police. A television crew from the London Weekend Television programme 'Black on Black' filming with permission on the estate around the Youth Association's premises, had the windows of their vehicle broken as they were about to leave. The second incident occurred when a local education officer was mistaken for a plain-clothes police officer and was threatened with a knife. During the scuffle that followed, his jacket was damaged.[58]

Senior management on Y District responded to the events of 1982 by setting up a dedicated team of one sergeant and ten constables to patrol the estate. It became known as the Broadwater Farm Estate (BWFE) Team. The intention was to provide a police presence on the estate between 8 am and 12 midnight for each of the seven days of the week. The officers were to patrol in pairs and, as a general rule, only one pair would be on duty at any one time. An initial trawl of Y District failed to produce any volunteers to make up this team and consequently officers had to be found from the existing divisional strength at Tottenham. It had been decided that the team would consist of officers young in service who, it was argued, were more likely to be susceptible to the changing values of society than their older colleagues. This was a bold step and not without its attractions provided that some choice was to be allowed from which to select the officers. It now appears that this was not the case. Five officers were struck off ordinary duty to form the permanent core of the team. Five others were to be drawn at two or three month intervals to partner them. Eventually, police action in relation to the estate was confined to this new team; other officers were discouraged from entering the estate.[59]

---

57. Ibid, 11 November 1982.
58. Tottenham Police Report, dated 17 November 1982.
59. Tottenham Divisional Instruction 7/83, dated 10 June 1983.

Symbolic locations

Sir Kenneth Newman moved from his post as Commandant at the Police Staff College to become Commissioner of the Metropolitan Police in the early autumn of 1982. One of the first things he did in his new post was to visit two of the most racially sensitive divisions, Brixton and Notting Hill. Afterwards he told the media that despite 'being spat at', 'gratuitously abused', 'having things thrown at them for no reason at all', and, sometimes, being 'enticed into ambushes' officers would continue 'to police those areas' and would 'enforce the law.' But, whilst he did not 'rule out large scale operations', he said, 'they would have to be efficiently and professionally organized,' and based on a more efficient system of gathering intelligence.[60]

In his preliminary assessment of the problems and priorities of the Metropolitan Police which he sent to the Home Secretary in January 1983, he pointed out that there were 'housing estates and streets where the law-abiding majority' suffered seriously 'at the hands of the lawless minority.' In such places, 'the lawless minority' tended 'to label every police intervention as harassment' and 'yet the majority' wanted 'more police presence and intervention rather than less.'[61] He went on to claim that 'in many ethnic areas' police encountered 'outright hostility and obstruction', and it was 'common place for a policeman making a legitimate arrest or intervention to be surrounded by a hostile crowd bent on "rescuing" the prisoner or interviewees.'[62] He continued:

> 'This brand of obstruction and hostility is at its height in such places as Railton Road, Brixton; All Saints Road, Notting Hill; parts of Hackney; Sandringham Road, Stoke Newington; Haringey and Finsbury Park. In areas like these confrontations with the police are often deliberately engineered either to make a

---

60. *Daily Express, Daily Mail, The Mirror, The Daily Telegraph, The Guardian, Morning Star, The Times* 27 October 1982.
61. Newman, Sir Kenneth (1983). Preliminary Assessment of Problems and Priorities: Report of The Commissioner of Police of the Metropolis to the Home Secretary. Typescript, p. 9, para. 24.
62. Ibid, p. 9, para. 25.

political point or to create a diversion to facilitate organized crime in relation to drugs or stolen property.'[63]

Finally, he claimed that:

'Locations with these characteristics assume symbolic importance—a negative symbolism of the inability of police to maintain order. The existence of these symbolic locations encourages law breaking in other parts of the Metropolis, affects public perception of police effectiveness and undermines police morale.'

Sir Kenneth emphasised that it was an 'important priority to restore order in such areas' but there was a need for sensitivity in doing so.[64] Thus the term 'symbolic location' was coined.

Newman re-affirmed his views on symbolic locations in his annual report for 1983, specifically naming the Broadwater Farm Estate as such a place.[65] The following year, he reported that the 'combined pressures of force policy together with local resentment of what [was] seen as disregard for the law' weighed upon the chief superintendents of the divisions concerned. But, he pointed out the dangers of creating 'no-go' areas and the effect that this might have on the morale of officers required to police such areas.[66]

Back to Haringey

By 1983 it was clear that resentment was growing amongst officers at Tottenham because of the way Broadwater Farm was being policed. One of the young officers posted to the team for three months in the early part of 1983 described how 'four residents of the estate were attacked by a gang of black youths and doused in petrol.' Emergency calls were received by both the police and the ambulance service but on their arrival they 'were

---

63. Ibid, pp. 9 & 10, para. 26.
64. Ibid, p. 10, para. 27.
65. Annual Report of the Commissioner of Police of the Metropolis for 1983 (Cmnd. 9268). London: Her Majesty's Stationary Office, p.47.
66. Annual Report of the Commissioner of Police of the Metropolis for 1984 (Cmnd. 9541). London: Her Majesty's Stationary Office, p. 13.

promptly ambushed by a gang of bottle throwing youths.' The officer then described how they

> '...all retreated with the victims of the assault, and District Support Units were summoned to deal with impending disorder. The senior officer who attended refused to allow police officers to enter the estate and there followed a catalogue of crimes committed against other residents.'

Although no riot ensued, the officer claimed that the day was lost 'to the mob of criminals' who had control of the estate at that time.[67]

National Front

The police were not helped by the activities of the National Front who insisted in holding an election meeting at High Cross School in Tottenham in May as it was entitled to do under the Representation of the People Act 1949. But under the Act, such meetings were public and anyone was entitled to attend. The argument invariably put forward by those groups opposing National Front meetings was that they were prevented from attending by the police, sometimes by force. On this occasion the meeting was opposed by approximately 1,000 anti-fascists. Trouble flared when the 40 National Front members arrived to go into the meeting and a number of the anti-fascists were arrested. Responding to a suggestion by one local councillor that innocent bystanders were amongst those arrested, Commander Dickinson claimed they were neither 'innocent' nor 'bystanders' but were involved in unlawful protest in that they physically tried to prevent people from entering the meeting and were therefore liable to arrest. Unfortunately, it seems that a National Front member died during this incident and, in late July, having accused the anti-fascists of murdering him,[68] wanted to hold a meeting in his memory at the spot where he died. There was a threat that the National Front would riot on this occasion and 'police from all over London were drafted into Tottenham'. In the event, around 250 members of the National

---

67. Ritchie, op. cit. 4, p.18.
68. There was no evidence to suggest the man had been murdered but had merely collapsed and died of natural causes.

Front were corralled at Tottenham Hale Railway Station and only four were allowed to lay a wreath at where the National Front alleged the murder had occurred.[69]

The National Front episode 'led to an increase in bottle throwing and injuries' on the estate as a result of which the number of officers patrolling it was temporarily increased. Nevertheless, according to Chief Superintendent David J Williams, the practice of selecting young officers just out of their probationary period so they were not 'set in their ways' and could be 'trained' began to show dividends:

> 'Despite a succession of bottle throwing incidents, abuse and other anti-police behaviour, great restraint was shown by the officers deployed which was rewarded in the short term by a dramatic reduction in the incidents.'

In the long term, he claimed that 'it manifested itself in closer contact with those who need us on the estate and major inroads in terms of arrests, particularly for burglary.'[70]

Some encouragement

With one exception, a number of events in the second half of the year suggested that things might be improving. Firstly, on the occasion of the second Lordship Lane Festival, officers mingled with the crowd, allowing the children to wear their helmets and were, according to Williams, generally welcomed. Secondly, when a week of Rastafarian concerts being held on the Lordship Lane Recreation Ground resulted in complaints by local residents of excessive noise, the Chief Executive of Haringey Council, Roy Limb, attended and cancelled the remainder of the concerts under local bye-laws. Despite the presence of at least 100 'rastafarian types', eight police officers were able to disperse them without disorder, simply because most of them

---

69. *Weekly Herald* (Tottenham and Wood Green), 4 August & 3 November 1983; *Policing London* No. 8, June/July 1983; *Searchlight*, No. 96, June 1983; Williams, D.J, op. cit. 3, p. 10, para. 2.14.
70. Williams, David J, op. cit. 3, p. 10, para. 2.15.

were strangers to Broadwater Farm, the residents of whom supported police action because of the noise generated by the concerts.[71]

The improvement continued in October. A group of senior officers from the Police Staff College, Bramshill, visited the estate where they were welcomed by Dolly Kiffin and spent time in a frank exchange of views on the premises of the Youth Association.[72] This was followed by a visit to Haringey by the head of the Metropolitan Police's Race and Community Relations Branch, Commander John Newing. Organised by Haringey Community Relations Council, Newing spent a day meeting with local ethnic community groups. This included a visit to the Broadwater Farm Estate, where, in answer to a question, he said:

> 'I don't know whether police harassment exists or not but I certainly wouldn't deny the possibility of it. There seems to be sufficient evidence to suggest that it does happen from time to time.'

Nevertheless, at a reception at the end of his visit, in a statement which smacked of political correctness for the time, he said:

> 'The working relationships between the police, local authority and Community Relations Council in Haringey appear to be as good as anywhere in London. It is a sound foundation to deal with the problems that do exist.'

Dolly Kiffin disagreed, claiming everyone was 'making the race problems in Haringey look petty' when they were not. The whole day had been contrived she claimed, so that he only met the 'converted' and had not met those at 'grass roots level'.[73]

Another event took place at the end of the month when Chief Superintendent David J Williams visited the estate at the invitation of the black youths and was shown the new Job Creation Initiatives and Youth Association facilities as well as the new Estate Offices. It ended with a frank exchange of views during which Williams agreed to encourage officers

---

71. Ibid, pp. 10–11, paras. 2.16–2.17(a).
72. Tottenham Police Report, dated 28 October 1983.
73. Ibid; *Weekly Herald* (Tottenham and Wood Green), 20 October 1983.

patrolling the estate to establish closer working relationships with the youths.[74]

Finally, at the beginning of December, accompanied by CLO, Chief Inspector Dick Stacey, and Community Involvement Officer, Constable Paul Gee, male and female youths, predominantly black, from the estate visited the Metropolitan Police Cadet Corps Training School at Hendon to play football and netball matches against the cadets. The youths lost at football but won at netball.[75]

The exception was a particularly nasty incident in August 1983. Two officers were questioning a woman living in Manston Block about a possible drug offence when a man intervened and was promptly arrested for obstructing the officers in the execution of his duty. The woman, meanwhile had pulled free. A crowd of between 50 and 60 people, many from a nearby disco being held in Moselle School, quickly congregated and the two officers called for assistance. Among the units responding was a police van, driven by Police Constable Geoffrey Betts, a 39-year-old officer with some 17-years-service but who had only been at Tottenham since the previous November. As he was standing by the van, waiting for the man arrested for obstruction to be placed in it, he was stabbed in the back. He was rushed to North Middlesex Hospital where he was initially admitted to the Intensive Care Unit but recovered.[76]

This could have led to a major confrontation. It was later learned that 'elements at the scene' were hoping for a large scale operation 'so that they could provoke a riot'. Indeed, 'missiles had been secreted at various locations in the vicinity'. Following the stabbing of the officer, a number of police units did respond but were kept out of sight nearby. Careful control at the scene resulted in such a small police presence that the youths 'abandoned' their plan. Additionally, the attendance of Chief Executive Roy Limb and two councillors persuaded the disco to close 'and there was a peaceful dispersal.'[77]

This was the position that had been reached when Chief Superintendent Colin Couch arrived to take command of the division.

---

74. Ibid.
75. Tottenham Police Reports, dated 28 October and 13 December 1983.
76. Tottenham Police Report, dated 5 August 1983;
77. Williams, David J, op. cit. 3, p. 11, para. 2.17(b).

CHAPTER FIVE

Policing the Estate from mid-1984 to October 1985

Arrival of Chief Superintendent Couch

In an interview with the local newspaper just over a month after his arrival, Chief Superintendent Couch pointed out that he had previously served in the London Borough of Camden. Claiming it was in many ways similar to Tottenham he said:

> 'There is some evidence of decline and deprivation in parts and a large ethnic population. In Camden the police managed to create good relations with the Bengali population and I will be looking to do exactly the same with ethnic groups here in Tottenham.'

A firm believer in community policing, he said:

> 'I want local people to feel that they are being given a quality service by their police force. They may not always get what they want, but they will always be promptly and professionally dealt with.'[1]

If quoted correctly, this was a somewhat naïve comparison to make. Anyone who had been closely involved with the policing of predominantly African-Caribbean communities will know that there is a huge difference between such communities and those from Asia.

Nevertheless, despite the fact that Y District already had a community liaison officer, Couch appointed one of his inspectors, Barry Day, as community inspector. Day described his job as being to 'get out in the community, get to know the current leaders and cultivate others with potential and introduce them to [Chief Superintendent] Couch'. He also became responsible for the home beat officers, which included the Broadwater Farm

---

1. *Weekly Herald* (Tottenham and Wood Green), 19 July 1984.

Estate (BWFE) team, was involved in the introduction of Neighbourhood Watch into Tottenham Division and more latterly, the setting up of the Police and Community Consultative Group.[2]

Expectations of the Broadwater Farm team

Kenneth Newman had told the Home Secretary in January 1983 that 'symbolic locations' would 'receive the highest priority' when it came to manpower allocation.[3] He also said district commanders would be 'directed to ensure more specific tasking of uniformed patrols'. This would include seeking specific intelligence, co-operating with other agencies in Priority Estate Projects[4] and addressing specific problems such as vandalism, racial harassment and hooliganism.[5]

Although all officers were made aware that Broadwater Farm was 'a thing apart, a place to be wary of' from the moment they arrived at Tottenham, the Williams Report claimed that 'none of the officers who had served on the dedicated team had ever been properly briefed as to his role or duty'; thus they were unaware of precisely what was expected of them. Given the sensitivity that was required in policing the estate if tranquillity was to be maintained, the report suggested that it was 'surprising' that those who were required to carry out the policy, such as it was, were not made more aware of it.[6] Indeed, such instructions as did exist, tended to relate to what they should not do, rather than what they should do. For instance, Couch felt it necessary to issue a written instruction on 8 November, that the Broadwater Farm Youth Association were 'not to be searched by police unless the offender' was 'actually seen to enter the premises' and even then it would only be done under the 'direct control' of the duty inspector.[7] Only two officers were likely

---

2. Day, Barry (2014). Correspondence with the author, dated 4 August.
3. Newman, Sir Kenneth (1983). *Preliminary Assessment of Problems and Priorities: Report of The Commissioner of Police of the Metropolis to the Home Secretary*. Typescript, p. 22, para. 54(b).
4. The Priority Estates Project has already been mentioned in *Chapter 2*. See Power, Anne (1999). *Estates on the Edge: The Social Consequences of Mass Housing in Northern Europe*. Basingstoke: Macmillan, pp. 197–200.
5. Newman, op. cit. 3, p. 24, para. 54(i).
6. Williams, David A (1986). *Internal Police Report on the disorders of the 6th October 1985 at the Broadwater Farm Estate, Tottenham*. London: Metropolitan Police, p. 73, para. 3.2.5.
7. Tottenham Instruction 6/84 dated 8 November 1984.

to be on the estate at any one time and any police action to prevent or detect crime or rowdyism was likely to precipitate some kind of threatening or violent response. It was therefore difficult to see what was left for them to do other than walk around ignoring everything that went on around them; in other words nothing more than a flag-waving exercise designed to avert any suggestion that it was a 'no-go' area.

Chief Superintendent Couch told the Williams Inquiry that he was under the impression that team members were being briefed by their immediate superiors but clearly they were not. Given that policy was formulated at Y District Headquarters, rather than Divisional Headquarters, one wonders how he formed this impression. How did their immediate superiors get to know what the policy was if it was not from him? And given the sensitivity of policing the Broadwater Farm Estate, why did he not attend such briefings to see what the officers on the front line were being told? Williams stated that the result of this 'oversight was the multiple interpretation by junior officers of the concept of policing by consent.'[8] Indeed, as the situation deteriorated from May 1985 onwards, officers were more concerned with 'their personal safety' rather than the prevention and detection of crime, as bottles, beer barrels, bricks and lumps of concrete were thrown from the first level walkways at the officers patrolling below. Thus, 'a stop in the street either on or near the estate by individual officers was rare, while the arrest of a black youth on the estate usually resulted in the officer being surrounded and jostled or worse, by groups of hostile young men.'[9]

The Williams Report claimed it was difficult 'to gain an accurate picture of what the police officers at Tottenham felt about the Broadwater Farm Estate', but, perhaps one of the most telling revelations, given the macho image of the police service at the time, was the admission by 'some of those who regularly patrolled the estate' that they were apprehensive and, in some cases, fearful of patrolling it. As the report stated:

---

8. Williams, David a, op. cit. 6, p.74, para. 3.2.7. During research for this book, the author received correspondence from five former officers who had been part of the Broadwater Farm Estate team and all claimed that they received no proper briefing; when they joined the team they were posted with someone who already had some experience of being on the team and it was a matter of being guided by them.
9. Ibid, pp. 73–74.paras. 3.2.6–3.2.7.

> 'Given the prevailing culture of the police service this cannot have been an easy admission by young male officers conscious of their image as policemen. Yet fear was an emotion which was most often mentioned by the officers interviewed. Consequently few patrolled where trouble could be expected.'

This 'was the area immediately surrounding Tangmere which housed the Youth Association, and, at certain times of the day, the ground level car park, where drug-dealing was suspected.'[10]

The report went on to suggest that 'lack of experience and inter-personal skills as well as fear may also have played their part in the failure to break down some of the more obvious barriers which existed between youths and police' and 'repeated attempts by the community liaison officer, Mrs Kiffin and others to encourage officers to visit the Youth Association were wholly ineffective.'[11] But it would not be right to create the impression that relationships between the police and black youth of the estate were constantly at a low ebb. Emotions rose and fell, with the cold winter months usually providing a welcome respite to police. The Gifford Report claimed that 'the Youth Association wanted, above all, to build a co-operative relationship with the regular patrolling officers'.[12] There was some evidence to suggest that attempts were made by Kiffin, in particular, 'to build good relations with the police' and she had a 'reasonable relationship' with the now promoted Superintendent Stacey who was the community relations officer for the district. Although she claimed that he always tried to respond positively to anything she said, she got 'the feeling that he was frustrated' because he did not get 'support from other officers'.[13] For a brief period some officers did start to visit the centre which Kiffin encouraged but, given the climate that existed for much of the time, it was unlikely that officers would have been very welcome and would themselves have been apprehensive. Added to which, given the apparent indifference shown by senior management at

---

10. Ibid, p.74, para. 3.2.8.
11. Ibid, p. 75, para. 3.2.10.
12. Gifford, Lord (1986). The Broadwater Farm Inquiry: Report of the Independent Inquiry into Disturbances of October 1985 at the Broadwater Farm Estate, Tottenham. London: Broadwater Farm Inquiry, p. 40, para. 3.14.
13. Williams, Paul (1994). Keeper of the Dream: The Story of Dolly Kiffin of Broadwater Farm. London: International Community Talk, p.30.

both Tottenham Police Station and Y District Headquarters to the dangers faced by officers on an almost daily basis, it led individual officers to query why they should put themselves at risk.

Complaints by the older residents of the Broadwater Farm Estate and those with young families were frequent. They complained about the apparent immunity from prosecution of the black youths and were not impressed when told that arrests were being made but in places that were least likely to arouse publicity. What those residents wanted was to see 'overt police action dealing with the law breaker at the moment of his law breaking—action almost certain to result in a heightening of tension and a grave risk of serious public disorder—the very condition it was supposed to prevent.'[14]

There was no means of predicting with any accuracy the sudden and dramatic changes in the behaviour of some of the black youths. Although an incident which had occurred nationally or internationally sometimes caused a rise in tension which led to bottle throwing in the estate, it was the general view of local officers that the troublesome element on the estate were only motivated by incidents which directly touched upon their lives. Thus while the death of Colin Roach at Stoke Newington Police Station in 1983[15] generated considerable publicity there was no appreciable rise in tension. Again, events internationally, in South Africa,[16] while used as an excuse by one or two youths for their criminal activities, caused little interest on The Farm. However, any attempt by police to tackle crime on the estate was invariably met with strong opposition by a hard core of about 50 black youths, on occasions supported by Mrs Kiffin.[17] By mid-1985, the situation had got much worse.

---

14. Williams, David A, op. cit. 6, p. 75, para. 3.2.10.
15. Colin Roach died of gunshot wounds inside the entrance to Stoke Newington Police Station on 12 January 1983. See Timmins, Nicholas (1983). 'Colin Roach shot himself inquest jury decides by eight two majority. *The Times*, 21 June, p. 3.
16. South Africa was still under minority rule and the African National Congress was still fighting apartheid.
17. Williams, David A, op. cit. 6, p. 75, para. 3.2.11.

Guidance for professional behaviour

In March 1985, Sir Kenneth Newman issued a booklet entitled *The Principles of Policing and Guidance for Professional Behaviour*. In ran to 60 pages but in the context of what occurred on 6 October 1985 the relevant parts read:

> 'In discharging the duty of maintaining The Queen's Peace, the Metropolitan Police will co-operate with others in maintaining a state of public tranquillity. Where a conflict arises between the duty of the police to maintain order and their duty to enforce the law, the solution will be found in the priority which is given in the last resort to the maintenance of public order, and in the constant and commonsense exercise of police discretion. Priority will also be given to dealing with those crimes which most harm or cause anxiety to the public.'[18]

The commissioner pointed out that there was 'an uncritical readiness' in some police officers 'to think poorly of the black community'. He went on:

> 'There is an over-generalised assumption, on occasions, of their involvement in violent crime, deceit and collaboration in avoiding detection and rescuing lawfully detained prisoners, lack of intelligence and the ability to articulate, and absence of motivation to work. Similarly, some black community comment on the police features allegations of racial prejudice, harassment and abuse, use of excessive force, falsification of evidence, and indifference to the problems of black people. Allegations of this nature, coming from both "sides", feed off each other. Examples of positive conduct both by police and by black community alike struggle for recognition against such a background and it is hard to persuade some that a rational assessment, rather than labels of convenience and generality, is both fair and just.'[19]

Such guidance is all very well but it does not tell young constables what they should actually do when confronted with the kind of incidents that were occurring weekly, if not daily, on the Broadwater Farm Estate.

---

18. Newman, Sir Kenneth (1985). *The Principles of Policing and Guidance for Professional Behaviour*. London: Metropolitan Police, p. 9.
19. Ibid, p.48.

Increasing difficulties in policing the Estate

Whether it was purely coincidental or not, a worsening of relationships between the police and the hostile element on the estate appears to have re-emerged with two events. In the first, on 3 May, a youth who was well-known on the estate and would figure prominently in the events immediately following the riot, Winston Silcott, was released on bail having spent three months in custody on a murder charge.[20] Described by one source as 'entirely disruptive in character' Silcott's influence amongst the youths of Broadwater Farm at that time should not be underestimated. He was disliked by Dolly Kiffin who it was alleged had, on several occasions, asked 'police to deal with him'. His three months absence from the estate had been a welcome relief to both police and the management of the Broadwater Youth Association.[21]

The second, at the end of May, was the closure of a nearby youth club, the Clapton Youth Centre by the London Borough of Hackney when disciplinary and criminal enquiries were instigated against those responsible for running the centre. A number of the youths who normally attended the centre gravitated towards Broadwater Farm but despite being denied access to the Youth Association, continued to hang around the area. At the end of May, member of the BWFE team, Constable Trevor Paice, noted there was 'an increasing number of unknown faces hanging around the estate with abuse coming from the deck of Tangmere'. Two weeks later, the same officer commented again on the number of new faces 'hanging around outside the Youth Association' and felt bound to remark 'I think in weeks to come we may have trouble as they are not in the club and seem to resent the idea.'[22]

Additionally, in May, Dolly Kiffin was personally involved, with other members of the Youth Association 'in the forceful removal from custody of a black deaf mute who had been arrested by local officers.' No action was taken against Mrs Kiffin other than she was seen by Superintendent Sinclair, the deputy divisional commander, and given 'appropriate words of advice'. Suggesting 'this was undoubtedly the only sensible course of action for police to take', the Williams Report pointed out that 'it did nothing for

---

20. *Weekly Herald* (Tottenham and Wood Green), 7 February 1985.
21. Williams, David A, op. cit. 6, p. 86, para. 3.7.3.1.
22. Ibid, p. 86, para. 3.7.3.2.

the morale of the officers of Tottenham Division and nothing to enhance the image of the service with any of the residents of the Broadwater Farm, black or white.'[23]

Nevertheless, Couch thought the link with Dolly Kiffin was working well and went so far as to suggest that Broadwater Farm Estate 'was a pleasant place to work' for police officers.[24] It is doubtful whether those who actually policed it on a day-to-day basis would agree, particularly from mid-June onwards when the situation began to deteriorate yet again. It started on 19 June, when there was another confrontation outside Tottenham Police Station. Between 50 and 60 youths, led by Mrs Kiffin, gathered following the arrest of a man on the estate who had hit an officer over the head with an iron bar. A rumour had quickly circulated that the arrested person had been beaten by police and this had been sufficient to persuade the youths to attend the station. To calm the situation, Mrs Kiffin was allowed to see the prisoner following which the group dispersed. The damage, however, had been done. The following morning, patrolling officers discovered five beer barrels on a first floor walkway which passed over one of the roads on the estate. Later that day, in the evening, late turn officers felt it prudent to leave the estate so as not to make worse an already tense atmosphere.[25]

Appointment of Sergeant Gillian Meynell

Sergeant Gillian Meynell was appointed to take charge of home beat officers at the end of June. As such, she also became responsible for the team of officers who policed Broadwater Farm, the BWFE team. A requirement of her job was to liaise closely with the Community Inspector, Barry Day, and through him, submit periodic reports to Chief Superintendent Couch, particularly with regard to the situation on the estate. From the outset, Sergeant Meynell quickly realised that members of the BWFE team experienced, 'almost as a daily occurrence' milk bottles being thrown at them, together with 'racial' and 'anti-police' abuse. If anyone was stopped on the

---

23. Ibid, pp. 79–80, para. 3.4.8.
24. Interview on the London Programme, 11 October 1985.
25. Williams, David A, op. cit. 6, p. 80, para. 3.4.9 and p. 86, para. 3.75.

estate, the officer or officers would quickly find themselves 'surrounded by a gang of black youths' who would intimidate the officers by 'jostling' them.[26]

There were several more bottle-throwing incidents between 20 June and 13 July, which was the date Dolly Kiffin and her party left for the Caribbean to take part in the twinning arrangement already mentioned in *Chapter 2*.[27] Nominal control of the Youth Association was passed to Dolly's son, Trevor Anderson, 'but it soon became clear that he did not enjoy his mother's considerable qualities of leadership and force of character.'[28]

The day after the party left, Police Constables Mark Nicholson and Dal Babu stopped two young men on the estate who were subsequently found to be in possession of cheque cards and credit cards. Both officers were immediately surrounded by a hostile crowd of black youths who racially abused particularly Babu, who was of Indian origin, and he was 'left in no doubt' that he would be the target of physical assault if he ever came onto the estate again.'[29] Babu went on to become the most senior Muslim officers in the Metropolitan Police, reaching the rank of chief superintendent before retiring in 2013.[30] He was awarded the OBE in the Queen's Birthday Honours List in 2010 for services to policing.[31]

Three days later, a police vehicle which chased a stolen vehicle onto the estate was attacked with milk bottles as a result of which the police vehicle suffered some damage. The duty inspector judged the situation 'to be so serious' that he instructed all police personnel to withdraw from the estate.[32]

Dolly Kiffin and her party had been away for about four weeks when, on 24 August, the fourth annual festival took place on Lordship Lane Recreation Ground. Senior management instructed police officers patrolling the event 'not to do anything about the drugs which would be seen at this festival as it would antagonise the black youths';[33] consequently, the event passed off

---

26. Report by Sergeant Gillian Meynell, undated, sent to the Police Federation of England and Wales, the content of which subsequently appeared in Burden, Peter, and John Passmore (1986). 'My Riot Warnings Ignored', *Daily Mail*, 21 January 1986, p. 6.
27. For further details see Williams, Paul, op. cit. 13, p.37.
28. Williams, David A, op. cit. 6, p. 87, para. 3.7.6.
29. Ibid, p. 87, para. 3.7.7.
30. *The Guardian*, 4 February 2013.
31. *The Telegraph*, 12 June 2010.
32. Williams, David A, op. cit. 6, p.87, para. 3.7.8.
33. Meynell, op. cit. 26, p. 3; Burden, op. cit. 26, p.7.

without incident. Whilst such an instruction can be questioned, it is one that has quite frequently been given to officers at the much larger Notting Hill Carnival. Most police officers would probably agree that there is no value in precipitating serious public disorder for the sake of arresting people in possession of small amounts of, particularly cannabis, for their own recreational use.

However, with Dolly and her party away, it became apparent that trouble was brewing. Following her departure, an increasing number of youths from outside had begun congregating on the estate. Two reasons for this were suggested. Firstly, they were possibly drawn by the 'cheap meals served' at the Youth Association. But by far the more serious reason was the build-up of 'a new set of traffickers', who had, by all accounts, been 'driven out of their former patches in Stoke Newington and Hackney by recent police operations.'[34]

During the six weeks following the festival, bottles were regularly thrown in the direction of home beat officers patrolling the estate and they were subjected to verbal abuse.[35] Of some additional concern was the widening of the attacks to include organizations other than the police. On 6 September, firefighters, extinguishing a burning car under Tangmere Block, were attacked and the following day a Local Authority Removal Team were physically prevented from clearing the area of abandoned vehicles, after only one vehicle had been removed. When the team attempted to remove the vehicles on a second occasion, bottles were thrown at them, forcing them again to abandon the attempt. Representations were made for the vehicles to remain on the grounds that they provided 'spare parts' and were a source of income to the youths. On another occasion, workmen carrying out repairs to the estate on behalf of the council were the target of bottle-throwing youths.[36]

---

34. Gifford, op. cit. 11, p. 57, paras. 3.55–3.56.
35. Taken from the Broadwater Farm Incident Book in which members of the BWFE team recorded any incidents that had occurred during their tour of duty.
36. Ibid, pp. 87–88, paras. 3.7.9–3.7.10.

Handsworth, Birmingham

The commencement of the string of events that led to the rioting in Handsworth on 9th and 10th September was strangely reminiscent with the lead up to the Broadwater Farm riot described in the next chapter. A police motorcyclist who questioned a black driver about his tax disc was surrounded by other black youths and assaulted. On this occasion the driver escaped but two youths were arrested. Just over an hour later, fire service personnel were attacked by stone-throwing youths as they tackled a fire in a disused bingo hall; petrol bombs followed. The police initially responded but were force to withdraw as the violence intensified. For over three hours, the rioters had full control of a substantial part of Lozells Road until the police eventually began to re-establish control. The following morning, two Asian brothers were found dead in the burnt out building which housed the post office they ran. Sporadic outbreaks of disorder continued the following day and the toll over the two days was substantial. Over 40 shops had been burnt, a garage had been destroyed, and a supermarket and a public house wrecked and looted. Over one thousand police officers from eleven forces had been deployed; 137 people were arrested.[37]

Effect of Handsworth on Broadwater Farm

The effect of the riot on the officers patrolling the Broadwater Farm Estate was almost immediate. On 11 September, Police Constables Mark Nicholson and Paul Morley were faced with what must have been, to them, an extremely frightening experience. They were patrolling the 4th level of Tangmere Block when they were confronted by a large gang of black youths, none of whom appeared to the officers to be local. Morley radioed through to Tottenham Police Station to say they were discreetly exiting the estate. The two officers went to the lift but found that it was being held at a lower level. So they decided to walk down some back stairs which would enable them to exit into Gloucester Road without going on the deck of Tangmere. However, they were intercepted by a small group of youths, their faces covered by masks who told

---

37. Brain, Timothy (2010). *A History of Policing in England and Wales from 1974: A Turbulent Journey*. Oxford: Oxford University Press, pp. 106–108.

them they would have to go down onto the deck and 'run the line'. At this point the duty inspector, David Hudson, came on the radio to ask whether they were alright. One of the masked youths began to draw an object from his pocket which Morley thought was a knife. As he did so, he said 'If you start to touch the radio you're dead.' Both officers were then physically pushed down the stairs onto the deck where about 60 black youths, some wearing masks and military fatigues, stood in two lines on either side of the walkway, armed with bottles, sticks and bricks and, Morley believed one had a bicycle chain. The youths started chanting 'Birmingham, Handsworth riot.' The two officers ran the line and were hit 'with everything'. Nicholson was struck on the head with a bottle, staggered and was grabbed by Morley, who urged him 'to keep running or we're dead.' Morley was hit a number of times on his back to the extent that some thirty years later he still suffers from 'back problems'. As they reached the grass which was between Tangmere Block and Gloucester Road — the very spot where Keith Blakelock would meet his death less than a month later — Morley radioed for 'urgent assistance' and an ambulance. In Gloucester Road the officers were met by Inspector Hudson, two District Support Units (DSUs) and the area car and other units were converging on the area. On the directions of Hudson, police withdrew without any attempt being made to enter the estate.[38]

The decision facing Inspector Hudson was a difficult one. Sufficient resources were available to him either immediately or within the following ten to 15 minutes to enable him to enter the estate and investigate the serious assaults on his officers. He fully realised, however, that his actions would, in all probability, lead to further outbreaks of disorder without much hope of successfully identifying the culprits. The alternative — to withdraw his officers — had implications for his own personal credibility with the men and the morale of the whole division. On balance, the Williams Report felt 'his decision was probably right, disloyal though it must have appeared to the injured officers.'[39]

There was support for Hudson's fears the next day when at three different locations on the estate, two beer barrels, a crate of milk bottles and an

---

38. Williams, David A, op. cit. 6, p. 88, para. 3.7.12; see also Burden, op. cit. 20, p. 7 and Morley, Paul (2014). Correspondence with the author, dated 11 August.
39. Ibid, p. 89, para. 3.7.13.

assortment of bottles were found on the first level walkways of the estate. Few can doubt that these objects were intended to be used against police and tension remained at a high level for several days.[40] The response by Chief Superintendent Couch was to issue an instruction to the BWFE team to patrol the periphery of the estate and keep well away from Tangmere Block whilst he attempted to sort the problem out. But he emphasised that The Farm was 'not a no-go area'.[41]

Most rank-and-file officers at Tottenham believed that black youths on the estate 'were above the law'; nothing was being done about the situation and, according to Sergeant Meynell, 'morale within the BWFE team' had become 'almost non-existent.' Nevertheless she claimed, 'despite this frightening attack and despite knowing that it could be repeated at any time', and 'knowing tensions were rising and trouble was expected,' the officers from the team recognised that the elderly and law-abiding residents of the estate still deserved police cover, and 'continued to patrol the estate.'[42] However, Constable Morley had had enough and requested a move from the BWFE team back to a relief.[43]

The senior management team on Y District tended to agree with the rank-and-file in that they saw it as 'an attempt by a hard core of perhaps no more than 50 to 60 criminals, to protect a lucrative trade in drugs and stolen property'. This was a similar situation that existed in other areas of London and some of the major cities outside the capital. Their response was to set up a robbery squad under the senior CID officer on Y District, Chief Superintendent Andy Gallagher and, at the time of the riot there was already some evidence that this hard core of criminals were involved in street robberies elsewhere in Tottenham.[44]

On 19 September, racial graffiti was daubed on a shop rented by an Indian on the deck of Tangmere. Four days later, 23 September, Dolly Kiffin returned

---

40. Ibid, p. 89, para. 3.7.14.
41. Taken from an entry made by Sergeant Meynell in the Broadwater Farm Incident Book, op. cit. 35, clearly at the behest of Chief Superintendent Couch.
42. Meynell, op. cit. 26, p. 4; Burden, op. cit. 26, p. 7
43. At that time, personnel for general police work were divided into four reliefs at most police stations in the Metropolitan Police District. On most days, three of the reliefs operated three shifts covering the whole 24 hours. The fourth relief was either taking rest days or was employed on a particular function.
44. Meynell, op. cit. 26, p. 2, para. 4.5.

to the estate after being away for eight weeks by which time the situation had 'really deteriorated.' According to Paul Williams

> '…beat police patrolling the estate could not understand why their superiors were holding them back from taking action against the blatant drug-trafficking going on. The responsible Youth Association leaders were equally baffled and frustrated by these tactics of "masterly inactivity".'[45]

Almost immediately, Superintendent Stacey visited Dolly Kiffin in her office, pointed out to her just how much the situation had deteriorated and the police feared there would be a riot. When she asked him why the police had taken no action, he is alleged to have told her that they were waiting for her to call them on her return. Kiffin was furious. She was aware that if she did invite them in and things went horribly wrong, she would be blamed and all her credibility would be lost and 'she felt strongly that while the police should keep responsible community leaders informed if they were about to take action, final responsibility for operational decisions rested with them alone.'[46]

Brixton

On 26 September, detectives from the Hertfordshire Constabulary visited an address in Southwark in South London looking for Michael Groce, a 19-year-old black youth wanted in connection with £10,000 jewellery robbery in their area. Unfortunately, he had recently had an argument with his girlfriend during which he had fired a shotgun into the wardrobe and left. Unbeknown to them at this time Groce was appearing at a local magistrates' court on an unrelated matter and had given the address of his mother in Normandy Road, Brixton, as his own. As a result, armed police raided the house in the early morning of 28 September, during which the mother, Cherry Groce, was shot by Inspector Douglas Lovelock.[47]

---

45. Williams, Paul, op. cit. 13, p.39
46. Williams, David A, op. cit. 6, p. 89, para. 3.7.16.
47. Inspector Lovelock was charged with manslaughter but was acquitted by a jury in January 1987. See Brain, op. cit. 26, p.116.

Attempts by the local commander to mediate failed and that evening eight hours of rioting occurred during which 'police were attacked; shops, garages, a supermarkets were looted and set on fire.' Press photographer David Hodge died as a result of injuries received during the rioting; 31 members of the public and 93 police officers were injured. Over 900 crimes, including the raping of two women, were reported. Damage was estimated to be £2.4 million. Over 300 people were arrested of whom 219 were charged. Accompanied by his solicitor, Paul Boateng, Michael Groce surrendered himself at Brixton Police Station the following morning.[48]

The effect of Brixton on Broadwater Farm

The following day, in the temporary absence of Couch, Superintendent Sinclair withdrew all police from the Broadwater Farm Estate as a precautionary measure. For the next week, an uneasy calm existed. In response to the events in Brixton, all District Support Units (DSUs) throughout the Metropolitan Police area were placed at 15-minute standby.[49] There were brief outbreaks of disorder in Toxteth, Liverpool, and Peckham, London, on 1 October but most people hoped that was the end.[50] Far from it. Pressure was building up on the Broadwater Farm Estate in Tottenham.

Drug problem

In response to the drug problem on the estate, Chief Superintendent Couch took advantage of the Metropolitan Police's mobilisation and instructed the local DSU to carry out selective 'stops' on the periphery of the estate in an attempt to combat the growing menace. It was not long before the unit was attacked by bottle-throwing youths and it withdrew. Acting Commander Ted Hodge immediately ordered that no further stops of this nature were to be made on the grounds that the operation was 'ill-conceived and lacked

---

48. Metropolitan Police (1986). *Public Order Review: Civil Disturbances 1981–1985*. London: Metropolitan Police, pp. 1–4; see also Brain, op. cit. 36, pp. 109–110.
49. Williams, David A, op. cit. 6, pp. 89–90, para. 3.7.17.
50. 'Riots erupt in Toxteth and Peckham'. BBC—On this day—1 October. See http://news.bbc.co.uk/onthisday/hi/dates/stories/october/1/newsid_2486000/2486315.stm (Accessed 6 November 2014).

planning and purpose'. He also took the view that the risk of a major confrontation was highly likely given the atmosphere that existed amongst black communities, post-Brixton.[51]

Mounting tension

On 2 October information was received from several sources which suggested young men were collecting bottles on a large scale and petrol bombs were being made on The Farm. One petrol bomb was actually found by police and taken for forensic examination. On 3 October there were only two minor incidents which, but for what happened at the end of the week, would have passed without comment. In the first, two members of the BWFE team attempted to stop a solo motor cycle near Tangmere Block which then drove straight at them making good its escape. The second incident was an attempt to lure police onto the estate. A telephone call was received in which it was suggested that 20 black youths were throwing bottles at two officers but brief enquiries revealed that the information was false and police did not respond. Otherwise the area was quiet.[52]

The estate was quiet on 4 October. Information was received that some petrol bombs had been moved from the greengrocer's shop on Tangmere Block, which was run by Winston Silcott, to vehicles parked below. In addition, two senior officials from the Post Office visited Tottenham Police Station to voice their concern over the harassment of postmen by black youths when delivering and collecting mail from the estate and informed police that if the situation did not improve the Post Office would consider suspending deliveries and collections.[53]

---

51. Williams, David A, op. cit. 6, p. 90, para. 3.7.18.
52. Ibid, p. 90, paras. 3.7.19–3.7.20.
53. Tottenham Police Report, dated 4 October 1985.

Chapter Six

The Death of Cynthia Jarrett and Build Up to the Riot

Arrest of Floyd Jarrett

As was the case in Brixton only one week earlier, the riot on the Broadwater Farm Estate was triggered by a serious incident involving the police and a woman of African-Caribbean descent.[1] It all started in Rosebury Road, Tottenham, at around 1 p.m. on 5 October, when Constable Casey saw the excise licence on a BMW coupé, driven by Jarrett, had apparently expired. Using his radio he requested the vehicle be stopped and it was, by Sergeant Parsons and Constable Allen, who were close by in a police car. A check on the Police National Computer revealed that the number plates on the car, UGX 50F, did not exactly match that shown on the exercise licence, WGX 50F and Constable Casey informed Jarrett that he would be arrested for suspected theft of the vehicle. Jarrett ran away but he was quickly caught by the officers at which time it was alleged that he punched Constable Christopher Casey in the face. Jarrett was taken to Tottenham Police Station arriving at about 1.30 p.m. where he initially gave the police a false name and address, but by 3.30 p.m. it was known who he was and, as a result of an invoice found in the car, it was believed that he lived at 25 Thorpe Road. According to the Gifford Report, there the matter should have ended and he should have been released. It was at this moment Detective Constable Michael Randall, who was officially off-duty but at the station completing some papers relating to a forthcoming trial, intervened and visited Jarrett in his cell. In evidence at the subsequent inquest into Cynthia Jarrett's death, Randall claimed that Jarrett had recognised him. However, Jarrett claimed

---

1. See Brain, Timothy (2010). *A History of Policing in England and Wales from 1974: A Turbulent Journey.* Oxford: Oxford University Press, pp. 109–110.

he had never met Randall and this version was apparently supported by the custody record.[2]

The events that followed were, to say the least, controversial, and, on the face of it, did not place the Metropolitan Police in a particularly good light. On his return from the cells, Randall claimed, it would appear on the basis of rumour and innuendo, that he knew Jarrett to be 'a major handler' of stolen goods and decided that the address at 25 Thorpe Road should be searched. This decision was approved by the duty officer, Inspector Ian Clarke, who instructed that a search warrant should be obtained from a magistrate who lived nearby.[3]

Search of 25 Thorpe Road

The four officers who were going to conduct the search — Detective Constable Randall, Sergeant Parsons and Constables Casey and Allan — were aware that there might be trouble and, in fact, Inspector Clarke was alleged to have commented that he hoped 'the search would not start any riots.' In any event he arranged for an area car and a DSU to stand by.[4] From thereon there are two different versions as to what happened. The four officers claimed to have arrived at 25 Thorpe Road at 5.45 p.m. and found four people in the house, Cynthia Jarrett, her daughter Patricia, a grandchild, aged two years, and a neighbour's young child. The time was disputed by the Jarrett family, Patricia in particular, who maintained it was just before 5 p.m. Initially, there was disagreement as to how the police gained entry into the house. Although Sergeant Parsons was the senior officer present it was clear that Randall had assumed command.[5] The police claimed they knocked three times before entering through an unlocked door. The Jarrett's maintained they did not knock and they would never have left the door open with young children

---

2. Gifford, Lord (1986). The Broadwater Farm Inquiry: Report of the Independent Inquiry into Disturbances of October 1985 at the Broadwater Farm Estate, Tottenham. London: Broadwater Farm Inquiry, pp. 66–68, paras. 4.5–4.12; see also Rose, David (1992). *A Climate of Fear: The Murder of PC Blakelock and the Case of the Tottenham Three*. London: Bloomsbury, p.58.
3. Gifford, op. cit. 2, p. 69, para. 4.14.
4. Ibid, p.74, para. 4.27; see also report in *The Daily Telegraph*, 'Jarrett "low key" order' dated 2 December 1985.
5. Gifford, op. cit. 2, p.74, para. 4.28.

in the house.⁶ Sergeant Parsons later admitted at the inquest into Cynthia Jarrett's death that he lied to Patricia Jarrett and they had, in fact, 'opened the door with keys taken from Floyd Jarrett'.⁷

A number of rooms had been searched when it was alleged that Detective Constable Randall went into the dining room, pushing aside Cynthia Jarrett as he did so. According to Patricia, her mother fell and broke a small table as she did so. She helped her mother to get up and managed to get her to a chair; Cynthia was gasping for breath. Patricia phoned for an emergency doctor but was told one was not available, so at 5.55 p.m., she telephoned for an ambulance. Cynthia's other son, Michael, who lived at the address, arrived. He made it clear to the officers that Floyd Jarrett did not live there⁸ and ordered them out of the house. By now Cynthia Jarrett had collapsed completely and another call was made for an ambulance at 6 p.m. Alerted by a radio message from Detective Constable Randall, Inspector Clarke arrived and Patricia Jarrett was persuaded to allow the officers to re-enter the house, where, for a time, Randall, a qualified first-aider, 'tried mouth to mouth resuscitation' and 'an airway device' was brought in from a police car.' However, 'when a mirror was put to Cynthia Jarrett's mouth, there was no misting of the glass.' An ambulance arrived at 6.11 p.m. and Cynthia Jarrett was taken to the North Middlesex Hospital but was pronounced dead on arrival at 6.35 p.m.⁹

The police officers' version of events as to what took place inside the house was at variance with that given by the Jarretts. The police claimed that Patricia was 'abusive almost from the start, shouting and swearing obscenities at the officers; that Michael Jarrett had joined in the abuse after he arrived; and that there had been no contact of any kind, accidental or deliberate, between DC Randall and Mrs Jarrett.'¹⁰

Cynthia Jarrett's death made a lasting impression on at least one of the officers. Nearly 20 years later, an emotional Mark Parsons subsequently told a BBC Documentary that he wished there had been a way that he could have expressed his condolences to the Jarrett family:

---

6. Ibid, p. 74–75, para. 4.28–4.30.
7. *Police Review*, 6 December 1985, p. 2459.
8. In fact he had been living at an address in Enfield for the previous six months.
9. Gifford, op. cit. 2, pp. 74–77, paras. 4.27–4.35.
10. Ibid, pp. 77–78, para. 4.36.

'I wish there had been some way in which I could have gone back and said I really am sorry about your Mum dying. We didn't do anything wrong.'[11]

The search warrant

There was considerable controversy as to how and when the warrant was obtained, leaving the Gifford inquiry, whilst accepting that 'people are frequently vague and inaccurate about times' to suggest that most of the evidence pointed to the fact that the search warrant was obtained after the search had been undertaken and not before. This was despite the fact that both Detective Constable Randall and Constable Casey claimed that the warrant had been read out loud to the occupants of the house. Patricia Jarrett was adamant throughout that it was not. However, the discrepancies in the times given by the four officers involved, Inspector Clarke, custody Sergeant Bowell, the magistrate and the magistrate's mother, as to the timings when the police attended the magistrates' house suggested otherwise.[12] Inspector Clarke was adamant that when the officers returned from the magistrates' house one of them held up the search warrant and he saw it had been signed. This was before the four officers went to Thorpe Road.[13]

There was also some controversy over the ease with which it had been obtained. Writing some 13 years before the incident, Humphrey suggested that the 'signing of search warrants' was 'hidden from the public gaze'. Either the warrant was applied for in a closed court, for the obvious reason that it would not be in the interests of justice to disclose the location that a warrant was to be executed, or police officers went to the home of a local stipendiary magistrate or justice of the peace and got one signed there. Most magistrates, he claimed, accepted what the police officer told them 'and [probed] no further'. Humphrey accused magistrates of not exercising 'their powers in this respect with responsibility', suggesting that police officers seeking search warrants should be subjected to a fairly rigorous questioning about the specific reasons for the search.[14]

---

11. Barling, Kurt (narrator)(2004). Who killed PC Blakelock? Documentary shown on BBC TV.
12. Gifford, op. cit. 2, pp. 70–73, paras. 4.19–4.26.
13. Clarke, Ian (2014). In correspondence with the author, dated 16 October.
14. Humphrey, Derek (1972). *Police Power and Black People*. London: Panther, pp. 167–168.

Charging and court appearance of Floyd Jarrett

Jarrett claimed that he had given a false name and address because he only had a provisional driving licence. Therefore he should have been accompanied by a qualified driver and the vehicle should have been displaying 'L-plates'. He was therefore charged with three motoring offences in addition to the assault on Constable Casey. When he finally appeared at the magistrates' court on 13 December 1985 he was acquitted of the assault charge and the court ordered the police to pay £350 costs which suggested the charge should never have been brought. He was, however, fined a total of £105 for the three offences of driving without insurance, no 'L-plates' and failing to have a qualified driver in the car to supervise him.[15]

The coroner's inquest

The inquest into Cynthia Jarrett's death took place in Hornsey from 27 November to 4 December 1985 before Dr David Paul and a jury. During the proceedings, the family, the police officers involved and witnesses gave evidence and were subjected to vigorous cross-examination.[16]

Medical evidence was given to the inquest by Dr Walter Somerville. He told the court that, unbeknown to the family, Cynthia Jarrett suffered 'from a very severe heart disease', although they were aware she had high blood pressure for which she was receiving treatment. As a result of the disease, 'death could have been triggered off by physical activity or an emotional upset'. The mere arrival of the police could have caused a certain amount of emotional stress on top of which 'a push by the police followed by a fall would have been "an important precipitating factor".'[17]

In his summing up, Dr Paul told the jury that there were four verdicts open to them, unlawful killing, accidental death, natural causes and an open verdict if they could not find, on the evidence, given, that one of the first three applied. The jury decided, unanimously, it was accidental death. This,

---

15. *The Times*, 14 December 1985; *Weekly Herald* (Tottenham and Wood Green), dated 19 December 1985.
16. Gifford, op. cit. 2, p. 81, para. 4.43.
17. Ibid, p. 77, para. 4.39–4.40.

claimed Gifford, meant that 'the jury was satisfied that there was a push but were not sure that the push was a deliberate act, but merely a consequence of someone going through a narrow place and brushing Mrs Jarrett aside.'[18]

A statement from the Jarrett family, released through their solicitor at the conclusion of the inquest, read:

> 'The verdict of the jury is a vindication of our complaint against the police officers who arrived at our house on 5th October. Our mother died as a result of a push by a detective during a careless and callous search by four police officers who during the inquest had been forced to admit to lying, to numerous breaches of their code of conduct and to a total inconsistency between the ambulance records and their fabricated story. We expect that apart from any other action, the officers concerned will be severely disciplined.'[19]

The role of the Police Complaints Authority

The Police Complaints Authority (PCA)[20] had been formed by virtue of the Police and Criminal Evidence Act 1984. Its aim was to bring an independent element to the whole question of complaints made against the police. In serious cases, a senior officer from another force would carry out the investigation under the direction and supervision of a member of the PCA.

It commenced its work at the beginning of January 1985, so the investigation into the death of Cynthia Jarrett was one of its early cases, just nine months after its formation. On this occasion when the case was referred to the PCA, the Chief Constable of Essex was asked to appoint an officer to head up the investigation and Assistant Chief Constable Peter Simpson was so appointed.[21] A solicitor acting for the Jarrett family, Bernard Carnell, made it clear to Simpson at the outset that the substance of the complaint extended from the reasons why Floyd Jarrett was stopped and had been taken to Tottenham Police Station in the first place, the grounds on which it was

---

18. *The Times*, 5 December 1985; see also Gifford, op. cit. 2, p. 80, para. 4.41.
19. Gifford, p. 80, para. 4.42.
20. The Police Complaints Authority was replaced by the Independent Police Complaints Commission (IPCC) in April 2004.
21. Metropolitan Police (1986). Public Order Review: Civil Disturbances 1981–1985. London: Metropolitan Police, p.8, para. 3.5.

decided to search Mrs Jarrett's house, the means by which they gained entry into the house, their behaviour and actions in the house and their failure to produce a search warrant.[22]

The Gifford Report was critical of the role played by the PCA claiming that the independence of the investigation was seriously in question when it became clear that statements given by members of the Jarrett family 'in confidence' to Simpson 'for the purpose of the investigation' had been passed to the Metropolitan Police prior to the inquest. Representing the Metropolitan Police Commissioner, barrister Michael Austin-Smith questioned Patricia Jarrett about two different versions of events she had given, firstly in a radio interview on the day following her mother's death and then to the Essex Police. Austin-Smith said Patricia Jarrett 'had waved her privilege to confidentiality by making a statement "inconsistent on a material point",' claiming also that the police 'had a duty to provide the coroner with all the available information.'[23] But the statements had been given to the Metropolitan Police without the knowledge of the PCA. The reason given was that the commissioner, as the disciplinary authority, was entitled to see them. Gifford disagreed, pointing out that, whilst he would have been entitled to them at the end of the investigation in order to make a decision as to any disciplinary offences that may have been committed, the investigation was by no means complete when the inquest was held — in fact it was not completed for a further four months. The PCA subsequently issued a statement expressing its concern that the statements 'had been used by the Metropolitan Police without their consent'.[24]

But Gifford's most serious allegation against the authority was reserved for its interpretation of the verdict given by the inquest jury. In its summary statement which was issued at the same time as the press release, in April 1986, the PCA said:

> 'The jury tended to accept neither party's version completely but implied, in accordance with the directions given by the Coroner, that DC Randall did not

---

22. Gifford, op. cit. 2, pp. 81–82, paras 4.44–4.45.
23. *Police Review*, 6 December 1985, p. 2459.
24. Gifford, op. cit. 2, p. 82, paras. 4.46–4.47.

push Mrs Jarrett but in all probability inadvertently brushed past her causing her to lose her balance.'

Gifford claimed 'this was a serious misreading of the jury's verdict.' He went on:

'On the essential issue of whether DC Randall pushed Mrs Jarrett, they accepted Patricia Jarrett's evidence and rejected that of DC Randall, who totally denied that he had any kind of physical contact with Mrs Jarrett. On the further question, was the push deliberate or unintentional, the jury decided that they could not be sure that it was intentional. This was not a rejection of Patricia Jarrett's evidence. Patricia Jarrett could only tell the jury what she saw DC Randall do; whether what he did was deliberate was a matter for the jury.'

By using the words 'inadvertently brushed past', Gifford accused the PCA of making too light of DC Randall's actions, pointing out that police officers who search people's houses have 'a duty of care' to the occupants. It followed that 'a pushing or brushing aside of a large woman standing in a doorway even if it was not intentional, was an act of carelessness and grave discourtesy', and as such, in Gifford's view, was 'a serious departure from the standards which the public [were] entitled to expect from police officers.' Secondly, Gifford found the PCA's decision as to how the search warrant was obtained before the search took place as 'unconvincing'.[25]

Finally, Gifford was critical of the fact that no disciplinary charges were brought, identifying six breaches of the Discipline Code contained in the Police (Discipline) Regulations 1985, including abusive authority, discreditable conduct, racially discriminating behaviour, neglect of duty, falsehood or prevarication and being an accessory to a disciplinary offence, which could have been brought against one or more of the officers involved.[26]

---

25. Ibid, p. 72, para. 4.24; p. 84, para. 4.51.
26. Ibid, pp. 84–86, paras 4.52–4.53.

Back to 5 October

Given the background of the Jarrett family and the unfortunate circumstances surrounding their mother's death, the late senior duty officer on Y District, Superintendent Buchan, felt there was a danger of a similar escalation of violence to that which had occurred in Brixton following the shooting of Cheryl Groce only a week earlier. As a result, he informed Chief Superintendent Alan Stainsby, who was standing in that weekend for Acting Commander Ted Hodge, and the new Area Deputy Assistant Commissioner, Mike Richards. That evening, the two officers visited the Jarrett household to express condolences. Nearly 20 years later, Stainsby described that visit:

> 'There was a whole range of emotions. Tears, anger, frustration, very anti-police, quite an intimidating atmosphere.'[27]

Stainsby also explained to the family that a senior police officer from another force had been appointed to enquire into the incident.[28] Immediately following the visit the Metropolitan Police issued a public statement expressing regret at the death of Mrs Jarrett.[29]

Later that night, shortly after midnight, members of the Jarrett family visited Tottenham Police Station to make further representation about the death of Mrs Jarrett. They were accompanied by between 20 and 30 black people who became involved in a noisy protest outside the police station. As the Jarrett family left, missiles were thrown at the police building from the crowd, breaking four windows. They were eventually persuaded to leave the area.[30]

---

27. Barling, op. cit. 11.
28. Richards, M.D (1985). Public Disorder in Tottenham 6th October 1985: A report to the Haringey Police/Community Consultative Group. London: Metropolitan Police (typescript), p. 5–6, para. 7.1.
29. Metropolitan Police, op. cit. 20, p. 8, para. 3.4.
30. Richards, op. cit. 27, p. 6, para. 8.1.

Police options following the death

Following the death of Cynthia Jarrett, Deputy Assistant Commissioner Richards recognised that events might escalate. On the face of it, the options open to him the next morning were:

    (a) With the assistance of community leaders, to defuse tension and thereby avoid disorder; *and/or*

    (b) To obtain information both from officers on the ground and from local sources about the intentions of the local community; *and/or*

    (c) To arrange for sufficient police reserves to be on hand should disorder occur.

Option (a)

Richards was faced with a problem insofar as option (a) was concerned because, for reasons which have been set out in *Chapter 3*, there were no formal arrangements under which the local police met with council officials and members of the community, although senior police officers did sometimes meet with council officials on an ad-hoc basis. This was such an occasion and, on what was the first of a number of significant events that day, he invited prominent members of Haringey Council and the community to a meeting which took place at Tottenham Police Station between 12.45 p.m. and 1.50 p.m. In attendance were the deputy mayor of Haringey, Councillor Andreas Mikkedes, who was accompanied by Eric Clark of the newly formed but yet to meet Haringey Community and Police Consultative Committee; Chris Kavallares from the Police Sub-committee of the Haringey Community Relations Council; Councillor Ernie Large; Jeff Crawford, Senior Community Relations Officer; and Council Chief Executive Roy Limb. Also present were Dolly Kiffin from the Broadwater Farm Youth Associations and Cynthia Jarrett's two sons, Floyd and Michael. For the police, Richards was accompanied by Chief Superintendent Couch and Superintendent Dorricott.[31] A key demand from those attending the meeting was that the officers involved in the search should be suspended from duty

---

31. Ibid, pp. 6–7, paras 9.2–9.3.

but, according to Chief Executive Roy Limb, Richards claimed it was out of his hands because the investigation was being undertaken by the PCA.[32] Indeed, Councillor Large, claimed that whenever a question was addressed to Richards relating to Cynthia Jarrett's death, he would invariably say it was the subject of the inquiry by the PCA.[33]

In responding thus, Richards was right — the investigation was out of the hands of the Metropolitan Police and was the responsibility of the PCA. However, he was wrong on the question of whether the officers should be suspended or not. This was a matter for the Metropolitan Police. Richards could have ordered their suspension under the Police (Discipline) Regulations in existence at the time; indeed, Roy Limb subsequently received a letter from the deputy chair of the PCA, Roland Moyle which stated the suspension of officers whilst an investigation was being conducted, was a matter for the Metropolitan Police, not the PCA.[34] After some discussion, the meeting agreed that:

(a) all parties would appeal for calm within the community;
(b) the enquiry into Mrs Jarrett's death would be completed as expeditiously as possible.

In addition, the community leaders demanded the PCA report be made public and that Deputy Assistant Commission Richards would pass this request to the Police Complaints Authority, which was supervising the investigation by Assistant Chief Constable Simpson.[35]

Richards was, by all accounts, reassured by the positive attitude of those present and their apparent willingness to do all they could to prevent any disorder. In fact, in response to questions at the subsequent Blakelock murder trial in early-1987 he agreed that he had been surprised that rioting had broken out, because of 'the optimistic feeling' he had taken away from the meeting. He denied a defence suggestion that he could have demonstrated goodwill by suspending the officers involved in the search of Cynthia Jarrett's house, saying that the police did not 'suspend officers to appease members

---

32. Gifford, op. cit. 2, p. 91, para. 5.5.
33. Ibid, p. 90, para. 5.4.
34. Ibid, p. 91, para. 5.5.
35. Richards, op. cit. 27, pp. 6–7, paras. 9.2–9.3.

of the public.'³⁶ But at least two people at the meeting were unhappy at the way things had gone. Councillor Large was annoyed, suggesting that 'if you want to defuse a situation, you have to defuse it by being open.'³⁷ Chief Executive Roy Limb, left in sombre mood, subsequently telling the Gifford Inquiry that he was 'extremely sad' and 'very concerned, because we had heard nothing that could help [them] to go and defuse the tension that was there in the community.'³⁸

The second significant event, if only because it should have alerted the police even more to the possibility of disorder, occurred shortly after the meeting ended when about 100 people, predominantly black, gathered in the road in front of the police station; some carried placards accusing the police of murdering Mrs Jarrett. For a time the crowd completely blocked Tottenham High Road and traffic diversions were set up. Police officers, under the command of Superintendent Sinclair, standing between the police building and the crowd faced a constant barrage of abuse, described in the internal report as 'the most abusive and hostile verbal attack that most of the police officers present had ever experienced' which included threats to 'kill' policemen or 'rape their families'³⁹ in revenge for the death of Mrs Jarrett. At one stage, both Eric Clark, leader of the newly-formed Haringey Community and Police Consultative Group, and Hyacinth Moody, black chair of the Haringey Police Sub-committee attempted to pacify them but they too were abused and threatened. It was also suggested quite forcibly to the police officers present that there would be trouble later that day on the Broadwater Farm Estate but, with the exception of two minor attacks on cars and the breaking of a window in the police station when a missile was thrown, no physical violence was offered by the crowd at that stage.⁴⁰

---

36. *Police Review*, 27 March 1991, p.631.
37. Gifford, op. cit. 2, p. 90, para. 5.4.
38. Ibid, pp. 91–92, para. 5.6.
39. Williams, David A (1986). Internal Police Report on the disorders of the 6th October 1985 at the Broadwater Farm Estate, Tottenham. London: Metropolitan Police, p. 14, para. 3.11; Metropolitan Police, op. cit. 20, p. 9, para. 3.10.
40. Sinclair, William (1990). In an interview with the author on 10 April.

Option (b)

Chief Superintendent Couch and other senior police officers who were present took the view that the threats were rhetoric arising from a release of anger and tension. However, many of the junior officers took a different view and were convinced that, at the very least, attempts would be made to attack police officers later in the day and that there was a very real danger of an outbreak of serious disorder. They were also aware that it was unlikely that any of those present at the meeting at Tottenham Police Station had any influence over the youths who frequented the estate with the exception, perhaps, of Dolly Kiffin. This should have provided the police with valuable information as to the intentions of a section of the community. Instead, it seems, the information being provided by those on the streets was ignored in favour of the impressions that senior officers got from that meeting.[41]

Option (c)

Richards did take a certain amount of action in respect of option (c). Yankee Control at Wood Green Police Station, about a mile away from Broadwater Farm, had been opened at 8 a.m. The appointed controller was Commander David Polkinghorne, who was regarded as one of the most experienced officers in the Metropolitan Police when it came to public order policing. As a chief superintendent, he had served for three years in the Public Order Branch (then known as A8) at New Scotland Yard before serving on Y District as Commander Dickinson's second-in-command. The control was staffed by a chief inspector as deputy controller, an inspector as team manager and five constables as the working team. During the day, it was arranged that a number of police units would be on standby either at Wood Green Police Station or Northumberland Park Police Section House from 10 a.m. but they were briefed that Wood Green High Road, where there was a large shopping centre, or Tottenham High Road were the likely areas of disorder. During the early part of the day, Yankee Control was monitoring both the

---

41. Ibid; see also Richard, op. cit. 2, pp. 7–8, paras 10.1 and 10.2.

Hornsey and Tottenham Police radio networks. Certainly it was aware of the demonstration outside Tottenham Police Station.[42]

Other significant events

Meanwhile, at 2 p.m., a third significant event took place at the West Indian Centre in Clarendon Road. Chaired by Martha Osamor, chair of the Haringey Police Sub-Committee, there was a meeting of black community leaders attended by about 40 people, amongst them William Trant, an officer of the West Indian Standing Conference and two councillors, Bernie Grant and Steve Banerji, a former chair of the police sub-committee. However, it was noticeable that there were very few young black people present. A resolution was passed which contained five demands:

- A full public inquiry into the death of Cynthia Jarrett;
- The resignation of Deputy Assistant Commissioner Mike Richards;
- The payment of the Metropolitan Police precept to be withheld by the council;
- The account given by the Jarrett family of how their mother died to be accepted.
- The four police officers involved in the search to be suspended from duty.[43]

The fourth significant event occurred even before the third one had finished. At around 3.15 p.m., two home beat officers, Constables Roger Caton and George Hughes went to a house in The Avenue after a complaint that an airgun had been fired at one of its windows. As they were about to leave, they noticed a group of black youths, some of whom were armed with bricks outside the house. The officers left the house and hurried away under a hail of missiles. One of the missiles, a section of a paving stone, struck Caton in the back and he was taken to hospital where he was found to be suffering from internal bleeding. He underwent major surgery during

---

42. Williams, David A, op cit. 38, p. 245, paras. 2:3 to 2:5.
43. Gifford, op. cit. 2, pp. 92–93, para. 5.8.

which his spleen, which had been ruptured beyond repair, was removed.[44] Off work for nearly five months, he finally returned to his home beat in mid-March 1986.[45]

The meeting outside the police station eventually broke up at about 3.30 p.m. and most of those who had taken part moved to the Broadwater Farm Estate for a fifth significant event, a meeting which commenced at around 4 p.m. in the Youth Association premises. Gifford described in some detail the apparent anger that was expressed at this meeting. Subsequently, at the Blakelock murder trial[46] Roy Limb agreed that 'in a very emotional atmosphere' there had been shouts of 'an eye for an eye'.[47] Two other prominent people were also present at that meeting, Bernie Grant and Martha Osamor. Osamor tried to introduce Grant who wanted to tell them what had been agreed at the Clarendon Road meeting but the anger in the room was such that she didn't get the opportunity to do that. Grant subsequently claimed:

> 'The fact that they didn't allow me to speak seemed to indicate to me that if I had spoken it wouldn't have made any difference at all. People were really hyped up. I have never seen anything like it. People were very, very threatening. They were very aggressive.'[48]

At the murder trial, Limb was asked whether any of the three 'had tried to dampen the tension at the meeting' to which Limb replied that they were not invited to speak and it would 'have been an intrusion' for him or for them 'to intrude upon what was really a very emotional scene.' He said that 'an outbreak of violence was not obvious at this time' claiming 'it was emotion and anger and distress that was there.' But Mr Justice Hodgson pointed out

---

44. Richards, op. cit. 27, p.8, paras 11.1–11.2; see also *Mail on Sunday*, 13 October 1985; and Williams, op. cit. 38, p. 14, paras. 3:13–3:15. A letter to the *Daily Mail* by a resident of Graham Road described Roger Caton as 'a highly respected officer and regarded with affection by many local people, who are shocked by the extent of his injuries'—*Daily Mail*, 18 October 1985.
45. *Hornsey Journal*, 21 March 1986.
46. The trial of Silcott, Rajhip, Braithwaite and three juveniles for the murder of Police Constable Blakelock which took place at the Old Bailey at the beginning of 1987.
47. Knight, Tim (1987). '"Calls for revenge" before Blakelock killing'. In *Police Review*, 6 March 1987, p.466: see also Rose, David (1987). 'Blakelock trial told of call for revenge'. In *The Guardian*, 3 March 1987.
48. Gifford, op. cit. 2, p.95, para. 5.12.

to Limb that he was unable to take his chosen exit from the estate after the meeting because it was blocked by a 'burning barricade.'[49]

Dolly Kiffin also rushed from the meeting in Clarendon Road to Broadwater Farm when she heard about the meeting at the Youth Association, with the intention of telling them what had been decided. However, when she arrived:

> '[S]he saw that the young man just out of prison seemed to be in charge. He was dressed out in army gear and seemed to be leading the meeting in a direction she did not like. There was talk of marching to the Tottenham Police Station.'[50]

She immediately left the meeting and went upstairs to her office.[51] She was then reminded by Roy Limb of a reception that evening at his home for the Jamaican Minister of Culture and others. She chose to go to the reception and left the estate, taking a taxi to Limb's house.[52] Eventually, the meeting broke up in the Youth Association between 6.30 p.m. and 6.45 p.m., and the intention was to return to the police station.[53] But, as will be seen in the following chapter, they were prevented from doing so.

For much of the time following the attack on Constables Caton and Hughes, there was an uncanny silence about the estate during which time the police received no calls. It was almost as though the Broadwater Farm Estate had ceased to exist. But it was the lull before the storm. From 6.10 p.m. the police received five emergency calls at Tottenham Police Station within an hour from people living on the estate. In each case, the police were told that about 100 youths, some wearing masks, were running through the estate banging on doors. Although it was established that the calls were genuine, no actual damage was caused, and Chief Superintendent Couch made a conscious decision not to respond for fear of provoking a confrontation. He was also mindful that it might be an attempt to suck police into an ambush. However, he did send the duty inspector, Dave Hudson to patrol

---

49. Knight, op. cit. 46, p. 466.
50. Williams, Paul (1994). Keeper of the Dream: The Story of Dolly Kiffin of Broadwater Farm. London: International Community Talk, p.42.
51. Gifford, op. cit. 2, p. 94, para. 5.12.
52. Williams, Paul, op. cit. 49, p.43.
53. Gifford, op. cit. 2, pp. 93–96, paras. 5.10–5.15.

the periphery of the estate to assess the situation but, as he was driving along The Avenue about 400 yards from the estate at about 6.25 p.m., two black youths on a motorcycle, both wearing helmets, pulled alongside his car and smashed a beer bottle through the window of the driver's door before riding away. Glass from the shattered window went into Hudson's eye and he was subsequently taken to Moorfield's Eye Hospital for treatment.[54] In the light of this latest attack, Chief Superintendent Couch decided that only protected vehicles would be deployed to answer calls to the estate and its periphery and the two local DSUs, Y31 and Y32, were instructed to patrol in the vicinity.[55]

Yankee Control

The response to these incidents was controlled from Tottenham Police Station. For reasons that are not apparent, Yankee Control were not monitoring the Tottenham Police radio network at this time and no one at Tottenham Police Station thought to report the incidents to the senior officers in Yankee Control. This was a significant omission which was to leave Commander Polkinghorne 'with the understandable impression that following the dispersal of the demonstrators from outside [Tottenham Police Station] all had become quiet.'[56] So Yankee Control began dismissing all those units that had been present since 10 a.m. and replacing them with around 250 men, mostly shield-trained, who had recently paraded for duty.[57] However, the sudden movement of police was seen by various people, some of whom were associated with the estate. Nick Wright and Debbie Wild, from the Haringey Police Research Unit, subsequently told the Gifford Inquiry that between 6 p.m. and 6.30 p.m., there had been a build-up of police traffic, some in police carriers, others in green coaches, in both directions.[58] The general belief on the estate was that the police were moving towards Broadwater Farm and a rumour immediately circulated round the area that

---

54. Richards, op. cit. 27, p. 9, paras. 12.2–12.3.
55. Williams, David A, op. cit. 38, p. 18, para. 3:32
56. Ibid, p.15, para. 3:18.
57. Ibid, p.17, para. 3:28(d). In addition, a further 450 men, in units which varied from properly equipped public order trained units to ad-hoc units that had to be kitted out centrally but were not necessarily trained in the use of shields, etc., available for deployment from elsewhere in the Metropolitan Police District.
58. Gifford, op. cit. 2, p.101, para. 5.31.

they were about to seal it off. This apparently had the effect of mobilising the youths on the estate.

Plan to deal with disorder at Broadwater Farm

A plan to deal with disorder on the Broadwater Farm Estate had been in existence for some time and it is relevant to quote from the document, particularly in the light of the events described in the next chapter:

> 'It is essential that in order to consolidate and isolate disorder, police should quickly gain control of the walkways connecting the blocks of flats on the estate. Unless this is carried out effectively, units at ground level may be subjected to missiles thrown from above and roaming crowds could move about the estate, thus rendering police mobility in vehicles ineffective.'

The document went on to describe how:

> 'Once the walkways have been secured, pockets of disorder may be contained and dealt with. In the event of disorder involving numbers of persons, efforts will be directed towards moving the participants towards the empty spaces to the west of the Estate for dispersal.'

The document also called for a forward control to be set up in the Car Park adjacent to the Lordship Lane Swimming Pool and for a local officer, equipped with a radio on the local frequency, to be assigned to all units not from Y District.[59]

---

59. Tottenham Police (unknown). Contingency Plans for the Control of Disorder on the Broadwater Farm Estate, Tottenham. Typescript, paras 6.1–6.3, 2.1 and 1.3.

CHAPTER SEVEN

The Riot

The riot starts

A telephone call was received by police at about 6.50 p.m. The caller claimed that a large group of African-Caribbean youths were throwing stones at houses in The Avenue but he refused to identify himself. The two District Support Units (DSUs),[1] Y31 and Y32, visited the area briefly but, although there were a number of youths present, they did not appear to be causing trouble. Both units withdrew. Four minutes later there was another call; this time the caller requested the urgent attendance of the police but did not say for what reason before ringing off. On this occasion, Y32 was sent to investigate but shortly after its arrival at 7.05 p.m., it was attacked by a large group of African-Caribbean youths—about 200 in number, 'dressed in combat jackets and masked with balaclavas, scarves or crash-helmets'—who had congregated under Stapleford Block near the Willan Road entrance to the estate. Sergeant Paul Nevens, the officer in charge of the unit described the scene:

> '[A] lot were carrying milk bottle crates which appeared to be full of bottles with tapers sticking out of them. I could see some holding machetes, various sticks, some of which could have been swords, and with shopping trollies full of bricks. They started running towards our carrier and began lighting petrol bombs and throwing them at us. [At one stage] they were trying to tip our carrier over. The vehicle was swaying from side to side and it was obvious that if they did get in we would be very seriously injured or killed.'

---

1. A DSU normally consisted of a sergeant and ten constables in a protected personnel carrier with an inspector in charge of two such units. Although dressed in ordinary uniforms whilst carrying out general patrols, the officers had protective equipment, such as flameproof overalls, NATO-style helmets and long or smaller round shields with them on the vehicles.

DSU Y32 withdrew eastwards along The Avenue to the junction with Mount Pleasant Road where they were joined by Y31. Officers from both units quickly put on their flameproof overalls and protective helmets before leaving their vehicles carrying protective shields, to confront the youths.[2]

The Gifford Report gives a slightly different version. According to people who gave evidence to his inquiry, three DSUs arrived in The Avenue on the second occasion; one turned into Willan Road, shortly to be followed by another two. It is likely that these were the two Y District DSUs and, if this version is correct, possibly X32. A group of youths, initially numbering only ten, rushed out in front of the first apparently intent on stopping it going into the estate. They had no weapons but banged on the front and sides of the vehicle with their fists. The ten youths were quickly joined by others and the three DSUs reversed up Willan Road to The Avenue and then drove eastwards to the junction with Mount Pleasant Road.[3]

In any event, it is clear what happened during the next few minutes. As the officers from the DSUs left their vehicles they deployed, facing west, towards Willan Road, across the width of The Avenue. By now the group of youths was somewhat larger. Some turned over and set fire to five cars that had quickly been pulled across the entrance to Willan Road, thus effectively making a burning barricade. Others knocked down a garden wall on the corner of the junction and used the bricks to bombard the 20 or so officers stretched across the width of The Avenue. As the Gifford Report succinctly puts it, 'the fighting had started.'[4]

---

2. This version of events was given by Sergeant Nevens, who was in charge of Y32, in evidence on 6 February 1987, at the trial of Silcott, Raghip and Braithwaite, who, together with three juveniles, had been charged with the murder of Constable Keith Blakelock. Reported in *The Guardian* on 7 February 1987 and in *Police Review*, 13 February 1987, p.310. Sergeant Nevens was accused by Michael Mansfield of 'totally exaggerating what had happened' but this was denied.
3. Gifford, Lord (1986). The Broadwater Farm Inquiry: Report of the Independent Inquiry into Disturbances of October 1985 at the Broadwater Farm Estate, Tottenham. London: Broadwater Farm Inquiry, pp. 102–103.
4. Ibid, p. 101.

The rioting worsens

At around 7.10 p.m., the police received messages that cars had been overturned and set on fire in Gloucester Road.[5] The events at this location, which was where Constable Keith Blakelock subsequently met his death, will be described in the next chapter. Meanwhile, Yankee Control deployed units[6] on standby to the Broadwater Farm Estate to assist the DSUs already present. The first ones arrived at 7.10 p.m. but they, too, came under attack in The Avenue, firstly at its junction with Drayton Road and then at its junction with Mount Pleasant Road. In addition, another car was overturned and set on fire in The Avenue approximately 50 yards from the junction with Mount Pleasant Road.[7]

By the time the first senior officer, Superintendent French, arrived there were approximately 50 police officers at the scene. Half were at the junction, whilst the other half were moving, crouched behind long shields, towards the burning vehicles. Youths, who had been throwing missiles at the police line withdrew behind the burning vehicles to join others and petrol bombs were thrown. The barrage of missiles intensified and the police units were forced to withdraw back to the junction.

At this point, French had two options. He could either:

(a) attempt to disperse the rioters; *or*
(b) remain where he was and attempt to contain the rioters in the vicinity of the estate whilst additional units were deployed.

After briefly consulting with the two inspectors present, Superintendent French discounted option (a) above as being untenable. No doubt still

---

5. Ibid, p.105, para. 5.40.
6. It is unclear whether these units were DSUs or ad-hoc units, referred to as serials in Williams, David A (1986). Internal Police Report on the disorders of the 6th October at the Broadwater Farm Estate, Tottenham. London: Metropolitan Police, p.219. Serials (an inspector, three sergeants and 20 constables) and half-serials (a sergeant and ten constables) had originally been put together for duty at other potential trouble spots in the Metropolitan Police District. The reason why deployment was subsequently so unclear was because the 'plot' [deployment board] in the control room was erased without being recorded and a Control Room Log, in which a chronological sequence of deployments should have been shown, was not kept, p. 41, para. 4:22. It is not clear from the Williams Report which of these ad-hoc units consisted of officers who had undergone public order training and were properly equipped.
7. Gifford, op. cit. 3, pp. 130–131.

concerned that the Wood Green Shopping Centre or Tottenham High Road were to be the principle targets for any attack, he advised Yankee Control that the entrances to the estate should be sealed off to prevent people leaving.[8]

Griffin Road

Meanwhile other units were arriving in Mount Pleasant Road. Within a short space of time a further 60 officers — No. 5 Unit of the Special Patrol Group[9] under the command of Inspector Dellow, and three DSUs under the command of Inspector Brooks, had arrived at the junction with Griffin Road where by far the worst and most sustained violence of the evening was to occur.

Griffin Road was about 100 yards long, running westwards from Mount Pleasant Road into the Broadwater Farm Estate. The roadway was about 20 feet across, with footpaths about six feet wide on both sides. Abutting onto each footpath were the side elevations of the houses of Mount Pleasant Road, Nos. 201 and 207, and brick walls nearly two metres high which enclosed the rear gardens.[10] An officer who was a member of DSU X32 described how when they arrived a lone black female walked from the estate in a way that was reminiscent of a scene in the film 'The Warriors'. In an 'eerie, menacing manner' similar to that which one of the characters in the film did at one point, she was chanting, 'Babylon. You're going to burn'.[11]

Immediately a group of youths, about 50 in number, standing about 50 yards west of the junction, at the entrance to the estate, started throwing missiles at the officers. Dellow and Brooks had the same options as French at this stage, either to:

(a) attempt to disperse the youths; *or*

---

8. French, David (1990). In correspondence with the author, dated 17 May. He had been directed to attend Hornsey Police Station on the morning of 6 October to take charge of the response to any disorder in Wood Green and was still there when he heard the messages emanating from Yankee Control.
9. A Special Patrol Group unit normally consisted an inspector, three sergeants and 30 constables. Transport consisted of a car for the inspector and three carriers, each carrying ten constables under the command of a sergeant.
10. Jeffers, Mike (1990). In correspondence with the author, dated 31 January 1990.
11. Lawson, Mark (2014). In correspondence with the author, dated 29 August.

(b) draw up a containment cordon in an attempt to keep the rioters from leaving the estate.

Because of the absence of any barricades at that stage,[12] and possibly because the two inspectors were unaware of the rumours circulating that the most likely target for rioting that day was elsewhere, they chose option (a). Leaving their vehicles the officers, dressed in protective overalls and carrying shields, charged westwards, driving the youths back into the estate. As they retreated, the youths split into two groups, half going under Rochford Block and half under Martlesham Block. Brooks led his men to the right under Martlesham Block; Dellow led his men left under Rochford Block. As each approached the basement areas of the respective blocks, they became aware that the two groups had doubled in size — there were now about 50 under each block. And then, almost as though a signal had been given, youths suddenly appeared above the officers on the first floors of each block and started bombarding the advancing officers with missiles, including pieces of paving-stones. Despite wearing a riot helmet, at least one constable was knocked unconscious and others were hit.

Realising that they had been sucked into an ambush both Brooks and Dellow ordered their men to withdraw and they retreated back to the edge of the estate, forming a cordon across the road. The total width of the road and footpaths meant only about twenty men could actually face the rioters and the front rank of police were immediately subjected to a ferocious attack from a crowd which, by now had reached about 200. Some were armed with clubs and machetes; others threw a variety of missiles, including petrol bombs.

To avoid further injuries, Brooks and Dellow, despite being under continuous attack, made an orderly withdrawal, westwards again, this time to the junction with Mount Pleasant Road. The youths advanced, and quickly moved a number of vehicles into the roadway before setting them on fire

---

12. This differs from the Richards Report which suggested that there were burning barricades already in place when the police first arrived. See Richards, M.D (1985). Public Disorder in Tottenham 6th October 1985: A report to the Haringey Police/Community Consultative Group. London: Metropolitan Police (typescript), p. 11, para. 14.2.

to form a barricade. It was now about 7.45 p.m.[13] In total, eight or nine cars were used in Griffin Road during the evening; as soon as one burned out, another was set on fire to take its place.[14] However, in the next five minutes, the police recovered some of the lost ground and, by 7.50 p.m. had driven the youths back behind the burning barricade.

Senior officer deployment

By now additional senior officers were beginning to arrive. Next after Superintendent French was Superintendent Sinclair, who arrived from Tottenham Police Station, and took over the Willan Road entrance to allow Superintendent French to go to Griffin Road. Chief Inspector Rowe, who was on standby at Northumberland Park, went to Adams Road.[15] On his arrival from Tottenham Police Station, Chief Superintendent Couch went to Gloucester Road.[16]

Adams Road

Meanwhile, a similar pattern to that which had been developing in Griffin Road was emerging in Adams Road, which also ran westwards into the estate from Mount Pleasant Road. Initially, at least one DSU from D District, arrived and deployed as two five-man long shield units across the width of the street. They were prevented from moving forward by a crowd of youths throwing missiles and, by 7.25 p.m., a barricade of burning vehicles had been erected which effectively prevented the officers from moving westwards

---

13. Dellow, Richard (1990). In conversation with author, dated 10 May. The Gifford, op. cit. 2, p.104, para. 5.38, supports Dellow's description of events but both are at variance with the Richards, p.11, which suggests that, in addition to the barricade at Willan Road, the police found blazing vehicles had been placed across the road at the three other vehicular entrances to the estate, at Gloucester Road, Griffin Road and Adams Road. .
14. Gifford, op. cit. 3, p.107, para. 5.46.
15. The role of Chief Inspector Rowe during the remainder of the evening is unclear. None of the reports on the riot mention him, other than his arrival.
16. French, op. cit. 8 and Sinclair, Bill (1990). In an interview with the author, dated 10 April. The information these two former officers gave to the author differs slightly from the deployment outlined by Williams, op. cit. 6, p. 20, para. 3:38.

towards the estate. They were also conscious of the possibility of being ambushed from Martlesham Block on their left flank.[17]

Ten minutes later, the officers came under attack from about 70 black youths who were already occupying the balconies of Martlesham Block and there was a request to Yankee Control for more units at that location. Serial 610, from H District,[18] was one of the units that arrived in response and immediately deployed, again as two five-man long shield units, parallel with but to the right of the D District unit. One of the youths, wearing a white crash-helmet, seemed to be the main instigator of petrol bombs; a shopping trolley full of broken paving slabs was dragged from Martlesham Block to supply the youths with ammunition. The police line moved forward, driving the youths back under Martlesham Block but, fearing an ambush, the line stopped at the stairwell. They were right to be wary because the group of youths quickly doubled in size as others waiting under the block joined them. The 20 or so police officers were in danger of being completely encircled by the youths and they therefore dropped back. However, as they did so, the number of youths increased until there were easily 150 or more. Serial 601 had, by this time, become separated from the D District DSU. It was then that the officer-in-charge of Serial 601, Sergeant Geoff Ervine, noticed that he had a man down in one of his five-man units and what followed was typical of the experiences a number of units underwent that night. Constable Keith Jeffries was picked up by Constables Arthurs and Harris and they started to drag him back, leaving Constables Garden and Johnson doing their best to protect them. Garden was then hit on the head with a paving slab which left him dazed; Johnson, hit by a youth wielding a wooden club and knocked down, pulled a riot shield over the top of his body to try and protect himself. Meanwhile, Arthurs and Harris, still trying to drag the injured Jeffries with them, were being struck by missiles. Johnson managed to get to his feet and retreated with one long shield; the other two long shields had been lost to the mob.[19]

The other five-man shield unit, with Paul Hogan on the left, Stewart Dawson in the middle and Jim Mahaffey on the right, supported by

---

17. Ervine, Sergeant Geoffrey (1985). Report, dated 21 October, in the author's possession.
18. Ibid.
19. Ibid.

Constable Fitzpatrick and Sergeant Ervine had been forced back against a builders' skip which was in the road behind them. The rioters were now so close that some were able to pull the shields aside, whilst others dropped or threw paving slabs at them. Ervine was hit fully on the visor, causing him to stagger back; Mahaffey was struck across the head with a metal pipe, causing him also to stagger backwards but in a dazed condition, and he had to be supported by Fitzpatrick and Ervine. Meanwhile, Hogan on the left of the five-man unit had also been hit by a number of missiles.[20]

By now Serial 601 along with the two D District DSUs, who were under a similar ferocious attack, had been forced back to a point only 30 yards from the junction with Mount Pleasant Road. This had been reduced to 15 yards when additional police units arrived to form a solid defensive line across the width of the road and they slowly began to push the crowd back towards the estate. Three of the officers who made up Serial 601, Mahaffey, Garden and Jeffries, were taken to hospital by waiting ambulances.[21] Some units were being deployed to the 'front line' who were not properly equipped because recently arrived officers 'frantically' attempted 'to equip themselves by "scavenging" uniform and equipment from injured officers.'[22]

Ervine re-grouped what remained of his unit, forming one five-man shield unit; the remaining officers were issued with short-shields to back up the five-man unit. He moved his men forward again into Adams Road, slowly replacing groups in front of them, as they too suffered casualties. At around 8.40 p.m. one of the houses caught fire. Whether it was an intentional act by the rioters or not was unclear. Certainly the youths deliberately set fire to private cars parked on both sides of the road as the police retreated; some were pulled across the road to replace the original barricade, which had nearly burned itself out, before being set alight; others were petrol-bombed where they were parked. A 'Royal Variety Sunshine' mini-bus which had been pushed out from one of the nearby schools, was driven by a youth towards the police line but crashed into a wall of the house that was on fire. The youth leapt out and ran away, leaving the engine running. After a relatively short period, Sergeant Ervine's driver, Constable Trevor Hanson, was able

---

20. Ibid.
21. Ibid.
22. Hogan, Paul (2014). In correspondence with the author, dated 30 June.

to leap into it and drive it away.²³

At one stage, DSU F30, under the command of Inspector Nigel Bailey, arrived in Moira Close outside William C Harvey School. Bailey realised that, with additional units, he could move in behind the youths in Martlesham Block but his radio call to Yankee Control asking for more units to enable him to do this got no response.²⁴

With the reinforcements having arrived, one eye-witness likened Adams Road unto:

> '[A] battleground, with 100 policemen in three ranks holding one end of the street against a constant barrage of missiles. Just in front of the police line...flames shot into the air from burning cars occasionally releasing deafening explosions. Bricks, pieces of paving-stones, bottles and petrol bombs rained on the police. The bricks battering into the shields sounded like gunfire. Black youths used the tower blocks on the estate as cover as they bombarded the police.'²⁵

The police responded to the house fire by advancing towards the barricade and establishing a cordon about halfway down Adams Road but were unable to advance further because of the ferociousness of the missile attack. Fortunately, it turned out that the house was unoccupied. Superintendent Boyall²⁶ arrived in Adams Road shortly before 8.40 p.m., just before the house caught fire. Things having quietened down in Griffin Road, Superintendent French, not realising Superintendent Boyall was already there, moved to Adams Road. The two senior officers discussed the situation and, as a result, an attempt was made to send officers through the rear gardens of the houses affronting Mount Pleasant Road, Nos. 225 to 227, to launch an offensive on the rioters behind the barricades but this was quickly abandoned because of the intense heat from the burning vehicles and the house fire at No.2

---

23. Ervine, op. cit. 17.
24. Bailey, Nigel (2014). In correspondence with the author, dated 8 August.
25. *The Daily Telegraph*, 7 October 1985.
26. Boyall, George (1990). Superintendent George Boyall was due to be on duty at Brixton on 6 October, following the rioting there on 28 September. However, as he was on his way there, he was re-directed to Wood Green, arriving at Yankee Control at sometime between 2 p.m. and 2.30 p.m. He was briefed by both Richards and Polkinghorne about the possibility of disorder in the area and the Wood Green Shopping Centre was the most likely location. Interview with author, dated 10 April 1990.

Adams Road. Therefore, French and Boyall decided on another ploy — to hide officers in the rear gardens and withdraw the police cordon back to the junction in an attempt to draw the rioters from behind the barricade towards them. The officers could then emerge from the gardens, cutting-off the retreat of the rioters back to the estate. The rioters failed to respond.[27]

The house fire in Adams Road was now intense and the flames became an increasing danger to the occupants of the houses nearby. Repeated requests by radio for the Fire Brigade and a JCB, to remove the burning vehicles, met with no response. Eventually, although still under intermittent attack from missile throwers, the police cordon moved towards the estate, stopping immediately in front of the burning barricade. This enabled officers to evacuate the houses in Adams Road opposite No.2.[28]

The Fire Brigade eventually arrived at about 9.30 p.m. and, under police protection, extinguished both the house fire and the burning vehicles. The rioters had largely vacated Adams Road by now although the occasional petrol bomb or piece of paving stone was thrown but it fell short of the fire engines. In the meantime, two vehicles had been set on fire in the car park under Martlesham Block and, again, protected by police officers, the Fire Brigade extinguished these fires. The JCB finally arrived in Mount Pleasant Road shortly before 10 p.m.[29]

Griffin Road again

Following his arrival in Griffin Road, French discussed the situation with Brooks and Dellow, and it was felt that it would have been an act of folly to have tried to advance past the barricade from their frontal position. They were unaware of how many youths were opposing them and the rioters were clearly in control of the balconies of Martlesham and Rochford Blocks from which they could launch a devastating attack on the police below if they came within range.

Within a relatively short time the tactics of the rioters became clear:

---

27. French, op. cit. 8.
28. Ibid.
29. Ibid.

'About 200–300 youths would emerge from under the tower blocks and attack one or more of the barricaded locations with bricks and petrol bombs...After each attack, when ammunition was exhausted, the rioters would withdraw to re-arm and then attack again either in the same location or at one of the others.'[30]

At the subsequent murder trial, Constable Ian Pyles described the barrage of missiles aimed at police as if 'someone [was] constantly pushing at our shields.' At one stage the rioters were able to pull down the shields and strike at officers over the top. He saw a barrel of burning material thrown at police from a balcony; he also saw a youth with a rifle, and another with a knife mounted on a long pole which he used to strike over the top of the shields. The injuries to police officers mounted and 'bloodstained officers were carried to ambulances waiting in side streets.'[31] Those with minor injuries were given first aid on the spot.

More disturbingly, at shortly before 8 p.m., came the first indications that firearms were being used by the rioters when a member of one of the DSUs, S32, announced that he had a bullet-hole in his shield. Shortly afterwards, Yankee Control was informed that an injured officer who had been taken to hospital had a bullet wound.[32] Police Constable Stuart Patt, from Rainham in Essex, had been trying to stop rioters turn over a car as part of the barricade when he was shot. He was rushed to hospital where he 'underwent two hours surgery to remove shotgun pellets from severe abdominal injuries.'[33] Before the night was over at least five more people had been injured by gunfire. Two were police officers[34] and the other three were from the media. Robin Green, a sound technician, and Keith Skinner, a cameraman, both working for the British Broadcasting Corporation, were both hit by shotgun pellets and taken to the Royal Middlesex Hospital. Also hit was Press Association reporter, Peter Woodman.[35]

At about 8.30 p.m., many of the youths behind the barricade in Griffin Road ran back into the estate. Although the police were able to advance

---

30. Richards, op. cit. 12, pp. 12–13, para. 14.7.
31. *Police Review*, 6 March 1987, p.466.
32. Richards, op. cit. 12, p.13, para. 14.9.
33. *The Times* 8 October 1985; see also *Daily Express*, 8 October, and *Daily Mail*, 9 October.
34. *The Times*, 8 October 1985.
35. *The Daily Telegraph*, 7 October 1985; *The Guardian*, 7 October 1985; *The Times*, 8 October 1985.

and establish a new protective cordon in line with the rear of the houses fronting onto Mount Pleasant Road, they went no further, fearing that the move by the rioters might have been yet another attempt to draw them into an ambush.[36]

Griffin Road remained fairly quiet for a period, but shortly before 9.15 p.m. the number of youths behind the barricade, which had, by this time, almost burned itself out, suddenly increased and launched a violent missile attack, which included a large number of petrol bombs on the police cordon. More vehicles were dragged across the road on the edge of the estate and set on fire. Some of the youths gained access to the rear gardens of Nos. 207, 209 and 211, Mount Pleasant Road. Using the walls as cover, this enabled them to get very close to the right flank of the police cordon. A number of officers were injured and at 9.25 p.m., Inspector Dellow suggested to Yankee Control that a senior officer was urgently required to consider the use of baton rounds and/or CS gas. Chief Superintendent Mike Jeffers was sent.[37]

He arrived at a time when the crowd was increasing and the sustained and ferocious attack on the police cordon was continuing. At this time, there were still only about 80 police officers actually deployed at the junction in rows four deep. Facing them between 40 and 50 feet away, the crowd was estimated at between 400 and 500, most of whom were involved in a 'horrifying, sustained and accurate barrage of broken paving-stones, bricks, canned food and petrol bombs' at the police lines. Occasionally, some of the more daring or reckless youths darted forward of the main group to deliver a telling attack.[38]

Individual officers subsequently described their experiences of what it was like in Griffin Road. A constable described how, although the kerbs were originally reasonably high, the rioters 'literally levelled the pavements' in their quest for weapons and, as a result, because of the rubble, it was 'difficult' for police officers 'to maintain [their] footing.' He went on:

---

36. *The Times*, 8 October 1985.
37. Dellow, op. cit. 13.
38. Jeffers, op. cit. 10.

'During the height of the rioting we were literally toe to toe with the rioters separated only by a thin sheet of Perspex. Rioters were literally climbing up the shields to smash lumps of concrete onto the officers' heads'.

He went on to describe how his unit, X32, was effectively disbanded as officers were used to individually replace those who had been injured in No. 5 Unit of the SPG and other DSUs.[39]

At one stage, a senior officer instructed 'snatch squads', officers with the smaller round shields, to run towards the rioters in an attempt to disperse them, but, at the same time, he told the long shield units to 'stand firm'. This was against established force practice and meant that the 'snatch squads' had no back-up. As a result, one officer described in a letter to the *Police Federation Journal* how he saw 'several officers fall to the ground injured as they were forced to run an unnecessary distance back to the relative safety of the long shields.'[40] When it was pointed out to the senior officer by an experienced inspector that this was contrary to public order training, the former ensured that the long shields did give support.[41] Another officer described how, as the police advanced slowly forward, the rioters came to meet them, ever bolder, getting within feet of the shields like a latter-day scene from the film *Zulu*. In turn, the police would dress back, sometimes having to turn and run, then someone would fall, to be unceremoniously dragged away by the front of his uniform.

'Flaming cars illuminated the rioters as they danced in the orange light like pagan silhouettes, as we prepared to drive forward again. They charged to meet us, and again we were forced to retreat. The bricks were thrown with an ever-increasing ferocity, which meant we could no longer turn our backs, having to drag the shields slowly away, keeping the bottom edge close to the ground.'[42]

---

39. Lawson, op. cit. 11.
40. *Police*, Vol. XVIII, No. 3, November 1985, p.11.
41. Dellow, op. cit. 13.
42. Cotton, Paul (1995). A 'Pagan' Nightmare. In *Police Review*, 6 October, p. 17.

Summary of activity in Adams and Griffin Roads

For at least two-and-a-half hours the police, particularly in Griffin Road and Adams Road, faced

> 'constant volleys of dangerous missiles. Slabs of pavement were broken up and thrown. When the available slabs from nearby were used up, young people were seen rushing through the estate carrying missiles in various containers.'[43]

These missiles included a shopping trolley, milk crate and a large communal rubbish bin. From an early stage, 'many petrol bombs were thrown' and, later, 'tins stolen from the supermarket became a common form of ammunition.'[44] The 'destructive power of these weapons' was enhanced by the use of the balconies 'as launching pads' for the rioters 'to drop [them] on the heads of the police below.'[45] Despite the presence of large numbers of officers, the narrow streets and fiercely burning barricades prevented their effective deployment. At both locations, a relatively small number of officers in the front rank, about 20 in each case, bore the brunt of the attacks. The remainder were merely drawn up in rows behind the front rank where, although they were targets for missile and petrol bomb attacks, lobbed over the front row of police officers, they were not in a position to confront the rioters. For most of this time, the police officers stood passively behind long shields, 'fending off the missiles which came at them.' From time-to-time 'they would advance a short distance, 40 or 50 yards, and then retreat again,'[46] as the next attack was launched from both ground level and the walkways and balconies above. One officer, Constable David Smith, who was at one time in the front rank of police officers in Griffin Road when he was hit by a brick thrown by a rioter and knocked unconscious, said:

---

43. Gifford, op. cit. 3, p. 106, para. 5.43.
44. Ibid.
45. Walsh, Mike (1989). A study of urban mob violence: the Tottenham riots, 1985. In Walsh, Mike (ed.) 1989. *Disasters: Current Planning and Recent Experience*. London: Edward Arnold, p. 142.
46. Gifford, op. cit. 3, p. 110, para. 5.52.

'We were just sitting targets. There was little we could do to protect ourselves or anyone around us, let alone stop the violence.'[47]

Some isolated attempts to enter the estate by police units acting on their own initiative have already been described. On another occasion, a unit managed to secure one of the balconies overlooking Adams Road but, lacking support and unable to advance further for fear of being over-exposed, it was forced to withdraw when the officers came under attack from a larger group of youths.[48]

Petrol bombs were manufactured with ease. One resident looking from the Rochford Block overlooking Griffin Road described the process. He saw

'people with bottles, then some people syphoning off fuel from cars, three or four people laughing and putting cloth inside. There was a white cloth, a large piece, and they were tearing it apart and then putting it into the bottles, and throwing it. But of ten bottles they threw, one of them would actually light up and land in the road. All the others would just be nothing.'[49]

A researcher from St Katherine's College, Oxford, Michael Keith, who was conducting a study of rioting at the time, went to Tottenham after hearing of the death of Cynthia Jarrett. He, too, saw just how easily and quickly petrol bombs were made:

'Two people, both Black, started shouting orders at the others: "we need more ammunition". Immediately five or six responded by running around the houses gathering up empty milk bottles, while four others turned over a car for petrol. In less than five minutes I counted more than 50 petrol bombs completed.'[50]

The burning vehicles became a major problem. Not only did they physically impede the police from entering the estate at Griffin, Adams and Willan Roads but the thick clouds of black smoke from burning tyres obscured

---

47. *The Times*, 8 October 1985.
48. Ibid, p. 110 para. 5.52.
49. Ibid, p. 106, para. 5.44.
50. Ibid, pp. 106–107, para. 5.44.

visibility and exploding petrol tanks were a hazard to anyone nearby and made a great deal of noise. Coupled with the shouting of the rioters, made worse by the echo effect of the high-rise buildings, this made verbal communication between police units and between those on the ground and Yankee Control extremely difficult.

Deployment of baton gunners at Griffin Road

A firearms team, consisting of nine officers, all trained in the use of baton rounds, under the command of Superintendent Peter Harris, had been on standby on Y District since about 4 p.m. At 9.40 p.m., 'the scale of the attack in Griffin Road had become so ferocious' that Deputy Assistant Commissioner Richards telephoned Assistant Commissioner McLean in the Special Operations Room at New Scotland Yard about eight miles away, seeking his authority to, if necessary, use baton rounds and/or CS gas. Permission was given for them to be used 'as a last resort should all else fail.'[51] Richards sought the advice of Superintendent Harris, who was at Tottenham Police Station. Harris went to Griffin Road to see for himself and quickly came to the conclusion that CS gas would cause as much if not more harm to police officers than it would to the rioters. However, he felt the use of baton rounds was an option and instructed the firearms team to attend. Both he and the on-scene commander, Chief Superintendent Jeffers, then spoke to Richards by telephone. It was now about 10.15 p.m. Jeffers apparently persuaded Richards that 'the severity of the attack had lessoned considerably, mainly it would appear because the Blakelock incident had drawn some of the rioters away to the other side of the estate'[52] and suggested to Richards that the police were doing what they had always done for 150 years and he saw no reason to move up a notch for the first time in history. Having convinced Richards that the use of baton rounds was unnecessary, the authority was withdrawn.[53]

Unfortunately, by this time the baton gunners had arrived and were in the

---

51. Williams, David A, op. cit. op. cit.6, p. 30.
52. Richards, op. cit. 12, p.16, para. 14.16; see also *Chapter 8*.
53. Waldren, Michael J (2007). *Armed Police: The Police Use of Firearms since 1945*. Stroud: Sutton Publishing, p. 114.

process of being deployed with the front shield serial, No. 5 Unit of the SPG who had trained regularly with baton gunners in exercises. The appearance of the baton gunners 'lifted' the morale of the officers who had, by this time, been under attack for well over two hours, 'so much so there was cheering, back slapping and general euphoria, not perhaps the correct behaviour for police in such a situation, but a clear indication that those baton gunners were needed by the men on the front line and had been so needed for some considerable time.' Having had the authority to deploy withdrawn, Superintendent Harris directed the baton gunners to withdraw, return to their transport and go back to the holding area. As they did so, the morale of the officers on the front line dropped; many looked 'dejected and abandoned.'[54]

Willan Road and the surrounding area

Willan Road runs, initially, from south to north from The Avenue into the estate but after about 40 yards turns westwards before continuing for approximately another 80 yards. Soon after his arrival at this location, Superintendent Sinclair became concerned that flames from the burning barricade would set light to a nearby house, No. 135, which was occupied by a black family and who were clearly reluctant to leave of their own accord for fear that they might be attacked and their home looted. Sinclair therefore had two options, either:

    (a) to attempt to evacuate the family, possibly through the back garden of the adjoining houses; *or*

    (b) to attempt to drive the rioters back from the barricade to enable the Fire Brigade to put the flames out.

Sinclair decided on option (b). At 8 p.m., a serial using long shields advanced, driving the rioters back into and northwards along Willan Road. This enabled Sinclair to take control of the junction and place a cordon across the southern end of Willan Road.[55]

For the next hour some activity did take place around Wimbourne Road,

---

54. Williams, David A, op. cit. 6, pp. 266–268; see also Waldren, op. cit. 50, pp. 113–114.
55. Sinclair, op. cit. 16; Richards, op. cit. 12 refers to blazing vehicles (p.13, para. 14.8). This was incorrect.

which was directly opposite Adams Road to the east of Mount Pleasant Road. Firstly, units came under attack from a group of youths in Wimbourne Road at its junction with Drayton Road at around 8.20 p.m. as they attempted to come up behind the police units facing the estate in Adams Road. When this was repelled, a second attempt was made about ten minutes later to come down Chandos Street into Wimbourne Road but this too was repelled; a third attempt was made at the same location at around 8.45 p.m. but this too, was repelled. The youths therefore confined themselves to taking bricks and rubble back to the estate, via a circuitous route that avoided the four locations at which the police were mainly concentrated. Also, police units were deployed to Moira Close after it was reported that youths were entering and leaving the estate from Lordship Lane. This continued for a period, the last group coming from Lordship Lane via this route at around 9 p.m.[56]

Shortly after 8.30 p.m., a number of youths who had gathered under Northolt Block moved quickly to Willan Road where they mounted an attack on the police lines. But it was relatively short-lived and petered out as the youths moved off elsewhere.[57] Thereafter, it was relatively quiet at this location until, at shortly after 10 p.m., a car suddenly appeared round the corner in Willan Road from the direction of the estate, followed by approximately 200 youths, and drove towards the police cordon, stopping half-way. Fortunately, the slight slope of Willan Road, which runs from a high point at the southern end, was in favour of the police but, fearing the vehicle might be driven at the police cordon, Sinclair instructed the driver of one of the attendant police vehicles, a personnel carrier, to be ready to ram it if it advanced any further. The vehicle then moved a short distance towards the police line but quickly reversed. This manoeuvre was repeated but on the third occasion the car suddenly came up the slope at speed. The police driver was ready and drove towards the oncoming vehicle, ramming it before it reached the junction and just after the driver leapt from it and made good his escape. The car immediately burst into flames and there is little doubt that it had been designed as a 'fire-bomb' with the intention of crashing it as close to the police lines as possible. The police vehicle although

---

56. Williams, David A, op. cit. 6, pp. 139–143.
57. Ibid, p. 142.

badly damaged was able to reverse back behind the police lines.[58]

Gloucester Road

The circumstances surrounding what happened at Gloucester Road and the fateful entry of Serial 502 into Tangmere Block is described in the following chapter. Suffice to say at this stage that Sergeant Pengelly, who was in charge of the unit, was instructed by Chief Superintendent Couch to accompany a unit of the London Fire Brigade into Tangmere Block. When they were attacked, the call for urgent assistance was heard over the police radio network.

Boyall's rescue attempt

In response to Serial 502's frantic calls for assistance at about 10.10 p.m. but, unbeknown to anyone else because it was impossible to get airtime on the only radio channel available, Superintendent Sinclair immediately despatched one of his units to Gloucester Road. Meanwhile, on the other side of the estate, Superintendent Boyall quickly agreed with French that he would try and lead some units to Tangmere. He collected together what he thought was six shield-trained DSUs[59]—about 70 officers—who had arrived outside the Nursery School in Moira Close, briefed them around a map of the estate that happened to be nearby—he could not find a local officer with knowledge of the area—and set off, at about 10.15 p.m., towards the general direction of Tangmere on a rescue mission, leaving French to hold Adams Road with the remaining 60 officers.[60]

Boyall led them forward through the basement underneath Martlesham Block. Unfortunately, although he could receive messages over his radio, he was unable to transmit because of a defect, but French informed Yankee

---

58. Sinclair, op. cit. 16. This version of the incident involving the car being driven towards the police lines was supported by the community relations officer, Superintendent Stacey, in his statement, dated 12 December 1985, who was called out from this home and was close by with Jeff Crawford and Fred Ellis, both members of the CRC Police Liaison Committee.
59. One of the units was DSU F30 mentioned earlier as having arrived outside William C Harvey School. Information from Bailey, op. cit. 20.
60. Boyall, George (1990). Interview with the author, dated 10 April 1990.

Control of Boyall's intentions. Using long shields for protection, Boyall realised before he had gone very far that some of the officers were not 'shield-trained' and some started to lag behind the others. Nevertheless, he pressed on, cutting across the front of Jeffer's area of activity in Griffin Road, but behind the rioters who were attacking that position.[61]

From his position in Griffin Road, Jeffers could see Boyall and his men in the estate. Despite the fact that he had about 240 men under his command at the time and the sustained attack mounted by the rioters on his forces at 9.30 p.m. had begun to subside, Jeffers decided he could not deploy units from Griffin Road to assist the advance and he advised Boyall to withdraw back to Adams Road with his men. Initially, Boyall did not respond to this advice. However, going beneath Rochford Block, he came under petrol bomb and missile attack from balconies and walkways as he emerged on the other side and began to suffer casualties. Realising that he could suffer even more as he passed under yet more balconies and walkways, Boyall decided to withdraw and the units fell back in good order to Griffin Road, arriving at about 10.35 p.m.[62]

The violence subsides

Shortly after the death of Police Constable Blakelock, for reasons which are not entirely apparent, the violence reduced in its intensity; it was almost as though the rioters considered the death of Mrs Jarrett had been avenged. Even so, there were a number of further incidents, particularly off the estate.

To the north, two schools and a day nursery all suffered damage and had equipment, such as computers, televisions and photocopiers, stolen. Until fairly late on, no police officers were deployed to prevent people entering or leaving along the footpaths which ran alongside the schools, between the estate and Lordship Lane in the north.[63]

At 11 p.m., a crowd of some 200 youths demolished a garden wall in Wimbourne Road, using the bricks to throw at police officers in Mount Pleasant Road. Some of the police units immediately formed a cordon to

---

61. Ibid.
62. Ibid.
63. Gifford, op. cit. 3, p.109, para. 5.50; Richards, op. cit. 10, p. 16, para. 14.17.

confront the youths who promptly overturned a car, tried to set it on fire and 'the battle ensued for over an hour with the police moving forward, then back, until eventually they dispersed them away from the estate into surrounding residential streets.'[64] At the same time, other police units patrolling around the periphery of the estate responded to reports of gangs of youths smashing windows and looting shops in Bruce Grove and Tottenham High Road, about half a mile away. Prompt action by these units prevented any of these incidents from developing into a serious outbreak of disorder.[65]

At 11.45 p.m., the police received a telephone call from a resident on the Broadwater Farm Estate who told them that a large group of youths were still assembled in the parking areas beneath 'the tower blocks', clearly lying in wait for the police. So, even at this late stage, and given that firearms had been used on a number of occasions against the police, Richards decided not to enter the estate.[66]

The police finally occupy the Estate

At about 1.30 a.m., Deputy Assistant Commissioner Richards ordered the senior ground commanders, Chief Superintendents Couch, Stainsby and Jeffers, and Superintendent French to a meeting at Wood Green Police Station, leaving the police cordons at the various entrances to the estate under the command of Superintendents Sinclair and Boyall, supported by a number of chief inspectors. At the meeting they were joined by Chief Superintendent Tom Jones and Superintendent Doug Hopkins of the Special Patrol Group, and Chief Superintendent Bob Wells, the officer commanding the Force Firearms Unit, and others. A plan to retake the estate evolved. The various senior officers then returned to brief units who would be under their command.[67]

At about 3.30 a.m., six units of the Special Patrol Group, nearly 200 officers, spearheaded the advance into the estate from the Gloucester Road

---

64. Gifford, op. cit. 3, p.120, para. 5.76.
65. Ibid, p. 120, para. 5.76; Richards, op. cit. 12, p. 16, para. 14.17.
66. Richards, op. cit. 12, pp. 16–17, para. 14.18.
67. Williams, David A, op. cit. 6, p.33, para. 3:87. With the exception of the two senior SPG officers, Chief Superintendent Jones and Superintendent Hopkins, Chief Superintendent Stainsby was the only one of the remaining senior officers who was 'public-order' trained.

entrance. Dressed in protective overalls and using long shields, the first two, led by Chief Superintendent Jones, moved at ground level along Gloucester Road, keeping Croyden, Debden, Hornchurch and Kenley Blocks on their left and Tangmere, Hawkinge, Lympne and Manston Blocks on their right. At the same time, Chief Inspector McCardle led two units into Tangmere Block and Superintendent Hopkins led a further two units at first floor level, covering Jones's right flank. As the SPG units advanced, DSUs, under the command of Chief Superintendent Couch and Superintendent Sinclair, occupied the ground behind them. At the same time, Chief Superintendent Jeffers, with 13 DSUs, 11 full serials and No. 5 Unit of the SPG, totalling around 400 officers, entered the estate from Willan Road, concentrating on occupying Stapleford, Rochford, Martlesham and Northolt Blocks. The units met little opposition. By 4.15 a.m., it was reported that the estate was firmly under police control.[68]

---

68. Hopkins, Doug (2014). In conversion with the author on 20 May: Riley, Steve (2014). In correspondence with the author, dated 14 May.

CHAPTER EIGHT

The Killing of Constable Keith Blakelock

Gloucester Road

Possibly because it was the least attractive from their point of view, the rioters paid little attention to the Gloucester Road entrance to the estate after setting fire to some vehicles at the outset. Indeed, as early as 7.30 p.m., it was reported that although the cars were still burning, no youths were present.[1] Here again, the initial police cordon was deployed level with the rear of the houses facing onto The Avenue. The only block of flats which afforded cover for the rioters was Croydon Block which was located on the left of the police cordon. But, being on the western edge of the estate, it would have been relatively easy for the police to have isolated any rioters using this as a base from which to mount attacks.

Although initially there were a number of units in attendance, the atmosphere, under Chief Superintendent Couch's command, was fairly relaxed. Not all police officers wore protective clothing or the NATO-style riot helmet, and people were still able to walk on and off the estate. Serial 502, which was to play a significant and tragic role in the events later, arrived at about 7.45 p.m. and, with other units, stood guard as the Fire Brigade extinguished the burning vehicles.[2]

Attempts were made to allow community leaders to mediate, particularly during the early stages. Those leaders who contacted Yankee Control during the evening were directed to the Gloucester Road entrance to liaise with Chief Superintendent Couch.[3] On one occasion, when Couch saw Arthur

---

1. Williams, David A (1986). Internal Police Report on the disorders of the 6th October 1985 at the Broadwater Farm Estate, Tottenham. London: Metropolitan Police, p. 131 (log of radio messages).
2. Gifford, Lord (1986). The Broadwater Farm Inquiry: Report of the Independent Inquiry into Disturbances of October 1985 at the Broadwater Farm Estate, Tottenham. London: Broadwater Farm Inquiry, p. 111, para. 5.55.
3. Polkinghorne, David (1989). In correspondence with the author, dated 2 November.

Lawrence and other members of the West Indian Council in The Avenue, he asked them to 'do something to help calm the situation'.[4] Their response was to ask for police units to be withdrawn but, as it had been in Notting Hill in 1976[5] and Brixton in 1981,[6] this was clearly not something to which the police could agree. The situation had already deteriorated and there remained the fear that, if they were given the opportunity, the rioters would leave the estate and attack targets elsewhere. Although Lawrence subsequently claimed that his group did 'secure an undertaking from the crowd at Willan Road that no property would be set on fire'[7] it was an undertaking that was not kept by the rioters.

Serial 502

At 2 p.m. on 6 October, ten constables under the command of Police Sergeant David Pengelly paraded at Hornsey Police Station. Those constables were Miles Barton, Keith Blakelock, Robin Clarke, Richard Coombes, Stephen Martin, Kenneth 'Gordon' Milne, Ricky Pandya, Maxwell Roberts, Michael Shepherd and Alan Tappy. Only Barton, Coombes, Milne and Tappy had more than five years' service. Three, Roberts, Shepherd and Martin were still in their probation.

Initially they remained on standby but, whilst they took a refreshment break at around 5 p.m., Sergeant Pengelly was directed to Yankee Control at Wood Green Police Station, where he was told to fit his unit out with protective clothing, riot helmets and shields from an equipment van that was in the station yard and go to Seven Sisters Underground Station, on the Victoria Underground Line to be on hand as 'large numbers of youths were arriving from other parts of London.'[8] At this time, another constable,

---

4. Disturbances of October 1985 at the Broadwater Farm Estate, Tottenham. London: Broadwater Farm Inquiry, p.111, para. 5.55.
5. Moore, Tony (2013). *Policing Notting Hill: Fifty Years of Turbulence*. Hook, Hampshire: Waterside Press, pp. 171–172.
6. Scarman, The Rt Hon The Lord (1981). The Brixton Disorders 10–12 April 1981. London: Her Majesty's Stationary Office, pp. 31–32, paras. 3.57–3.60.
7. Gifford, op. cit. 2, p. 111, para. 5.55
8. Fiennes, Ranulph (2011). Going Back into Hell. In *My Heroes: Extraordinary Courage, Exceptional People*. London: Hodder & Stoughton, p.48.

Martyn Howells, was allocated to Serial 502.⁹ Their transport was a Sherpa van, hired from a commercial outlet, which had not been designed for use in public order situations. In terms of shields, Pengelly chose three long shields and six smaller round shields. Two officers did not have shields; they would be crouched immediately behind the three with long shields to bind them together. However, the officers 'had never trained or worked together as a single unit';¹⁰ indeed, some had received no shield training other than a very rudimentary introduction during initial training. Constable Coombes, for instance, normally drove police response cars and had never been trained to use a riot shield or had to don a riot helmet—until that night. Coombes recalled some 19 years later, how Constable Blakelock had laughed at him as he struggled into the fire-retardant overalls.¹¹

After being at Seven Sisters Underground Station for a short time—there was no sign of the youths—Pengelly was ordered to take Serial 502 to the Broadwater Farm Estate. As they approached along Mount Pleasant Road, the officers saw lines of police with shields and cars on fire. Constable Miles Barton likened the noise unto the aggressive roar of a crowd in a football stadium. He said: 'As we drove along Mount Pleasant Road, overturned and blazing cars were piled across pavements and petrol bombs rained down.'¹²

Directed to Broadwater Farm

Pengelly was instructed to take his unit to the Gloucester Road entrance where he found two DSUs already present, under the command of Chief Superintendent Couch. Also present was a fire appliance from the London Fire Brigade under the command of Assistant Divisional Officer Graham Holloway; they were extinguishing some burning cars. Responding to calls for assistance from Superintendent Sinclair at Willan Road, Chief Superintendent Couch sent the two shield serials away, leaving just Serial

---

9. Editorial (1988). 'Met' honours its Broadwater Farm heroes.' *Police*, Volume XX, No. 6, February, p. 32.
10. Fiennes, op. cit. 8, p.48.
11. Craig, Olga (2004). 'They butchered Keith Blakelock and they wanted to butcher me.' In *The Daily Telegraph*, 3 October 2004.
12. Fiennes, op. cit. 8, pp. 48–49.

502. Unbeknown to any of them, a large group of youths on the estate were planning 'a careful trap' to 'ensnare' some police officers in Tangmere Block.[13]

Pengelly lined his men along the road. Between them and Tangmere Block was a short stretch of grass on a gentle downward slope away from the road. By now the last of the cars had been extinguished and Pengelly, Couch and Holloway were deciding what next. Constable Dick Coombes recalled:

> 'The visibility was good and we saw a group of men on a high balcony of the Tangmere block. They shouted at us that the supermarket on the mezzanine floor of their block was on fire. This, to me, smelled like a trap. They had probably lit the fire to lure us in. I heard the superintendent on the van radio saying, "Whatever you do, do not go into The Farm."'[14]

Initially, Holloway and another fire officer, Divisional Officer Stratford, decided to 'take a closer look at the fire and assess the potential hazard.' Police Constables Coombes and Martin accompanied them across the grass area between Gloucester Road and Tangmere Block and waited whilst the two fire officers climbed the stairs to the deck. They were able to see the extent of the fire 'but were then attacked by youths throwing bricks' and forced to descend the stairs rapidly where they met up with Constables Coombes and Martin, and together they returned to the police location in Gloucester Road. The fire officers reported to Couch that 'the fire posed a potential threat to the lives of the tenants living nearby.'[15] Consequently, the original policy not to go into The Farm was reversed.

Pengelly was assured by Couch that back-up would be requested, but he remembers thinking 'this did not seem to me to be like a great assignment.'[16] Pengelly then described what happened next:

> 'Off we went, single file over the grass, looking for a way up to the shop-level of the block. We moved as quietly as possible, the firemen dragging their hose,

---

13. Ibid, p. 49.
14. Ibid, pp. 49–50.
15. Editorial, op. cit. 9, p. 32.
16. Ibid, p. 50.

into the dark stilted parking zone under the ground floor and then up a series of concrete stairways.'

As they went up the stairs, Constable Blakelock mentioned to Pengelly that if they all went up to the deck they would be vulnerable to attack via the hallways on the intermediate level. Sergeant Pengelly therefore assigned Blakelock, along with Constables Pandya and Howells to stay at that level and guard the hallways. The remainder of the serial continued upwards, with the five-man long shield unit in front,[17] then the firemen, then Constables Tappy and Barton with smaller round shields. When they reached the open area where the shops were, Pengelly looked over the balcony at the ground thirty feet below, and although he thought he 'saw moving shadows' all appeared to be 'quiet.'[18]

Thick smoke was coming out of some of the smashed windows of the supermarket. The deck was littered with food tins and debris. Above the entrance, in thick black letters, were the words that had been daubed there on 19 September, 'Tandoori shit get out. Niggers Rule.' The firemen began to tackle the blaze but then Coombes distinctly heard 'the clang of a handbell', albeit from some distance away. He glanced over the balcony and described how, for the first time in his 16 years' service, the hairs on the back of his neck rose. Below he could see a large number of youths, many wearing balaclavas, moving quickly and silently towards the stairs where Blakelock, Pandya and Howells were stationed. Suddenly, he said, they became a baying mob. He continued:

'They were yelling, waving knives, blowing whistles and ringing bells. I knew in that moment that we were in deep trouble.'[19]

Groups of youths then emerged from various corridors and stairwells, all of which were in darkness. Many were armed and wore masks to conceal their faces. They encircled the small group of police officers who, by this

---

17. A long shield unit consisted of five officers. The three in front would have long shields. The two behind would hug the waists of the three in front in order to keep them bound together so there were no gaps between the shields.
18. Fiennes, op. cit. 8, p. 51; see also *Police*, February 1988, p. 32.
19. Ibid.

time had surrounded the firemen and begun to retreat. Sergeant Pengelly stepped to the front of the group, raised his hand and in a loud voice, told them that all they were doing was protecting the firemen and when the fire was out they would leave. Recalling the incident 25 years later, with the typical humour of many police officers of the period, Pengelly said: 'This was clearly not the right password.' Although there was a short pause, a brick was suddenly thrown and, 'with howls of anger, the youths rushed forward in an attempt to cut the group of police and firemen off from the stairs.'[20]

Over one hundred rioters, most, but not all, black, closed in for the kill. Coombes heard yells of 'Fuck off, pigs', 'This is The Farm!' 'No pigs here' and 'You'll never get out alive'. The individual chants soon merged into a steady booming chant of 'Kill, kill the pigs'. Petrol bombs exploded, chunks of paving-stones smashed against helmets, sharpened machete blades sliced into the shields, and Sergeant Pengelly screamed out orders for his group to retreat down the stairs. He also sent the radio message for urgent assistance. The mob above was the main threat, so Serial 502, the firemen in their midst, slowly moved backwards down the stairway, the three long shields locked together as best they could under the circumstances. But, as they retreated, the fire hose which stretched up the stairs and was still full of water proved to be a hazard. Using 'swords, javelins and stakes with knives attached', the youths 'tried to get over the police shields'.[21] Constable Miles Barton described how one masked youth in particular kept bringing a machete

> '...down on the shields trying to get over the top of the shields to our heads or around the sides to our bodies. I can remember numerous knives coming through the gaps in the shields.'[22]

A new chant suddenly went up: 'Burn the bacon' and Coombes saw a youth, through the scarred plastic of his visor, trying to light a flame-thrower. The police were now soaked in fuel from a number of unlit petrol bombs that had been thrown at them. Now he knew why. Fortunately, the

---

20. Ibid: see also *The Times*, 23 January 1987.
21. Ibid: see also *The Times*, 22 January 1987.
22. *The Times*, 27 January 1987.

flame-thrower failed to ignite[23] but he subsequently recalled:

> 'The staircase seemed much narrower on our way down—the fire hose had been flat on our way up, but now it bulged with water and we kept tripping on it. Every man held the belt of the man in front. We had to keep together. The noise was deafening. They screamed in our ears, "Kill them. Kill. Kill." In the dim light I could barely see, for the Perspex visor of my helmet was old and scratched. I had a tiny, short truncheon. Crazy. We were woefully under-equipped.'[24]

By then Chief Superintendent Couch, who had remained in Gloucester Road by the Sherpa van, had requested additional units, and it was at this point that Superintendent Boyall accessed the estate from Moira Close in a desperate attempt to provide the assistance Pengelly so desperately needed. But, as described in the previous chapter, he was unable to get there.

Despite the terrifying situation that confronted them, officers of Serial 502 'displayed remarkable courage and discipline in the manner in which they first and foremost protected the firemen.'[25] The retreat whilst under such a ferocious attack would have tested even the best-trained pubic order units in the Metropolitan Police. That this ad-hoc unit, thrown together for the first time on the day of the riot, managed it with such discipline was testament to that courage.

The group reached the concrete car park at the bottom of the stairs only to be met by more rioters, estimated by some to be between 100 and 200,[26] 'intent on cutting them off from the road a hundred yards above the grassy slope.' Away from the narrow stairway, the three long shields were now useless. Some of the officers were already bleeding from stab wounds.[27] Vulnerable to attack from all directions, the police officers and firemen made a run for the relative safety of the road but Blakelock slipped on the grass and fell.[28] To his flank, Coombes saw him go down and

---

23. *The Times*, 22 January 1987.
24. Fiennes, op. cit. 8, p. 52.
25. Editorial, op. cit. 9, p. 33.
26. *The Times*, 22 January 1987.
27. Fiennes, op. cit. 8, p. 52.
28. *The Times*, 22 January 1987.

> '[T]hirty masked men literally dropped onto the struggling body, hacking at it with their knives and screaming, "Kill, brothers, kill. We've got a beast".'

The mob tore away Blakelock's shield, truncheon and helmet. His arms were slashed, his fingers half-chopped off, stakes and knives were plunged into his chest and neck, but he did not die.[29]

Constable Coombes saw the crowd 'like a flock of murderous birds in a feeding frenzy, hacking and jabbing.' Running back to help him his route was blocked by a large group of youths and he was knocked to the ground by a vicious blow across the face with an iron bar. They tore off his visor and slit his neck open with knives. His jawbone was shattered by a machete and he lost consciousness. Another officer, Constable Michael Shepherd, who had turned back with Coombes, was hit with an iron spike; he fell to the ground next to Coombes 'and put his shield over him to protect him from a crowd of youths who were now kicking and striking both of them' as they lay on the ground.[30]

Serial 502 was now well and truly split. Sergeant Pengelly found himself on his own being hunted by a separate mob. He thought, initially that a fireman had fallen. He described how he ran back, shouting:

> 'After covering a distance of about 15 yards I hit the nearest of them with my truncheon on the head. He was about 45 to 50 years, with short, curly black hair, going grey. As he fell away to my right I hit another coloured person to my left and the group broke up and ran off. I could see it was a police officer lying motionless on the ground by a fire hydrant coupling. Defending with my shield, I tried to drag him away, shouting for assistance...I was facing youths and stumbled over the ground, I believe having been hit in the right knee by a stone or brick. I regained my footing quickly as I saw someone with a sword or machete, amongst others, running about. A coloured youth threw a rock, which hit me full on the visor of my helmet, partly stunning me. I continued retreating, facing off the youths following me. I could not see any of my officers and I believed there was one left behind. I was trying to check the ground for bodies. A coloured youth then caught

---

29. Fiennes, op. cit. 8, pp. 52–53.
30. *Police Review*, 27 March 1987, p. 630.

hold of my truncheon, and I tried to pull it away from him without success. To effect escape I released the thong from my hand and he ran off.'[31]

Meanwhile, Divisional Fire Officer Stratford and 19-year-old Constable Maxwell Roberts also managed to reach the severely wounded Blakelock[32] but both were themselves under attack. Roberts said Blakelock was so badly injured that he failed to recognise him at first. He said:

> 'I tried to help him up. I grabbed hold of his clothing but it came apart in my hands' so he told him, "Get up and run, bloody run." I helped him to his knees. He was still alive at this point. He tried to take two or three strides and just collapsed. I tried to help him to his feet again but he was a dead weight.'[33]

Stratford's spine was smashed with a brick, and Roberts was stabbed.[34] But together the three of them, Pengelly, Stratford and Roberts managed to drag the collapsed body of Blakelock up the grass slope as quickly as they could to the relative safety of the road and the vehicles. Even at this stage, Roberts did not realise who it was because 'his face was covered with blood. He did not have a helmet on. His face was a mass of red.' Only when they lowered him to the ground at the top of the slope did Roberts realise

> '[T]hat it was Keith because I saw his moustache. I saw a bread knife sticking in his neck.'[35]

The officers ringed the van against the rioters. The firemen tried to revive Blakelock. Assisted by Fireman Raymond Barrington, Divisional Officer Stratford tore off some of Blakelock's clothing; put his ear to his chest and announced that he had stopped breathing. Stratford massaged his heart and managed to get him breathing again before the ambulance arrived. His face

---

31. Rose, David (1992). *A Climate of Fear: The Murder of PC Blakelock and the Case of the Tottenham Three*. London: Bloomsbury, p.72.
32. *The Times*, 27 January 1987.
33. Ibid.
34. Fiennes, op. cit. 8, p. 53.
35. *The Times*, 27 January 1987; David Rose, op. cit. 31, makes no mention of Divisional Officer Stratford, claiming that it was Chief Superintendent Couch who assisted Constable Roberts to drag Constable Blakelock free of the mob, see pp. 72–73.

was a bloody mess. The handle of a serrated knife driven four inches into his neck stuck out from beneath one ear, and a gaping wound ran from his lips to the back of his shoulder.[36] Later it was discovered he had forty-two stab wounds on his chest, back and limbs.

Coombes was rushed to hospital in the back of a fire engine, with two firemen, James Ryan and David Kwai treating his injuries.[37] Accompanied by Divisional Fire Officer Stratford, who continued to try to resuscitate him en route, Blakelock, too, was rushed to hospital by ambulance but was, unfortunately, found to be dead on arrival. At this point some 60 constables arrived to extricate Serial 502. But they were too late.

It was the most brutal and sustained attack on an individual officer on the British mainland since the formation of the Metropolitan Police in 1829. Blakelock died

> '…from multiple injuries, including a severe wound across the right cheek from the mouth to the back of the neck which was accompanied by fractures of the lower jaw. There was a knife with a six-inch blade buried in his neck up to the hilt, five stab wounds in his sides, three of which had penetrated the lungs, and a hand wound probably sustained when he tried to defend himself. He had numerous other injuries including grazing of the type which could be caused by stamping feet, and 13 cuts to his back.'[38]

The immediate aftermath

Meanwhile, Sergeant Pengelly and the constables that remained sat in their van in silence unable to move. The keys were in Dick Coombes' pocket. When they did eventually get back to Wood Green, they felt that 'they were "on show" to the rest of the force.' There were no immediate counselling facilities available and 'several of the officers made their own way home in a state of shock.' When one of the officers of Serial 502 was later discharged

---

36. *Daily Star*, 23 January 1987.
37. *In Attendance*—Volume Three, Edition Eight—April 1989, p.3.
38. *Police Review*, 27 March 1987, p. 630.

from hospital, there was no-one to take him home; instead he left in the car of the wife of an officer visiting her injured husband in the same hospital.[39]

And later

Assistant Divisional Fire Officer Graham Holloway subsequently recalled that he was 'absolutely petrified' and had never been so frightened in his 22 years with the London Fire Brigade. Describing the attack on Constable Blakelock he said:

> 'I was aware of the crowd descending on him with various weapons. There appeared to be machetes, carving-knives, and a pole with a blade set at right angles. There appeared to be a frenzied attack going on where the person had fallen.'[40]

Another fireman saw Blakelock go down:

> 'He was totally engulfed. The last I saw of him was his head and his hand above his head trying to fend of blows. I didn't stop running. You can imagine the fear we were experiencing.'[41]

Fireman Alan Briars recalled:

> 'All hell was let loose. I was one of the lucky ones. I managed to get away. I ran like mad, frightened out of my life.'[42]

Review of Couch's decision to send Serial 502 into Tangmere

Whilst the main analysis of the Metropolitan Police's response to the riot will be discussed in the next chapter it might be appropriate to examine the decision of Chief Superintendent Crouch to send Serial 502 into Tangmere Block at this point. A key question asked by the surviving officers of Serial

---

39. Williams, David A, op. cit. 1, pp. 225–226, para. 6.
40. *The Daily Telegraph*, 22 June 1987.
41. Fiennes, op. cit. 8, p.53.
42. Ibid, pp. 52–53.

502 at a subsequent debriefing session organized by the Williams Inquiry team was why 'a part shield trained unit of probationers and home beat officers' was sent into the estate 'without back-up' for what turned out to be a 'highly dangerous operation?'[43]

The fact that Serial 502 was at Gloucester Road in the first place was almost certainly down to Yankee Control. Unfortunately, as will be mentioned in the next chapter, with some exceptions, e.g. units with '30', '31' and '32' call signs, Yankee Control was unable to recognise from the call signs allocated to units whether the unit was made up of fully trained public order officers or was an ad-hoc unit as was Serial 502. So blame for the fact that they were at Gloucester Road cannot be placed on Couch.

The Williams Report suggested 'Couch was the man on the spot' and 'he had to balance his wish to protect the residents of Tangmere' against the risk to Serial 502. The report went on to describe how:

> 'His perception of the degree of risk may have been influenced by the fact that nothing had happened at Gloucester Road for two and a half hours, that he had personally walked into the estate as far as Tangmere block without meeting resistance and that the rioters appeared to pre-occupied with the attack on police on the other side of the estate.'[44]

In its review of the disturbances of 1981 and 1985, the Metropolitan Police stated that 'it was recognised that incursion by the police at that time into the estate had an element of risk, but this was outweighed by the danger to the public if the fire was allowed to burn unchecked.'[45] Nevertheless, the Williams Report suggested that in hindsight 'it would have been prudent to await the arrival of additional resources.'[46]

As is often the case, the senior management team of an organization seeks to absolve itself from responsibility and, even in some cases, accountability, for actions taken at the 'coal face' in 'the heat of battle'. But, in this case, there is no doubt that part of the blame for what happened that night to

---

43. Howe, Sean (1991). Riot Hero's Farewell. *The Job*, Volume 14, Issue 609, 26 July)
44. Williams, David A, op. cit. 1, p.224, para. 4iv).
45. Ibid, p. 29, para. 3:68.
46. Metropolitan Police (1986). Public Order Review: Civil Disturbances 1981–1985. London: Metropolitan Police (typescript), p. 12, para. 4.11.

Keith Blakelock must rest with the senior management in the Metropolitan Police. Chief Superintendent Couch was 'relatively inexperienced in operational command' having only held the rank for 15 months and having spent his career as a superintendent as a community liaison officer.[47] In addition, he had undergone no specific training in the operational command of officers in riot situations as recommended by Lord Scarman in 1981.[48] The Williams Review examined the radio messages that passed between him and Yankee Control during the riot and found that, on at least two occasions, he sought 'support and endorsement' for actions he wanted to take[49] but, as will be seen in *Chapter 9*, Yankee Control, perhaps with one exception early on in the evening, issued no command decisions throughout the entire period of rioting. Despite being the Commander of Tottenham Division and presumably having knowledge of the plan to be followed in the event of disorder on the Broadwater Farm Estate, Couch neither queried Yankee Control's failure to implement it nor did anything to resolve the position as to who was the ground commander.[50]

All the evidence on that fateful night points to Couch being overly concerned with trying to involve community leaders in bringing the riot to an end.[51] But history has shown that once serious disorder has broken out, there is little community leaders can effectively do.[52] The subsequent review into the disturbances of 1981 and 1985 stated that:

> 'Command responsibilities of a police operation dealing with serious public disorder requires an awareness of considerations which will include not only the tactical options available but the impact of their use on the community—and equally the effect of failing to use those options.'[53]

So the question that needed to be asked of the senior management team in the Metropolitan Police was why an experienced operational commander

---

47. Williams, David A, op. cit. 1, p.29, para. 3.68
48. Ibid, p. 24, para. 3.65.
49. Scarman, The Rt Hon The Lord (1981). The Brixton Disorders 10–12 April 1981. London: Her Majesty's Stationary Office, p. 83, para. 5.29.
50. Williams, David A, op. cit. 1, pp. 24–25, para. 3.65.
51. Ibid, p.25, see the exchange of radio messages.
52. Gifford, op. cit. 2, pp. 116–119, paras. 5.67–5.74
53. For a greater explanation of this, see *Chapter 10*.

was not appointed to a division which was known to be volatile? After all, the commissioner, Sir Kenneth Newman, had in 1983 identified Haringey as one of the areas in which there existed 'a negative symbolism of the inability of police to maintain order' and it was 'an important priority to restore order in such areas.'[54] It might have been better to appoint, as divisional commander, an experienced operational officer who was sensitive to community needs, rather than one who had little operational experience and was likely to over-concerned with community sensitivities[55] to the extent that men under his command were placed in danger. Additionally, having appointed Couch to command this volatile division, none of his senior officers felt the need for him to undergo public order training so that he would at least be aware of the tactical options available for dealing with outbreaks of disorder should it occur.[56]

Funeral

The funeral service for Keith Blakelock was held at St James's Church, Muswell Hill. The Metropolitan Police Engineers' Department extended the seating capacity of the 600-seat church to 800 and installed a closed circuit television system to allow a further 300 police officers to join in the service at a nearby British Legion Hall. Another 500 people stood outside the church listening to the service over a public address system which had also been installed by the engineers. The coffin was carried, through a guard of honour consisting of Metropolitan Police officers and representatives from the London Fire Brigade, into the church by former colleagues at Muswell Hill. The service was conducted by the Rt. Rev. Brain Masters, Bishop of Edmonton, the Rev. Michael Bunker and Archdeacon Bob Coogan. Amongst those attending the service was Home Secretary Douglas Hurd,

---

54. Metropolitan Police, op. cit. 46, p. 18, para. 4.5.
55. Newman, Sir Kenneth (1983). Preliminary Assessment of Problems and Priorities: Report of The Commissioner of Police of the Metropolis to the Home Secretary. London: Metropolitan Police.
56. Arguably, in the Spring of 1986, such a person was appointed to head up the policing of Tottenham, Chief Superintendent Alan Stainsby. Stainsby was the only fully-trained public order commander available on the day of the riots with the exception of Chief Superintendent Tom Jones and Superintendent Douglas Hopkins of the Special Patrol Group.

Commissioner Sir Kenneth Newman, Assistant Commissioner Geoff McLean and Deputy Assistant Commissioner Mike Richards.[57]

Following the service, Keith Blakelock was buried at the East Finchley Cemetery and Crematorium. His headstone reads:

> IN
> ETERNAL MEMORY
> of
> KEITH BLAKELOCK
> BORN JUNE 28th 1945
> DIED OCTOBER 6th 1985
> The Much Loved Husband of
> ELIZABETH
> And the adored father of
> MARK, KEVIN and LEE
> Never more than a thought away

In November 1986, a memorial was erected on his home beat at the Roundabout in Muswell Hill. It reads:

> HERE SERVED
> PC
> KEITH
> BLAKELOCK
> 16 MARCH 1981 to 6 OCTOBER 1985

Bravery awards

In his book *My Heroes*, in which he devotes a chapter to Richard Coombes, Ranulph Fiennes suggested that 'the natural and sensible instinct for self-preservation at such a moment of terror after the escape from within the Tangmere trap was all-consuming.' And yet, in what he described as 'a defining moment of true courage, some of the men of 502, seeing Blakelock's plight, gave up their own slim chance of survival from an equally horrific fate

---

57. *The Job*, 13 December 1985, p. 1.

by turning back into the heart of that screaming mob of killers in order to save Keith.'[58] He went on to quote Nelson Mandela's definition of courage:

> 'I learned that courage was not the absence of fear, but the triumph over it. The brave man is not he who does not feel afraid, but he who conquers that fear.[59]

Whilst it could be said that all the officers of Serial 502 conquered that fear in the disciplined way they withdrew from Tangmere Block whilst under attack, David Pengelly, Richard Coombes, Michael Shepherd and Maxwell Roberts, together with Trevor Stratford conquered fear for a second time by going back for Keith Blakelock. It was an outstanding example of courage.

In January 1988, Commissioner Sir Peter Imbert, awarded all the members of Serial 502 with High Commendations. Sergeant Pengelly's was for 'his exceptional leadership, outstanding courage and devotion to duty.' The constables of Serial 502 received theirs for 'outstanding courage and devotion to duty'. Keith's commendation was received by his widow, Elizabeth Blakelock.[60]

The officers, Sir Peter said, had acted in the highest traditions of the Metropolitan Police in putting 'the safety and protection of the members of the public and the firefighters before their own well-being'. They had 'unhesitatingly entered a building which they knew could prove difficult to escape from, fearful that they were being led into a trap, with the sole purpose of protecting fire officers, who, in turn, were intending to extinguish a potentially very serious fire.'[61]

Meanwhile, the Chief Fire Officer of the London Fire Brigade, Gerry Clarkson, awarded Commendations for outstanding bravery to Assistant Divisional Officer Graham Holloway and Divisional Officer Trevor Stratford. In addition, Leading Fireman James Ryan and Fireman David Kwai, who treated the injuries to Constable Coombs, were awarded the Chief Fire Officer's letter of congratulations.[62]

Eight months later, in August, all the eleven constables of Serial 502 were

---

58. Fiennes, op. cit. 8, p. 53.
59. Quoted in Fiennes, op. cit. 7, p. 41.
60. Editorial, op. cit. 9, p.33.
61. Ibid.
62. *In Attendance*—Volume III, Edition 8, April 1989, p.5.

awarded the Queen's Gallantry Medal for their actions that night. The citation in the *London Gazette* announcing the award described their actions as 'outstanding bravery and devotion to duty'. For his outstanding leadership, Sergeant Pengelly was awarded the George Medal.[63] At the beginning of December, Sergeant Pengelly and the ten surviving constables were presented with their awards by Her Majesty The Queen at Buckingham Palace. Before the main ceremony, Elizabeth Blakelock had a private audience with the Queen at which she was presented with her husband's posthumous Gallantry Medal.[64] Also awarded the Queen's Gallantry Medal was Divisional Fire Officer Trevor Stratford.[65]

Two heroines

There are also two heroines of that awful night who must not be forgotten. For both Keith Blakelock and Richard Coombes were married, Keith to Elizabeth and Richard to June. Keith and Elizabeth had three children, Richard and Pauline, two. Interviewed two days after her husband's death, his wife, Elizabeth, struggling for composure, spoke of the moment that she was told he had been killed:

> 'I was watching the news of the riot on television and seeing how rapidly the violence seemed to be progressing. When I heard that a policeman had been killed, I got in touch with the information people at Scotland Yard. I just had a horrid feeling right through me that it was my husband.'[66]

A short while later, Acting Commander Ted Hodge, accompanied by Woman Constable Sheila White, arrived at her house with the fateful news. Constable White stayed with Elizabeth and her sons throughout the remainder of the night and over the next two years was frequently at her side when she was asked to do television interviews.[67]

---

63. Hasler, Terry (1988). Queen's tribute to the brave. In *The Job*, Vol. 21, Issue 536, September 2.
64. Hasler, Terry (1988). Palace Date for Officers of 502. *The Job*, Vol. 21, Issue 544, December 9; see also Police, Vol. XX, No. 12, August 1988, p.4.
65. *In Attendance*—op.cit.62.
66. *The Times*, 8 October 1985.
67. White, Sheila (2014). Correspondence with the author, dated 9 June.

Four days later, Lee Blakelock celebrated his ninth birthday. He received a birthday cake in the shape of a footballer with the icing in Arsenal colours, his favourite team. Arsenal Football Club sent a football, signed by all the players. Blakelock's colleagues sent a 'stack of gifts' and, in addition, Lee received hundreds of cards, many from complete strangers.[68] But he would have given all this up just to have his father present. Elizabeth Blakelock remarried to become Elizabeth Johnson and moved back to the North East from whence both she and Keith had originally come. In 2000, Lee Blakelock followed in his father's footsteps and joined the Durham Constabulary. Three years later he was awarded a chief constable's commendation after he and another officer had tackled a man who was threatening his former partner with a knife and was also in possession of an air pistol and a can of petrol.[69]

Following the trial and acquittal of Nicky Jacobs in 2014,[70] surrounded by her three sons Elizabeth expressed her feelings about the night Keith died in an interview broadcast by Independent Television News, and, in doing so, addressed the people who had killed him:

> 'We lost Keith but then learning how we lost him, I find that very, very difficult and not right. It isn't right. You know that something happened to trigger anger and ill feeling so you go out looking for a uniform, a policeman such as Keith, who all his career just helped people. He went into Muswell Hill and tried to build bridges between all ethnic minorities and he was a friend to them. And this friend who was helping the firemen put out fires, you know, that night trying to save people — trying to save people's lives. Because he did that you do what you did to him. You know, you wouldn't do that to an animal, let alone a human being. And that human being was lying there and begging you, begging you for his life.'[71]

Two weeks before, Richard Coombe's wife, Pauline, a speech therapist, finally spoke to Frances Hardy about that fateful day and just how difficult it had been. Pauline, Richard, and their two children, Louise, then three years old and Matthew, only recently born, had been to a harvest festival

---

68. *The Job*, 18 October, 1985, pp. 2–3; *Daily Mail*, 10 October 1985.
69. BBC News, 16 April 2003.
70. The trial and acquittal of Nicky Jacobs is described in *Chapter 11*.
71. Independent Television News, 14 May 2014.

service at their local church before returning home to 'a lovely Sunday lunch'. Richard then went off to do a late shift at Hornsey Police Station on what turned out to be the day that changed their lives. At around 12.30 a.m., she had given Matthew a late feed, turned on the television, saw pictures of the rioting and wondered if Richard was there. Then two police officers accompanied by her neighbour knocked at the door to tell her that her husband had been injured and was in hospital. The neighbour stayed with the children whilst her neighbour's husband drove her to the Whittington Hospital. When she saw him she fell to her knees. With his jaw completely smashed, a number of missing teeth and awful gashes on his badly swollen face, she hardly recognised him.[72]

Richard, a former captain of the Metropolitan Police cross-country running team, eventually returned to part-time work nine months later, in July 1986,[73] but deteriorating health, particularly the onslaught of epilepsy, forced him to retire in 1991 by which time he had still not received any compensation from the Criminal Injuries Compensation Board (CICB). In February 1992, a 'derisory offer' was made and he appealed. Fourteen months later, in response to a letter from his solicitor, the CICB wrote back to say that his claim was 'in a queue with other claims'. Nearly 18 months later, in September 1994, he wrote to his local Member of Parliament and, at the same time, his solicitor wrote to the CICB to say that it was intended to lodge a formal complaint. As a result, ten months short of ten years after being brutally hacked down at the Broadwater Farm Estate, Dick Coombes finally received an acceptable offer of compensation.[74]

But his inability to work left him without a purpose in life and he fell into a deep depression. The family moved to Oundle in Northamptonshire but his depression worsened. Finally, in 1998, Pauline bought him a Labrador dog, Bracken. This assisted in lifting the worst of the depression. When Bracken died, she was replaced and he now has three Labradors. Nearly three decades on, Richard's injuries continue to plague him. At night, the pain in his back and legs can be excruciating and is only reduced by attaching

---

72. Hardy, Frances (2014). The other wife left grieving by PC Blakelock's murderers: Pauline's husband was left for dead by the Broadwater Farm rioters. 30 years on, she tells how he—and their marriage—still bear the scars. *Mail Online*, 23 April 2014.
73. *Hornsey Journal*, 4 July 1986.
74. Blagg, Keith (1994). To Hell and Back. In *The Job*, 9 June.

morphine patches to his skin. He also suffers from sleep apnoea during the night—and wears a mask to assist him in breathing—and he still has nightmares. He is prone to fall asleep without warning, his fingers have lost their dexterity and his legs are so weak he cannot stand for any length of time. Brain damage has precipitated the onset of blindness, his muscles are degenerating and, since 2010 he has worn a pacemaker because of an erratic and weak heartbeat.[75]

Pauline has stood it all stoically. She lost the 'jokey, sunny, popular' husband, the man she had loved since she was a teenager, on 6 October 1985 and 'acquired a trickier, darker, needier partner'. Although he was still her 'committed, kind and loving husband' she did not know how he would be when she came 'through the door each evening.' He started having 'explosive, unpredictable moods' which would come out of nowhere. Although he never hit Pauline or the children, he would 'thump the wall or a door'. When they were young the children were frightened of these outbursts which saw him switch from 'kind, fun-loving dad to ogre' but as they grew up they understood that their father had never stopped loving them. There were occasions when she thought she could not stay in the marriage but they passed. Sometimes she went for long walks or for a drive; parked the car, and had a little weep and a 'shout'![76]

For neither Elizabeth Blakelock nor Pauline Coombes has there been any closure. The acquittal of Nicky Jacobs[77] means that it is unlikely that those who killed Keith Blakelock and seriously injured Richard Coombes to the extent that it changed the lives of two families, will ever be brought to justice.

The final word

Normally, perhaps, the final part of this chapter would be the presentation of the bravery awards by Her Majesty the Queen. But there is a need to ensure that such an event does not occur again. So, the penultimate word is left to one of the young constables on Serial 502 that night. Giving evidence at a murder trial some sixteen months later, Constable Robin Clarke said:

---

75. Hardy, op. cit. 72.
76. Ibid.
77. See *Chapter 11*.

'In retrospect, we should not have been sent in without a serial (police group) at the foot of the stairs and on the first landing to protect the escape route, and Keith Blakelock died needlessly.'[78]

But, as has already been mentioned, given all the public order-trained units that were on standby, it can be strongly argued that Serial 502 should never have been deployed so close to the estate in the first place.

The final word is left to another of Blakelock's colleagues. Stephen Martin. Speaking on a BBC documentary nearly 20 years after the event he said:

'Why were they so angry that they had to kill somebody who was married with children and just went to work like we all do to earn money to support his family. He was another human being. He didn't deserve to die like that.'[79]

---

78. *The Guardian*, 29 January 1987.
79. Barling, Kurt (narrator) (2004). 'Who killed PC Blakelock?' A documentary shown on BBC TV. In an interview with Constable Martin.

CHAPTER NINE

Analysis of the Response to the Riot

Introduction

The first major review of the response to serious public disorder took place in the United States of America in 1968 following serious riots in a number of American cities. In its report to President Johnson, the Kerner Commission suggested that 'the capability of a police department to control civil disorder [depended] essentially on two factors: proper planning and competent performance.'[1] Unfortunately, the Metropolitan Police failed on both counts at Broadwater Farm on 6 October 1985.

In words that were strangely reminiscent of the Kerner Report, Lord Scarman claimed that the rioting in Brixton in April 1981 had 'revealed weaknesses in the capacity of the police to respond sufficiently firmly to violence on the streets'[2] and he made a number of recommendations aimed at improving operational performance. These will be referred to as the chapter progresses. In addition, in August 1982, the Metropolitan Police published a small manual entitled *Public Order—Notes of Guidance for Senior Officers*. Part of the foreword to it suggested that it had been necessary 'to conduct a radical review of the commitment to public order especially with regard to:

    (i) Information gathering and assessment;
    (ii) The ability to respond quickly and effectively to outbreaks of spontaneous disorder;
    (iii) The need for a positive strategy and carefully formulated tactics.'[3]

---

1. Kerner, Otto (1968). *Report of the National Advisory Commission on Civil Disorders*. New York: Bantom, p.486.
2. Scarman, The Rt Hon The Lord (1981). The Brixton Disorders 10–12 April 1981. London: Her Majesty's Stationary Office, p.71, para. 4.90.
3. Metropolitan Police (1982). Senior Officers Public Order Guidance Notes. London: Metropolitan Police (Typescript).

The Metropolitan Police failed on all three counts at Broadwater Farm. There was no system to gather or assess information about the rioters and their tactics. Consequently 'some far-reaching operational decisions were made by senior officers who were not in possession of accurate assessments of all the relevant facts.'[4] The plan for dealing with disorder on the Broadwater Farm Estate, plus the mobilisation of human resources before rioting occurred, arguably provided for a quick and effective response. But the plan was never implemented and the deployment of human resources was almost wholly reactive. In addition, although a number of senior officers were present, they did not possess the necessary skills to either formulate an effective strategy to bring the disorder to an end nor to implement many of the tactics currently being taught during public order training. These failures will be explained in greater detail as the chapter progresses.

As one of his goals in a preliminary assessment of the problems and priorities of the Metropolitan Police submitted to the Home Secretary at the beginning of 1983, Commissioner Sir Kenneth Newman identified 'the maintenance of public order' to be 'a major priority'. He continued, 'any failure in this responsibility' reflected 'adversely on the standing and reputation of the force'; encouraged potential rioters to believe they could succeed; undermined 'stability in the Metropolis'; and lowered 'police morale.'[5] This was certainly the case on 6 October. It adversely affected the reputation of the force, encouraged rioters to such an extent that they were able to brutally hack to death a police constable, and the morale of the force was adversely affected by this totally inadequate performance, as has already been described in the previous chapter.

His annual reports stressed the importance of responding effectively to disorder. In the report at the end of 1983, he stated his 'determination that the Metropolitan Police' would 'never tolerate serious disorder on the streets of London' and would 'react rapidly, firmly and professionally to deal with any

---

4. Williams, David A (1986). Internal Police Report on the disorders of the 6th October 1985 at the Broadwater Farm Estate, Tottenham. London: Metropolitan Police, p.34, para. 3:89 (i).
5. Newman, Sir Kenneth (1983). Preliminary Assessment of Problems and Priorities: Report of The Commissioner of Police of the Metropolis to the Home Secretary. London: Metropolitan Police, p.26, para. 55.

such incidents.'⁶ His annual report for 1984 released only a few months before the Broadwater Farm riot stated that in the event of 'large-scale disorder', the Metropolitan Police 'must retain, through practical training and effective equipment, the necessary skills and determination to bring it quickly to an end.'⁷

Six months before the riot, Newman issued a booklet, *The Principles of Policing and Guidance for Professional Behaviour*, which was circulated to every officer in the force. In it he had this to say in relation to the policing of potential riot or disorder:

> '[P]olice will think first in terms of mediation, short term intervention and the prevention of physical conflict. If, despite these efforts, disorder erupts, police will act firmly and decisively, meeting force with such force as is necessary and reasonable in the circumstances to prevent crime and protect life and property.'⁸

Mediation was tried. Deputy Assistant Commissioner Richards met with community leaders, both official and unofficial, at lunchtime on the day of the riot.⁹ However, the question to be asked is how representative where those leaders of black youth on the estate? Only Dolly Kiffin arguably had any sway with some and she absented herself from the estate before the riot started and did not return until the disorder had subsided.

The remainder of Newman's undertakings were not implemented. Police did not act firmly and decisively, and did not meet force with such force as was necessary and reasonable to prevent crime and protect life and property. Despite the passing of six months since the issue of the booklet and two outbreaks of major disorder, in Handsworth and Brixton, those senior officers deployed to respond to the events that unfolded on the Broadwater Farm Estate generally did not possess the 'professional skills' necessary to

---

6. Annual Report of the Commissioner of Police of the Metropolis for the year 1983. London: Her Majesty's Stationary Office, p. 52.
7. Annual Report of the Commissioner of Police of the Metropolis for the year 1984. London: Her Majesty's Stationary Office, p. 67.
8. Newman, Sir Kenneth (1985). *The Principles of Policing and Guidance for Professional Behaviour.* London: Metropolitan Police, p.13.
9. Richards, M D (1985). Public Disorder in Tottenham 6th October 1985: A report to the Haringey Police/Community Consultative Group. London: Metropolitan Police, pp. 6–7, paras. 9.1–9.3.

contain the disorder and police casualties were, arguably, must greater than they should have been.

It was not as though the Metropolitan Police was unaware of the defects in its ability to respond to serious public disorder; it was just that whilst edicts had been made from the top of the organization, little had been done to implement the necessary courses of action to ensure that they were capable of being carried out. With this in mind, an analysis of performance on 6 October follows. For ease it has been broken down into a number of factors.

Failure to implement the plan for the Broadwater Farm Estate

A plan for seizing control of the estate in the event of potential or actual outbreaks of serious public disorder had been devised some years earlier. A copy of that plan was in Yankee Control at the time of the riot.[10] Two main actions were to be taken. The first called for the police occupation of the walkways. Richards claimed it was considered but, according to him, the threat of disorder 'encompassed many more possible theatres of confrontation throughout the Borough of Haringey.'[11] The second was the setting up of a forward command post about which more will be said later in the chapter.

Lack of training amongst senior officers

Kerner pointed out that the 'standard training for police operations [was] basically different from that required for riot control.' He continued:

> 'Traditional police training [sought] to develop officers who [could] work independently and with little direct supervision. But the control of civil disturbances [required] quite different performance—large numbers of disciplined personnel, comparable to soldiers in a military unit, organized and trained to work as members of a team under a highly unified command control system.'[12]

Kerner also pointed out that two of the most serious deficiencies in most

---

10. See Richards' letter in *Police*, Vol. XVIII. No. 4. December 1986, p.13.
11. Ibid.
12. Kerner, op. cit. 1, p.485.

police departments was, firstly, the failure to train realistically for such events and, secondly, the almost total absence of riot control training for command-level officers.[13] This was a theme taken up by Lord Scarman. Whilst he praised the leadership displayed by some individual senior officers at Brixton in 1981, his most damning criticism was made of police commanders generally. He pointed out that officers untrained in the command of men carrying shields had been 'thrust into the front line'[14] Kerner had said that riot training 'must include all levels of personnel within the police agency, especially commanders.'[15] Likewise, Scarman recommended that 'training in the handling of public disorder' should be provided 'for officers of all ranks up to and including commander or the equivalent (assistant chief constable) in the provinces.' In making this recommendation he suggested that the most appropriate training for senior officers was 'in the command of men and in the strategy and tactics for handling disorder'.[16]

Some effort was directed towards the implementation of Scarman's recommendations in London. From early in 1982, the Metropolitan Police ran a series of three-day courses for commanders and chief superintendents.[17] In addition, from 1983 onwards, all officers of the rank of commander and assistant chief constable were required to attend a one-week course on the management of public order at the Police Staff College[18] but, with a few exceptions, the Metropolitan Police opted out of this programme claiming it had its own arrangements. Unfortunately, as the memory of Brixton 1981 receded, so did the enthusiasm for a continuing training public order programme in London for senior officers. Consequently, when the riot occurred at Tottenham, with one exception, none of the senior officers on the ground were familiar with current public order tactics.[19] And yet, only six months previously, Newman had announced:

---

13. Ibid, p.327.
14. Scarman, op. cit. 2, p. 71, para. 4.91.
15. Kerner, op. cit. 1, p. 490.
16. Scarman, op. cit. 2, p. 83, para. 5.29.
17. The author attended one of these courses in April 1982. By the end of that year all senior officers had gone through the programme. Thereafter officers promoted to chief inspector underwent the three day programme as part of their chief inspectors' course.
18. The author was responsible for developing and running this course from October 1983 to April 1986.
19. Williams, op. cit. 4, p.34, para. 3:89 (iii).

'It will be the policy of the Force to develop professional skills with a view to containing disorder with the least possible injury to all the people involved. The safety of citizens is paramount, but the police response will be governed also by the policy that police casualties will be avoided, as far as possible, by the use of reasonable force against people who threaten to injure police officers.'[20]

Failure to appoint an overall ground commander

Whilst the general criticism of the ability of senior officers to handle serious public disorder was valid, some of the criticism of individual ground commanders was ill-informed and unwarranted. It was not their fault they had been ordered for duty that day. It was an organizational problem. As Scarman said of the senior officers of Brixton in 1981, some of them performed bravely and were struck by numerous missiles themselves. Whilst it could be argued that individual senior officers, particularly those posted to areas where rioting might occur, had an obligation to ensure they underwent appropriate training, it was an organizational problem in that the senior management in the Metropolitan Police posted senior officers to such areas who had little or no public order experience and, having done so, failed to ensure that appropriate training was undertaken. Unfortunately, the police service still believed in the omnicompetent constable and this was particularly apparent in senior ranks. But, writing shortly after the events at Broadwater Farm, Moore suggested it was a fallacy to believe that every senior officer or middle-ranking police officer would make a good public order commander.[21] Although they may be perfectly good at their job for 364 days of the year, Kerner suggested, it required a different kind of mentality, almost a military mind,[22] to perform effectively when there was an outbreak of serious public disorder on what was effectively the 365th day.

Despite their lack of training in 1981, Scarman said senior officers had performed bravely and were themselves struck by numerous missiles. Interviewed afterwards, each of the senior officers at Tottenham felt they

---

20. Newman, op. cit. 8, p.13.
21. Moore, Tony (1986). Public Order: the police commander's role. In *Policing*, Vol. 2, No. 2, Summer 1986, p. 89.
22. Kerner, op. cit. 1, p.328.

had done all they could at their particular locations.[23] Some were hit by missiles on multiple occasions. To have attempted to enter the estate, other than in an operation which was properly co-ordinated would have been foolish in the extreme. Although some rank and file officers were critical of the lack of action, a number of the inspectors in charge of units were in agreement. Evidence of the difficulties likely to have been experienced in an individualistic approach was highlighted by Superintendent Boyall's failed effort to reach Tangmere Block at the time Serial 502 came under attacked and Constable Blakelock was killed.

The two most senior officers, Richards and Polkinghorne, remained in Yankee Control throughout the riot. Quite clearly, if he did not intend to do so himself, Richards should have appointed somebody to co-ordinate the efforts of the senior officers on the ground. Indeed, the Contingency Plans for the Control of Disorder on the Broadwater Farm Estate stipulated that a Police Forward Control should be set up in the nearby Lordship Lane Swimming Pool Car Park, and the confidential internal police report on the riot suggested that 'the failure to establish a forward control' was 'one of the most serious weaknesses of the whole operation.'[24]

In the absence of an appointed ground commander, it is arguable that Chief Superintendent Couch, as the officer in charge of the division on which the riot was taking place, should have assumed that role. He did not. Indeed, he remained at the quietest of the four locations throughout the evening and, but for the tragic death of Police Constable Blakelock, would have played a very minor role in the whole incident. For most of the time, he was in the best position to mount diversionary tactics to take the pressure off some of his colleagues. However, at about 8.30 p.m. he reported to Yankee Control that, in his opinion, to go forward would heighten tension on the estate—as if tension was not already heightened enough by then—and when Superintendent French asked Yankee Control for permission to mount an offensive on rioters at Adams Road at about 9 p.m., he was advised

---

23. During 1989 and 1990 the author interviewed or exchanged correspondence with David Polkinghorne, Mike Jeffers, David French, Bill Sinclair, Tom Jones (in command of the Special Patrol Group at the time of the riot) and Bob Wells (head of the D.11 Firearms Branch at the time of the riot) as part of a Master of Philosophy (M.Phil) research degree he was doing at the University of Southampton into public order policing.
24. Williams, op.cit. 4, p.29, para. 3.67.

against such action, not by Yankee Control, but by Couch. Fifteen minutes later, French asked Couch if it would be possible for units to enter into the estate from the west but got no response.[25] But, if blame for indecision and the lack of clear instructions is to be apportioned, then it must lie within Yankee Control, where the overall commander was, and not with Couch, who, despite what other senior officers on the ground may have thought, was merely one of four individual sector commanders.

Strategy

Three years previously, in an address to the Association of Chief Police Officers shortly before he took over as commissioner, Sir Kenneth Newman said:

> 'It is important that if the initiative has been lost to the rioters in the early stages it should be recovered by the police as quickly as possible. Rioting spreads quickly. Any successes gained by the rioters or any apparent reluctance of police to put down rioting will serve to encourage rioters and encourage others to join them.'[26]

But it would appear that the ferociousness of the attacks and the existence of firearms on the estate influenced the police strategy for much of the evening. In describing it as one of containment, Deputy Assistant Commissioner Richards suggested that:

> 'Any concerted effort to advance into the body of the estate ... could have resulted in death or serious injury to police and/or members of the public, whilst a withdrawal from the defended locations would have permitted the rioters to spill out into the side streets around Mount Pleasant Road, where fires in the old terraced houses could have been easily started by petrol bombs and could quickly have got out of control.'[27]

---

25. See the exchange of radio messages between Superintendent David French and Chief Superintendent Colin Couch in Williams, op. cit. 4, p.25.
26. Newman, Sir Kenneth (1982). 'Civil Disorder—Planning and Strategy: A paper containing an abbreviated version of a talk given to the Association of Chief Police Officers at the Police Staff College, Bramshill, on 22 March'. Unpublished.
27. Richards, op. cit. 9, p. 14, para. 14.11.

As the evening wore on, two other factors apparently influenced him in maintaining this strategy. Firstly, it had been reported to him that there were 'lakes of petrol'[28] on the estate waiting to be ignited by the rioters should the police mount an offensive. Secondly, although few arrests were being made, he was satisfied that many of those taking part in the riot could be arrested later as a result of the large numbers of photographs being taken by police photographers.[29]

Richards' strategy of containment was clearly not understood by senior officers on the ground, all of whom, it seems, took it to mean that the police 'were surrounding the estate in an attempt to prevent the rioters leaving.' This was not the case. What Richards actually meant by a strategy of containment was 'containing the attack on police to a limited number of defensible locations.'[30] In defending his strategy of containment afterwards Richards pointed out that:

> 'Unlike most other recent riots, all of the energies of the rioters were directed to the attack on police. There was little gratuitous violence to the person or property of others—unlike Brixton where there was widespread looting and a number of assaults, including rapes, upon members of the public.'[31]

But, unbeknown to him at the time, in adopting this strategy, Richards played into the hands of the rioters because it was subsequently suggested in the internal police report that their three main objectives were to:
- provoke a confrontation with the police;
- injure as many police officers as possible; and
- keep the police out of the estate.[32]

---

28. Ibid, p. 14, para. 14.2.
29. Richards had arranged for police photographers to attend earlier on the day of the riot. The intention was that photographs of the rioters would enable retrospective arrests to be made. A number of successful prosecutions did follow but the investigators were hampered in terms of identification by the fact that many of the rioters were masked and dressed in similar 'army fatigues'. Unfortunately, no photographers were in the vicinity of Gloucester Road when the attack on Constable Blakelock occurred.
30. Richards, op. cit. 9, p.14, para. 14.12.
31. Ibid.
32. Williams, op. cit. 4, p.22, para. 3.48.

The rioters achieved all three of their objectives and, in this, they were assisted by Richard's strategy of containment. Had they wanted to leave the estate to create mayhem elsewhere, the rioters could have done so at any time. Indeed, throughout the evening, many people did come and go across Lordship Lane Recreation Ground which lay to the west of the estate and was, by and large, un-policed throughout the evening. Pointing out that it was 'a massive area' and would probably have taken 'one thousand police officers to make a meaningful cordon', Commander Polkinghorne realised from the outset that he 'never had enough men to control Lordship Lane Recreation Ground'. As there was no evidence coming back to Yankee Control that it was necessary to control any escape route through the recreation ground, he 'concentrated all efforts in dealing with the rioters.'[33]

It was, without doubt, a difficult and dangerous situation both for the senior officers and those who faced the rioters in the front line. Indeed, The *Sunday Times* suggested it was 'the most vicious riot on the mainland within living memory.'[34] However, whilst the police, in general, received much sympathy in the aftermath of the riot, the police commanders came under severe attack for their inability to bring the riot under control sooner. Indeed, David Rose claimed that it soon became 'shockingly clear' that 'the one thing lacking from the police operation as the riot developed was any clear idea of what to do.'[35] But some of the most virulent criticism came from many of the junior officers who had faced the onslaught that night. They accused senior officers of 'incompetence' for what they saw as 'a succession of disastrous strategic blunders'.[36]

A strategy of the more commonly held understanding of containment, i.e. surrounding a location in an attempt to prevent people from leaving a location is a perfectly acceptable option in order to, for instance, keep opposing groups of demonstrators from confronting one another or to prevent a particular group from going on the rampage to attack property. It is not, however, an appropriate strategy when confronting a violent crowd which is

---

33. Polkinghorne, David (1989). In correspondence with the author, dated 2 November.
34. *Sunday Times*, 13 October 1985.
35. Rose, David (1992). *A Climate of Fear: The Murder of PC Blakelock and the Case of the Tottenham Three*. London: Bloomsbury, p.65.
36. Judge, Tony (1985). 'The "battle" of Broadwater Farm: Why the men behind the shields are angry.' *Police*, Vol. XVIII, No. 3, November, p. 10.

intent on attacking and maiming police officers, although it may be necessary in the short term whilst the police build up their resources.

But a strategy of containment should not be seen as an excuse for inactivity because it becomes increasingly dangerous for the officers on the front line the longer it goes on, as, indeed, it did at Tottenham. But, if Richards did consider an alternative strategy as casualties mounted, no mention of it is made in any of the police reports. Given the areas in which the rioters were mainly concentrated, a properly co-ordinated operation from the western side of the estate was probably the best option to go on the offensive. Another alternative was to implement some diversionary tactic to draw the rioters away from the main areas of rioting, particularly in Griffin Road. Ultimately, of course, a divisionary tactic was set up inadvertently and with tragic consequences by Chief Superintendent Couch when he sent Serial 502 into Tangmere Block to support the Fire Brigade.

In subsequent correspondence with the author, Commander Polkinghorne, claimed that a plan was formulated during the evening for officers under the command of Chief Superintendent Couch to enter the estate from Gloucester Road and, by 10 p.m., between 115 and 140 men (five or six full serials) had, according to Yankee Control, been sent to that location.[37] But Couch was unaware of the plan because, although some units failed to arrive, he had given away some in response to requests for assistance elsewhere until he was left with only half a serial, 502. Even so, the attempt to implement this plan was painfully slow for the riot had been in progress for over three hours when Police Constable Blakelock was killed. And, a little earlier, when there was a danger of the police lines being over-run in Griffin Road at about 9.30 p.m., Richards response was not to speed up any planned entry from Gloucester Road but to deploy a section of the Force Firearms Unit with baton rounds.

Tactics

A problem in responding to serious public disorder during the second half of the 1980s was not that the police units lacked enthusiasm or fitness or even equipment but it was rather an absence of tactical vision by police commanders. There was much criticism of the inability of police commanders

---

37. Polkinghorne, op. cit. 33.

to use the resources they had in a constructive way. In an article in *Police*, the Police Federation were quick to pick up on this point:

> 'The tactics employed at Broadwater Farm defy understanding. It is, after all, four years since the Federation was assured by the force hierarchy, that never again would officers be required to crouch behind static lines of long shields to become Aunt Sallies of the petrol bombers. Yet Broadwater Farm appears to have been a re-run of all the tactical mistakes of the 1981 riots.'[38]

The Head of Community Services for the London Borough of Haringey, Howard Simmons, who was in Mount Pleasant Road between 8.30 p.m. and 9 p.m., later told the Gifford Inquiry that he:

> '…was staggered to find them standing shoulder to shoulder about ten deep in receipt of all these missiles, but clearly they were going to sustain substantial injuries. God knows what their senior officers thought they were doing.'[39]

The huge disadvantage of a purely defensive posture meant almost total compliance with the crowd's initiative. It gave them the freedom to concentrate and strike as they wished. More importantly, lessons had not been learned from some of the 'inner city' riots of the early 1980s. In both Brixton and Toxteth, the police 'formed static or slow moving cordons that were unable to stem the disorder and resulted in unsustainable levels of attrition from injuries to officers.' But in Moss Side, the police 'adopted ad-hoc aggressive mobile tactics that swiftly brought an end to the disorder.'[40] Indeed, James Anderton, Chief Constable of Greater Manchester at the time of the Moss Side riot in 1981, said: 'Police should avoid static and "stand-off" postures which are now virtually useless in most outbreaks of disorder.'[41]

Writing five years after the riot after he had spent two years embedded in

---

38. Judge, op. cit. 36, p.15.
39. Gifford, Lord (1986). The Broadwater Farm Inquiry: Report of the Independent Inquiry into Disturbances of October 1985 at the Broadwater Farm Estate, Tottenham. London: Broadwater Farm Inquiry, p. 112, para. 5.56.
40. Waddington, P A J, and Martin Wright (2008). Police use of force, firearms and riot-control. In Newburn, Tim (2008). *Handbook of Policing*. Cullompton: Willan, p. 472.
41. Anderton, James (1981). 'Normal service will be resumed' In *Police*, the monthly magazine of the Police Federation, Vol. XIV, No. 2, October 1981.

the Metropolitan Police, Tank Waddington, himself a former police officer for a brief period before entering academia, accused the police of failing 'to appreciate the nature of the task of quelling serious disorder.' He went on, 'they, and many others remain blinded by their traditional image of policing public order without recourse to overtly aggressive tactics', concluding that 'from the vantage point of 1990, the development of police public order tactics [was] confused and out of touch with reality.'[42]

Mobilisation

Mobilisation is all about having the right resources in the right place at the right time. It is the act of assembling and effectively deploying police resources in response to the threat of, or an actual outbreak, of serious public disorder. This includes having a command team in place. On the face of it, the mobilisation of resources went well, despite the unfortunate dismissal of many of the units at around 6.30 p.m. But there are two parts to successful mobilisation. The first is getting sufficient trained units to the scene; the second is deploying them effectively.

As it had done at Brixton only a week previously, the mobilisation of resources and manpower had gone well; so, too, had the deployment, in theory. In practice, however, many of the units, for reasons discussed below, failed to reach the locations to which they were deployed. Additionally, for reasons that are not entirely clear, only one of the eight Special Patrol Groups units, at that time, still the best equipped—they had their own radio channel—and trained to respond to serious public disorder, was deployed at the height of the rioting.

At the height of the worse rioting, in addition to the SPG, 20 District Support Units (over 400 officers trained and equipped to deal with public disorder) were on standby locally but had not been deployed, but some 25 half-serials, some of which, like Serial 502, were ad-hoc units put together for general patrol, were.[43] Scarman had criticised the use of unprotected vehicles

---

42. Waddington, P A J (1991). *The Strong Arm of the Law: Armed and Public Order Policing.* Oxford: Clarendon Press, p. 159.
43. This information was gleaned from Williams, David A, op. cit. 4, Appendix H, pp. 122–191.

and officers untrained in the use of shields, at Brixton in 1981.[44]

Confusion

No police commander 'should allow his units to "drift" aimlessly into a public order confrontation or become involved in disorder itself piecemeal.'[45] But this is exactly what happened at Broadwater Farm. In the confusion that existed that night it is difficult to be precise about the deployment of manpower. By 10 p.m. approximately 760 police officers, including inspectors and sergeants, had been deployed. Nearly all had been briefed, to a greater or lesser extent, and assigned to specific locations in and around the estate before leaving the two main standby areas, Wood Green Police Station or Northumberland Park. However, the only designated approach route to the riot area was via Mount Pleasant Road, scene, for the greater part of the evening, of the most violent disorder. Consequently, many of the units assigned to Willan and Gloucester Roads, either because they were unfamiliar with the area and seeing the disorder in Adams Road and Griffin Road thought they had arrived at their destination, or thinking they would be of more use there, failed to arrive at the southern end of the estate.[46] In addition, as was evident when Chief Superintendent Couch sent units under his command at Gloucester Road to assist at other locations, police commanders on the ground were re-deploying units without notifying Yankee Control.

Police communications

Effective communication is essential if serious public disorder is to be managed; indeed, Kerner went so far as to say that 'effective command and control' in such situations depended 'upon communications.'[47] Unfortunately, history is littered with cases where the police have been handicapped by inadequacies in their communication systems. In London, on the occasion of pre-planned public order events, such as large-scale demonstrations, marches

---

44. Scarman, op. cit. 2, p. 71, para. 4.91.
45. Moore, op. cit. 21, p. 91.
46. Williams, op. cit. 4, p.24, para. 3:63.
47. Kerner, op. cit. 1, p.486.

and the Notting Hill Carnival, the Metropolitan Police had, for a number of years used two or more radio channels, one of which has always been designated a 'command' channel on which senior officers could communicate with the overall commander and with one another; the other channels would be 'working' channels on which units could be deployed and be given directions. But the events at Broadwater Farm were policed using only one radio channel.

The Metropolitan Police Public Order Review subsequently reported that 'the failure to create "command" and "support" channels at an early stage and as a matter of routine led to considerable congestion.'[48] Commander Polkinghorne had asked for a separate command channel to be allocated, well before the rioting started, but was told that continuing tension in Brixton and other events in London that day, meant it was not available.[49] In hindsight, it was a gross error of judgement on the part of those who failed to comply with his request but, given the serious and prolonged nature of the rioting, it is strange that an additional channel was not made available during the evening.

The failure to arrange for a 'command' channel resulted in two major problems. Firstly, throughout the evening, Yankee Control received no intelligence and very little information about the overall situation on the ground.[50] Secondly, neither Richards nor Polkinghorne spoke to the ground commanders during the riot except on the rare occasions when the latter left their positions to communicate with them by public telephone.[51] Therefore, whilst Yankee Control deployed resources to them, the senior officers on the ground were left to fend for themselves during the evening and they did this from their four locations, for the greater part, in isolation of one another.[52]

The net result of all this was, whereas Richards and Polkinghorne in Yankee Control thought there was a balanced distribution of units at the four locations around the estate, the reality of the situation was a complete imbalance

---

48. Metropolitan Police (1986). Public Order Review: Civil Disturbances 1981–1985. London: Metropolitan Police, p. 20, para. 9.3.
49. Polkinghorne, op. cit. 33.
50. Williams, David A, op. cit. 4, p. 34, para. 3:89.
51. Jeffers, Mike (1990). In correspondence with the author, dated 31 January, he described how he used a telephone in a nearby house to talk to Deputy Assistant Commissioner Richards.
52. Williams, David A, op. cit. 4, p. 20, para. 3:38 and p.35, para. 3:89 (vii).

between the two locations in Mount Pleasant Road and the two locations in The Avenue. At Griffin Road there were approximately 275 police officers and at Adams Road approximately 265, whereas there were only about 70 in Willan Road and 12 at Gloucester Road at the crucial time Constable Blakelock was killed. In addition, nearly 140 were operating around the periphery of the estate under the command of Chief Inspector Freeborn.[53]

Baton rounds

There was criticism also of the way the 'baton rounds' issue was handled. Although Richards had not spoken to or sought the advice of his ground commanders, he obviously believed their use might be of value when the police lines in Griffin Road were in danger of being over-run. They were to be used as a tactic of last resort but he failed to take into account that, at that time, the guidelines relating to the use of baton rounds and CS gas had not been distributed to officers below the rank of commander. Therefore, none of the senior officers on the ground, with the exception of Superintendent Harris, were aware of these guidelines.

Had they been fired, there is little doubt that the rioters would initially have retreated into the estate to escape being hit by the baton rounds. This would have left the police with two principle options, viz:

   (a) They could merely stand their ground; *or*
   (b) They could have pursued the retreating rioters into the estate.

Option (a) would have been relatively easy. Creating a gap between themselves and the rioters would have reduced injuries to police officers but it would not necessarily have put a stop to the rioting. Option (b), on the other hand, would have been far more difficult. Unless it had been mounted as a cohesive offensive from a number of different directions the pursuit of the rioters into the estate with the intention of making arrests and putting a stop to the rioting, would have placed officers in considerable danger from ambush attacks

The whole question of whether or not it was appropriate to use baton rounds that night was probably best summed up by an unnamed firearms

---

53. Ibid, p. 23, para. 3:61.

officer who told a BBC documentary team that the rioters had beaten the Metropolitan Police at Broadwater Farm. He went on to explain:

> 'They had firearms; we didn't. We got it back to front. The plastic bullet is there to keep the crowd away from you. I think if they had a few plastic bullets put down on them they would have panicked.'[54]

Failure to use the Special Patrol Group

The Metropolitan Police had a group of officers that night that could have made a significant contribution to bringing the disorder to an end. The Special Patrol Group, approximately 240 constables with appropriate supervisors from sergeant to chief superintendent, was the best equipped and most highly trained of any officers to handle public disorder. And yet only No. 5 Unit, which happened to be on duty that day anyway, was involved. The remaining units it seems were mobilised but kept on standby until 3.30 a.m. the following morning when they were used as part of the force to re-occupy the estate.

To understand why this might have been the case it is necessary to go back to the formation of the SPG in 1965. It was 'to provide a centrally based mobile squad for combatting particularly serious crime and other problems which could not be dealt with locally by divisions.' However, 'as time went by, because of their ready availability, the SPG were increasing used in connection with demonstrations and disorders.' As a result they were involved in countering disorder at Red Lion Square (1974), Grunwick (1976–1977), Lewisham (1977) and Southall (1979), where unfortunately a demonstrator, Blair Peach, died, probably as a result of being struck with a blunt object by a member of the group. Following this, the group came in for some severe criticism and a thorough review of its role was carried out by Deputy Commissioner Pat Kavanagh, as a result of which it 'could only be committed to public order duties with the express authority of a deputy assistant commissioner or someone more senior.'[55]

In his report to the Home Secretary in 1983, the new commissioner, Sir

---

54. *Police Review*, 17 October 1986, p. 2102.
55. McNee, Sir David (1983). *McNee's Law*. London: Collins, p. 87–89.

Kenneth Newman, emphasised the role of the DSUs as the first wave of response to civil disorder. Insofar as the SPG was concerned he told the Home Secretary that he intended to 'redefine their role to make anti-burglary patrols their prime function and public order as their secondary function'.[56] So, arguably, Newman had relegated the SPG in the order in which public order commanders should deploy units to respond to serious public disorder despite the fact that they were better trained than DSUs, where officers tended to be posted only for three months before being rotated, had their own set of senior officers who they worked under regularly and had their own separate channels of communication. Nevertheless, Newman continued to express the importance of the SPG in responding to disorder in his annual reports for 1983 and 1984. In 1983 he wrote 'a ready reserve of officers is essential to deal quickly and effectively with any outbreaks of disorder which is beyond the capabilities of local officers on duty at the time' before pointing out that 'the Special Patrol Group and the district support units (formerly called immediate response units)' were 'trained to a level which will do more to ensure a rapid and professional response to spontaneous disorder.'[57] He wrote in a similar vein the following year, pointing out that the SPG and DSUs were available to bring 'large-scale, serious disorder ... quickly to an end.'[58]

Given at one stage that Richards was thinking of using baton rounds for the first time on the British mainland it is somewhat surprising that he did not think it appropriate to commit the SPG into mounting an offensive operation to relieve the pressure, particularly on officers in Adams and Griffin Roads.

Lakes of petrol

In addition to the presence of firearms, one of the principle reasons given for not entering the estate was the so-called 'lakes of petrol'. The phrase 'lakes of petrol' conjures up a picture of the whole area or certainly a large part of it being flooded with petrol; all the evidence points to this not being the case. Indeed, some police officers suggested that it was merely an excuse thought

---

56. Newman, op. cit. 5, pp. 27–29, para. 56.
57. Annual Report, op. cit. 6, p. 50.
58. Annual Report, op. cit. 7, p. 67.

up after the event as a reason for not entering the estate and allowing an existing stand-off situation to continue.[59]

Having said that, there was petrol on the ground throughout the riot area, particularly around Griffin Road and Adams Road, either as a direct result of spillage as it was taken from motor vehicles or because many of the petrol bombs thrown by the rioters failed to ignite. Indeed, the Fire Brigade recorded that in Adams Road at 9.20 p.m., there were 'copious amounts of petrol spread on the road unignited'[60] and a *Times* journalist, Andrew Moger, who attached himself to one of the police units throughout the riot, reported that at one stage 'youths poured petrol across the road ready to be lit' should 'his' unit advance towards them.[61]

The failure to use the Force helicopter

The failure to make use of the powerful 'Nitesun' lighting equipment fitted to the Metropolitan Police Force helicopter was also the subject of critical comment. The helicopter was available from 7.30 p.m. onwards. Twenty minutes later, Superintendent French was asked by Yankee Control whether he wanted the helicopter and he responded to the effect that it was of no use to him personally.[62]

The helicopter was eventually deployed—whether at the request of Yankee Control or on the initiative of the Special Operations Room at New Scotland Yard is unclear—but it did not arrive over the estate until about 11.30 p.m. when things were much quieter. Its effect was quite dramatic. Fearing they would be easily identified, it drove the rioters from the balconies and walkways to seek cover from where they were waiting to ambush the police on the ground should they venture too close.[63]

---

59. See editorial 'Who poured the lakes of petrol' in *Police Review*, 17 January 1986.
60. Quoted in Gifford, op. cit. 39, p.114.
61. *The Times*, dated 7 October 1985.
62. According to a transcript of radio messages in the possession of the author, Superintendent French was asked by Yankee Control if he required the helicopter at 7.51 p.m. and he replied that it was of no use to him.
63. Williams, David A, op. cit. 4, p. 43, para. 4:33.

Degree of organization amongst the rioters

Finally, there was the question of whether or not the rioters were organized to the extent that individuals were exercising control over those taking part. Leaving aside an initial claim made at a press conference on the 7th October by the commissioner that 'groups of Trotskyists and anarchists had been identified as orchestrating' the riots[64] it was clear that the rioters were so effective in what they did that there must have been an element of organization by certain individuals and the evidence from all sides of the spectrum tends to support this view. In describing some of the tactics used by the rioters, Richards claimed that 'particular individuals were observed on several occasions giving directions to others by word or gestures.'[65]

The police also claimed that the speed with which the initial incident in Willan Road developed into a full-scale riot covering four separate locations, suggested 'a degree of planning and organization.'[66] Indeed, Sergeant Nevens saw crates of petrol bombs when he arrived in Willan Road shortly after 7 p.m. and petrol bombs and paving-stones were already in position on the first floor of Rochford House when Inspector Dellow led his men towards the basement during the very early stages of the riot.[67] Chief Superintendent Jeffers, too, felt that the way 'the mob appeared and disappeared' at Griffin Road 'obviously moving in a group to other parts of the estate showed some definite leadership and the steady supply of missiles showed organization.'[68]

However, the Gifford Inquiry concluded 'there were no generals' amongst the rioters and that people were merely 'supporting each other in a loosely organized way.'[69] But there is clear evidence, in addition to that put forward by the police, to suggest that the degree of control was greater than that suggested by Gifford. An eye-witness told the inquiry that when one group were running out of missiles to throw, two people shouted that more ammunition was required. Immediately, 'five or six responded by running round

---

64. Quoted in Gifford, op. cit. 39, p.124. This claim was subsequently withdrawn by a Scotland Yard spokesman according to a report in the *London Standard* on 17 October 1985.
65. Richards, op cit. 27, p. 13, para. 14.7.
66. Metropolitan Police, op. cit. 48, p.11, para. 4.3.
67. Sergeant Nevens in evidence at the Blakelock murder trial. *The Guardian*, 7 February 1987; *Police Review*, 13 February 1987, p. 310.
68. Jeffers, op. cit. 51.
69. Gifford, op. cit. 39, p. 109, para. 5.49.

the houses gathering up empty milk bottles, while four others turned over a car for petrol.'⁷⁰ In less than five minutes this group manufactured more than 50 petrol bombs. There was also evidence that 'some people had whistles, and one person had a bell.'⁷¹

One report suggested that 'the rioters tended to have small groups of agents provocateurs attempting to lure the police into ambushes' and 'small groups were also active behind the main mass of rioters.'⁷² Another went further, suggesting that the Broadwater Farm Estate 'with its elevated walkways and underground car parks was a perfect setting for guerrilla warfare', concluding that there was evidence that the riot 'was organized on military lines.'⁷³ A third report suggested that 'as the evening wore on ... it became clear that there was an inner group among the rioters who were waiting for ... an opportunity to hit out at the police.' The report went on to say that 'the organizational abilities of this inner group were skilfully deployed to prepare the petrol bombs' and suggested that they may have been responsible for 'bringing in the guns.'⁷⁴

Conclusion

Writing in *The Spectator*, Andrew Brown, summarised what happened when 'the wheel came off' at Tottenham:

> 'The external noise and what seems to have been a collapse of radio discipline made communications unusable: the control room at Wood Green, a mile away to the west, was convinced that the rioters' purpose was to get at the shopping centres around and did not for several hours realise how serious the situation was at Broadwater Farm. The senior officers at the front were strangers to each other, and to the men they commanded, which in an organization as personal as the Met makes a great difference.'⁷⁵

---

70. Ibid, p. 107, para. 5.44.
71. Ibid, p. 109, para. 5.49.
72. Walsh, Mike (1989). A study of urban mob violence: the Tottenham riots, 1985. In Walsh, Mike (ed.) 1989. *Disasters: Current Planning and Recent Experience*. London: Edward Arnold, p.142.
73. *Daily Express*, 8 October 1985.
74. *The Observer*, 13 October 1985.
75. Brown, Andrew (1986). 'Arming for the Next Riot'. In *The Spectator*, 19 July, p.10.

He went on to suggest that 'the most serious damage done at Broadwater Farm was inflicted on the trust of PCs for their supervising officers.'[76] The crucial sections of the Public Order Review that followed were not those which dealt with weapons and equipment, which so many people commented upon, but those concerned with command and control:

> 'Effective command and control of resources deployed at the scene of disorder is a key factor in determining the success or failure of any policing operation. The benefits of leadership qualities, expertise and directions of individual commanders deciding strategy and tactics can be realised through a clearly defined chain of command linked by clear and effective communications.'[77]

But perhaps one of the most telling statements in the context of whether or not the riot was organized came from the then chair of the Haringey Council, Bernie Grant. At an open air meeting outside Tottenham Town Hall on 8 October, he suggested that the riot proved 'black youth can successfully organize themselves and outsmart and outmanoeuvre' the police.[78] It is extremely unlikely that the rioters would have been so effective, even given the police shortcomings, had not a degree of organization been imposed by some individuals. Of one thing there is no doubt. Despite the claims by Deputy Assistant Commissioner Richards to the contrary, the police commanders were, on this occasion, outsmarted and outmanoeuvred by the rioters.[79]

The Police Federation was complimentary of the review carried out by Chief Superintendent David A Williams and his team[80] and also the Public Order Review published by the Metropolitan Police which covered the period 1981 to 1985[81] save in one respect. Both, it said, were on weak ground 'in putting forward the apologia of top management in that district for the major errors in decision-making which occurred over that weekend.'[82] Of

---

76. Ibid.
77. Metropolitan Police, op. cit. 48, pp. 19–20, paras 8.1 and 8.2.
78. Quoted in Gifford, op. cit. 39, p. 126, para. 6.6.
79. In a letter published in *Police*, Vol. XVIII, No. 4, December 1986, p. 18.
80. Editorial, 'Broadwaters run deep' in *Police*, Vol. XVIII, No. 11, July 1986, p. 3, in referring to Williams, David A, op. cit. 4.
81. Ibid, in referring to Metropolitan Police, op. cit. 48.
82. Ibid.

course, much was written 'in hindsight' about the riot (as indeed has been this book). Richards was quick to point out that it was easy 'in the cold light of day with the benefit of hindsight' to condemn 'senior management both before and during the riotous events of 6th October 1985.'[83] But, the Police Federation accused the Metropolitan Police of dismissing 'criticisms of police tactics and strategy at Tottenham as being inspired by hindsight', suggesting that it was 'always the first refuge of those who [had] no real answer.'[84]

---

83. In a letter published in *Police*, op. cit. 79.
84. Editorial, op. cit. 80.

CHAPTER TEN

The First Murder Investigation

Introduction

There have been three investigations into the killing of Constable Keith Blakelock. Seven people have been charged with his murder and although three were convicted at the end of the first trial, they were subsequently acquitted. Thus, despite all the scientific aids now available, as was so in the cases of Constable Culley in 1833 and Station Sergeant Green in 1919, no-one stands convicted of his murder.

The first investigation

The investigation into the murder and other criminal offences committed on the Broadwater Farm Estate on the evening of 6 October are described in some detail in David Rose's book, *A Climate of Fear: The Murder of PC Blakelock and the Case of the Tottenham Three*.[1] Whilst it is not intended to repeat much of what Rose said, in the context of this book it is necessary to outline what occurred which ultimately resulted in six people, three adults and three juveniles, appearing at the Central Criminal Court charged with murder.

As the senior detective officer on Y District at the time, Detective Chief Superintendent Gallagher was the obvious choice to lead the criminal investigation but it was quickly recognised that the work-load of investigating Constable Blakelock's murder and all the other crimes, some of them extremely serious, would be too much for one person. Therefore, to work with Gallagher, the Metropolitan Police's International and Organised Crime Squad (C.1) was asked to appoint an officer to undertake the investigation into the murder of Constable Blakelock. As a result, Detective Chief

---

1. Rose, David (1992). *A Climate of Fear: The Murder of PC Blakelock and the Case of the Tottenham Three*. London: Bloomsbury.

Superintendent Graham Melvin was telephoned at home by Commander Ron Dowling, the head of C1, and told to go to Tottenham the next morning. Much of his first day was taken up attending the post-mortem, putting a team together and briefing them and, together with Gallagher, setting up a joint headquarters at New Southgate Police Station, which, at the time, was not an operational police station but home of a number of the support functions on 'Y' District such as the community liaison officer, the Juvenile Bureau and the local crime prevention officer. Offices had to be cleared to enable a fully–computerised incident room to be set up. The snooker room became the exhibits room and the basement became a briefing room. There was not even a canteen on the premises so a temporary one had to be installed. Melvin was joined later that morning by another officer from C1, Detective Inspector Max Dingle. Eventually over 100 officers were drafted in. Most were detectives but they also included officers trained in the use of firearms, to accompany search and arrest teams when it was believed the occupants might be in possession of firearms, computer operators amongst whom were eight members of the civil staff, and other ancillary workers. Gallagher subsequently explained to the bi-weekly newspaper of the Metropolitan Police, how the length and complexity of the inquiry was dictated by the 'mixture of information and intelligence' that was received.[2] Over 1,000 photographs had been taken of the riot and local Tottenham officers, together with those who had responded to the events were asked to view them to assist in the identification of those who had taken part.

Writing a few years later, in 1991, the former Deputy Chief Constable of Greater Manchester Police, John Stalker, pointed out that 'the murder of a police colleague brings investigative pressures few detectives have experienced.'[3] Promoted to Detective Chief Superintendent in March 1985, Melvin was an experienced detective who had spent almost his whole career in the Criminal Investigation Department. It has been suggested that, because of the anger felt throughout the force at what people saw as Blakelock's unnecessary death, he was under considerable pressure to solve the murder.[4]

---

2. *The Job*, 13 December 1985, p.4.
3. Stalker, John (1991). 'It's time we accepted that policing is too important to be left to the police.' *The Sunday Times*, 21 December.
4. Rose, op. cit. 1, p. 76.

But Melvin had already led an investigation into what was thought to be the murder of a police officer earlier in the year. On this occasion, Police Constable George Hammond had stopped at a sweet shop in Dulwich to buy some cigarettes just as a robbery was taking place and was stabbed in the stomach with a ten-inch knife. He was in a coma for two months and required five major operations which included kidney transplant and heart bypass operations. It was only the skill of the surgeons that kept him alive. Melvin was eventually successful in bringing charges of attempted murder against a 17-year-old youth Christopher Ogleton, who was sentenced to nine years' youth custody.[5]

Following the completion of the inquiry into the murder of Constable Blakelock, Melvin went on to successfully investigate a series of murders committed by Kenneth Erskine. Known as the Stockwell Strangler. Erskine strangled seven elderly people, predominantly in South London, between 9 April 1986 and 23 July 1986 before being arrested on 28 July. He was convicted of murder and sentenced to life imprisonment which was subsequently reduced by the Court of Appeal to manslaughter in 2009 on the grounds of diminished responsibility.[6]

Melvin and, indeed Gallagher to a lesser extent, faced two significant hurdles from the outset. Firstly, the ultimate success or failure of a criminal investigation, particularly where murder is involved, will invariably depend on the thoroughness exercised at the crime scene in preserving, collecting and recording all the available evidence. In the immediate aftermath of the attack on Blakelock there must have been 'a wealth of evidence' as Rose explained:

> 'The wounds suffered by Blakelock must have sprayed blood over many of his attackers; their clothes would have been stained, or drenched. Other forensic evidence lay all around; objects or weapons with fingerprints, and all manner of clues.'[7]

But despite the presence of two former senior detectives in the Y District

---

5, 5 January 1996.
6. BBC News, 14 July 2009. http://news.bbc.co.uk/1/hi/england/8149050.stm accessed 17 October 2014.
7. Rose, op. cit. 1, pp.86–87.

Control Room at Wood Green,[8] the murder scene was not under the control of the police until they re-took the estate at around 4.30 a.m., over six hours after the murder had occurred. Given that, in addition to the killing of Constable Blakelock, serious criminal offences had occurred in different parts of the estate during the rioting, it is arguable that the whole of Broadwater Farm should have been treated as a crime scene. Even after the police had retaken the estate, little thought was given to the preservation of evidence. Instead, the police stood by whilst workmen from Haringey Council removed the debris created by the riot, in case there was a second night of rioting. Even the rubbish bins, in which weapons could have been thrown and on which there might have been fingerprints, were emptied. Indeed, as Gifford pointed out, 'the physical damage and mess was cleared up' with such 'remarkable speed' that all that could be seen of the events of that evening by the end of 7 October was 'the burnt scorch marks on the roadway and smoke on the pillars of the blocks.'[9] As Detective Chief Superintendent Melvin subsequently told a BBC documentary:

> 'We failed to put a cordon round [the scene] and therefore we lost much evidence in those first hours. It's true to say that much was burnt, that much clothing from the rioters was burnt and knives were thrown into bins. We lost a great deal.'[10]

The result was very few prosecutions were founded on physical evidence, be it forensic or otherwise. Occasionally, people were found to be in possession of items of stolen property on the basis of which a charge could be made but serious charges into the riot itself tended to be brought as a result of admissions those arrested had made under questioning, although, in some cases, photographic evidence existed of people carrying weapons or in the act of throwing them.

There has been huge advancements in the identification and use of forensic evidence in the last 30 years. DNA (Deoxyribonucleic acid), genetic

---

8. There were two, Deputy Assistant Commissioner Richards and Acting Commander Hodge.
9. Gifford, Lord (1986). The Broadwater Farm Inquiry: Report of the Independent Inquiry into Disturbances of October 1985 at the Broadwater Farm Estate, Tottenham. London: Broadwater Farm Inquiry, p.120, para. 6.13.
10. Barling, Kurt (2004). 'Who killed PC Blakelock?' A documentary shown on BBC Television. Interview with Graham Melvin.

fingerprinting, which shows similarities and differences between the DNA of the same family, and profiling, which can distinguish one individual from another from traces left on an article, were in the early stages of development for forensic purposes at the time of the riot. Additionally, the preservation of clothing, which may have been worn in the commission of an offence, was not of the same standard as it is today. Given the number of petrol bombs thrown that night and the number of cars set on fire, the clothing worn by some of those who took part would have reeked of petrol. And yet none was found.

One reason for a climate of fear

The second major difficulty both Melvin and Gallagher had was that, for reasons, some of which have already been identified, the investigation took place in an environment that was extremely hostile to the police. The Greater London Police Committee and Haringey Council, together with some of those who resided on The Farm at the time, subsequently claimed that, during the course of the investigations a climate of fear existed because the police treated everyone who had been on the estate that night as a potential criminal. Consequently, it was argued, people who were not involved and might have been able to provide some evidence of offences that had been committed, were turned off from being witnesses.[11] However, given that most, if not all, the law-abiding citizens on the estate had locked themselves in during the riot and, in any event, had they seen anything, were fearful of coming forward because of possible reprisals from the criminal element, it was unlikely that witnesses would have come forward on a voluntary basis. As a result 'throughout the autumn and winter' the investigation developed into a 'daisy chain' in which each arrest tended to be made as a result of what had already been gleaned from those in custody.[12] A number of those arrested were either juveniles or vulnerable people, e.g. educationally sub-normal, which again presented the police with problems as will be seen when it came to the trials. Suffice to say at this stage it was suggested that such people tended to say what they thought the police wanted to hear rather than what actually

---

11. Ibid.
12. Rose, op cit. 1, p. 116.

happened.¹³ Consequently, a number of those arrested gave the police a list of names of people who were alleged to have been present or had committed some offence, but this frequently turned out to be untrue.

Funded by Haringey Council, the Broadwater Farm Defence Campaign was set up and quickly complained that people living in the area were experiencing 'the most repressive policing methods', including daily raids on homes, which sometimes involved the use of sledgehammers to gain entry and the use of armed officers. But, as Deputy Assistant Commissioner Richards explained just over two months later, on each occasion property had been damaged, the police had arranged for it to be repaired. He admitted that some of the searches were conducted by armed officers but, in addition to one officer being brutally murdered, others, together with civilians, had been shot and the police had not yet recovered any firearms used by the rioters that night or the flame-thrower that was reportedly seen.[14]

An alternative reason for the climate of fear

Melvin, on the other hand, claimed that the climate of fear existed because those involved 'in the riot and the crimes of that night were petrified' that the police would find out they were present on the night of the riot. So the climate of fear was created as a result of the 'fear of detection' and 'fear of discovery.'[15] But, in relation to the murder investigation, Melvin had another problem in addition to the lack of forensic evidence. Although over 1,000 photographs had been taken many of those taking part wore military-style fatigues and were masked. Therefore even local officers had difficulty in identifying people from the photographs. Most of the military-style fatigues were destroyed in the immediate aftermath of the riot. Nevertheless, a number of those interviewed, but who refused to give evidence at court, told remarkably similar stories, e.g. 'that Silcott stood over Blakelock whilst he was on the ground and struck him with a machete or sword.'[16]

The difficulties the police were up against in their investigations was

---

13. Gifford, op. cit. 9, p. 141, para. 6.38.
14. *The Job*, 13 December 1985, p. 4.
15. Barling, op. cit. 10.
16. Chittenden, Maurice (1990). 'Blakelock murder: did they convict the real killers?' *The Sunday Times*, 22 April.

exemplified by the case of Andrew Pyke, a youth of 15-years-of-age, who attend a school for educationally subnormal children, as did a number of those who were questioned. He was arrested on 8 October, just 36 hours after Blakelock's murder. In his first interview with Detective Sergeant Kenneth van Thal, Pyke claimed to have been at the riot with his friend Mark Pennant, one of those subsequently charged with murder, who he alleged was in possession of a knife. Pyke admitted he was present but claimed he did not know about Blakelock's death until he saw it on the television news. However, in a subsequent interview, Pyke claimed to have seen a man he knew as Sticks, a name by which one of the main suspects, Winston Silcott, was known, with a machete. He said he had seen the police officers and firemen run down the stairs and was subsequently told by Pennant that 'Sticks and some other guys' had stabbed a policeman. The police were keen to use him as a witness and, although 'he admitted throwing ten rocks', for which others were being charged with affray, he was merely charged with threatening behaviour for which he was sentenced at the magistrates' court to two months youth custody. However, in answer to further questions, he then claimed the stabbing had occurred 'on the stairs.' A theme of Rose's analysis of the evidence subsequently presented at court was that officers undertaking the questioning of suspects did not appear to have been well-briefed as to precisely how and where Blakelock was murdered; otherwise, in Pyke's case, the officers would have known that 'this account was worthless' because Blakelock was not stabbed until he was some distance from the stairs.'[17]

At the committal hearings at Tottenham Magistrates' Court, Pyke attempted to retract his whole story about the riot and was treated as a hostile witness. Following this he was seen by police officers who, under a witness protection programme, offered him a new identity, asked him where he would like to live, and offered to arrange a training place for him in a motorcycle workshop. Arrangements were made for Pyke to be placed in the care of a local authority in the suburbs but Haringey Council refused to agree to his transfer. He failed to appear at the trial and a warrant was issued for his arrested. He was eventually found in a flat after three men were arrested for robbery but it could not be substantiated that he was being held against his will. When he was eventually brought before the court,

---

17. Rose, op. cit. 1, pp.100–102.

prosecuting counsel, Roy Amlot, QC, decided there would be little value in calling him as a witness.[18]

A second example arose early in 1986 which led to the arrest of Mark Braithwaite. On 16 January, Bernard Kinghorn was arrested. He initially denied being involved in the riot but, during a second interview, claimed to have seen a man he knew by sight as Mark Braithwaite 'stab PC Blakelock repeatedly with a long kitchen knife.' Kinghorn was eventually convicted of affray, theft, deception and fraud and sentenced to four-and-a-half years' imprisonment. Whilst he was in prison, the police tried to persuade him to give evidence but, after toying with the idea, he refused. His refusal was put forward by the police as just one of the many examples of the climate of fear that prevented witnesses from giving evidence. But Kinghorn's version of the murder bore little resemblance to the truth of what actually happened and some years later, he admitted 'his allegations against Braithwaite had been false all along.'[19]

Refusing access to a solicitor

Much publicity was given to the fact that a number of those arrested, including juveniles, were refused access to a solicitor. Of the 359 that were eventually arrested, according to the Metropolitan Police only 77 people were so refused but a further 232 were alleged to have signed a form indicating they did not require a lawyer. Rose claimed that some of these 'were unaware of what they were doing, others were later to claim they had been deceived.'[20]

It is unclear precisely what rules investigators were operating under, Judges Rules or the Police and Criminal Evidence Act (PACE) 1984. Judges Rules, which gave guidance to police officers and others when questioning people who were suspected of or had been charged with a crime, had first been introduced in 1912. They were due to be replaced by PACE, on 1 January 1986, some three months after the riot. However, at the time of the riot, the police were conducting a trial run on Tottenham Division using the procedures laid down by PACE.

---

18. Ibid, p. 103.
19. Ibid, pp. 169–176.
20. Ibid, p.110.

Judges Rules stated every person had the right to communicate and consult privately with a solicitor even if he was in custody, provided 'that in such a case no unreasonable delay or hindrance [was] caused to the processes of investigation or the administration of justice by his doing so'. Section 58 Police and Criminal Evidence Act 1984, together with the accompanying codes of practice, gave a suspect under interrogation an absolute right to have a solicitor present but this could be over-ridden on the authority of an officer of the rank of superintendent or above if he believed it would (a) lead to interference with or harm the evidence connected with serious arrestable offences or lead to interference with or physical injury to other persons; or (b) lead to the alerting of other persons suspected of having committed such an offence but not yet arrested for it; or (c) hinder the recovery of any property obtained as a result of such an offence.

At the murder trial Detective Chief Superintendent Melvin was, on more than one occasion, asked why he denied defendants access to solicitors and he responded by saying:

> 'In this wholly exceptional case, there was great pressure on solicitors and their friends which might interfere with the course of justice...there were many outstanding witnesses, suspects and evidence. I believed that the presence of a solicitor would allow those suspects, either wittingly or unwittingly, to be informed.'[21]

Later, he suggested that 'incidents' had 'cropped up' which led him 'to believe that the integrity of some firms of solicitors left a lot to be desired', suggesting that some were a party to 'a conspiracy to pervert the course of justice.' He added:

> 'My belief was that there was a possibility that they were being advised by persons who had an interest in what the suspects were actually saying. I had a firm who tried to blackmail me over the release of a person's property, otherwise they would not agree to the release of Keith Blakelock's body for burial. There was an incident where a solicitor...instructed a defendant to make allegations of assault when that person had given a full and frank confession.'[22]

---

21. Ibid, p. 135.
22. Ibid, pp. 174–175.

A similar view was expressed by Detective Chief Superintendent Gallagher at the second trial of Gary Potter, who was charged with causing an affray—the first trial ended in a hung jury, as, in fact, did the second. When he was cross-examined as to why Potter was denied access to a solicitor, he told the court that lawyers might '"wittingly or unwittingly" disclose information which might lead to further evidence being concealed.'[23]

In making such statements, Melvin and Gallaher were merely expressing what many police officers had observed over the years. The subject of 'crooked lawyers' had first been put into the public domain by Metropolitan Police Commissioner Sir Robert Mark in the Dimbleby Lecture in November 1973. Mark, who had made huge efforts to rout out corruption in the Criminal Investigation Department of the Metropolitan Police, has been variously described as 'arguably the most important individual to emerge from 20th century policing'[24] and 'probably the most accomplished post-war commissioner'.[25] In his lecture, he claimed that, for the most part, defence lawyers were 'only doing their job'. However, there were 'a small minority of criminal lawyers' who produced

> 'off the peg, the same kind of defence for different clients. Prosecution witnesses suddenly and inexplicably change their minds. Defences are concocted far beyond the intellectual capacity of the accused. False alibis are put forward. Extraneous issues damaging to police credibility are introduced.'[26]

Speaking some seven months later, Lord Salmon said:

> 'I cannot think why Sir Robert thought it worthwhile to make an allusion to the small minority of criminal lawyers whom he vividly described as dishonestly inventing spurious defences and alibis for their clients, suborning witnesses and doing very well out of highly paid forensic trickery.'[27]

---

23. Ibid, p.123.
24. *Independent*, 5 October 2010.
25. *The Guardian*, 1 October 2010.
26. Mark, Robert (1977). Minority Verdict in *Policing a Perplexed Society*. London: George Allen & Unwin, pp. 64–65)
27. Mark, Sir Robert (1978). *In the Office of Constable*. London: Collins, pp. 147–148.

The response the following day in the *Times* leader was succinct: 'There is a very simple reason. It is true.'[28] Writing in 1978 after completing his term as Commissioner, Mark pointed out that 'experienced and respected metropolitan detectives' could 'identify lawyers in criminal practice'[29] who were 'more harmful to society than the clients they [represented].' But, he claimed, unfortunately 'corrupt practices' amongst a small minority of lawyers continued because 'no satisfactory machinery' existed 'to prevent them' and 'the criminal justice process [was] only too willing to let sleeping dogs lie'.[30]

But Mark went further suggesting that there was 'no doubt that a minority of criminal lawyers [did] very well from the proceeds of crime.'[31] Such lawyers exist today. In July 2013, a 'criminal defence solicitor was branded an "enemy of justice"' and jailed for two years after being found guilty of 'telling a wanted drugs suspect of how best to flee the UK.'[32] Three months later, another 'criminal defence solicitor' was jailed for three years after being found guilty of tipping off the leaders of a major drug cartel after two of the gang had been arrested in possession of cocaine, the street value of which was estimated to be £50,000.[33]

Charges of murder

Melvin's investigation eventually led to the appearance of three adults, Winston Silcott, Engin Raghip and Mark Braithwaite appearing with three juveniles, Mark Pennant, Jason Hill and Mark Lambie, at the Central Criminal Court on 14 January 1987. All were charged with the murder of Constable Blakelock, riot and affray. In addition Lambie was charged with throwing petrol bombs. The trial began on 19 January 1987 before a jury of two black women, two white women and eight white men.[34] There was witness evidence against only one of the three juveniles. In the remaining five

---

28. *The Times*, 28 June 1974.
29. Mark, op. cit. 27, p. 155.
30. Ibid, p. 148.
31. Ibid, p. 155.
32. *Liverpool Echo*, 22 July 2013.
33. *The Mirror*, 1 November 2013.
34. *The Guardian*, 20 January 1987.

cases, the only evidence consisted of admissions made to detectives whilst undergoing interrogation.

The three juveniles

The three juveniles were arrested early on in the investigation, Pennant, aged 15, and Lambie, aged 14, on 10 October; and Hill, aged 13, on the following day. Pennant's arrest at school, which Detective Constable Lockwood claimed was 'unavoidable', was criticised by the trial judge, Mr Justice Hodgson, who remarked that it was 'difficult to escape the conclusion that the purpose was to prevent his mother finding out.' At the police station, he was told that his mother had refused to attend; in fact she had not been told of his arrest, and he was denied access to a solicitor on the grounds that it might 'interfere with the investigation'. He was interviewed on five occasions during which, in one of the interviews, he admitted being involved in the murder and he 'ascribed a significant role to "sticks".' He also named other people who had been present, including Mark Lambie and Nicky Jacobs.[35] As it turned out, he was the last of the three juveniles to be discharged, partly because his defence counsel, Michael West, QC, was keen to mount a defence based on evidence from two psychologists. The first claimed that Pennant was of low intelligence and subject to suggestibility and the second explained how vulnerable people could make unreliable confessions.[36] After an application from West to disallow the confession, Mr Justice Hodgson ruled his statements inadmissible. He continued:

> 'I have no doubt whatsoever that there was no justification for withholding this youth access to a solicitor...the idea that this youth might have passed coded messages, or, indeed, messages in clear [words], via his solicitor, does not seem to me to hold water. One would have thought that by now the dangers of interviewing a juvenile in the absence of legal advice were too well known to require my repetition. In my judgement, the number of times when refusal to allow access to a solicitor by a juvenile is justified are so few as to be non-existent. To

---

35. Rose, op. cit. 1, pp. 106–109.
36. Ibid, p. 177.

tell him that he was not to have anyone informed of his whereabouts was, in my judgement, an almost greater impropriety.'[37]

Lambie, aged 14 at the time of his arrest, was questioned, in the presence of his father, by Detective Inspector Maxwell Dingle 'with impeccable fairness'. He 'made rigorous efforts to ensure that Lambie knew what was going on and understood the caution.' In response Lambie admitted to 'playing a minor role in the disturbances.'[38] However, unlike the other five, the police produced a witness at the trial who claimed that Lambie was prominent amongst the group clustered around the fallen Blakelock, although he had not mentioned this when first interviewed. Lambie was defended by Michael Mansfield, the only one of the six leading barristers acting for the defence who was not (then) a Queen's Counsel but who was extremely well-known to the police.[39] Unknown to the witness, Jason Cobham, Mansfield was in possession of correspondence sent by Cobham to a friend which revealed a number of things that occurred during the riot.[40] This suggested that Cobham had done sufficient during the riot to lead to a charge of affray, but in return for becoming a witness against Lambie, he had only been charged with 'stealing a bottle of Cherryade and threatening behaviour' for which he was fined a total of £200 at Tottenham Magistrates' Court. He also agreed that the police 'had fixed him up with a flat, on which they paid the rent, and had given him money to buy groceries.' Finally he admitted under Mansfield's cross examination that he had lied to the police and had agreed to give evidence because he did not want to go to prison. With that, Roy Amlot, on behalf of the prosecution, withdrew the charges of murder and riot.[41] However, Lambie admitted throwing stones at the police and was convicted of affray for which he was sentenced to 120 hours of community service.[42]

Jason Hill had been seen 'looting the shop' in Tangmere Block, along with

---

37. Ibid, p. 183.
38. Ibid, p. 136.
39. Mansfield was made a Queen's Counsel in 1989. He was involved in many high-profile cases, including those of the Angry Brigade, Price Sisters, Guildford Four, Birmingham Six and Orgreave miners. He also represented the parents of Stephen Lawrence, the family of Jean Charles de Menezes and, more recently insofar as Tottenham is concerned, of Mark Duggan .
40. Mansfield, Michael (2009). *Memoirs of a Radical Lawyer*. London: Bloomsbury, pp. 215–216.
41. *Police Review*, 27 February 1987, p.414; see also Rose, op. cit. 1, pp. 136–139.
42. *The Guardian*, 26 February 1987; *Police Review*, 27 March 1987, p. 621.

his younger brother. When the police came to the flat where the Hill family lived, not only did they arrest Jason and his brother but also their parents after they found goods worth about £100 that had been stolen from the shop. Hill was refused access to a solicitor but was eventually interviewed by Temporary Detective Constable Perry Cockram in the presence of social worker Joe Heatley. In the four-hour interview he admitted stealing. This amounted to 'a *prime facie* case against him for the offence for which he had been arrested' and, under Judges Rules, he should have been charged and taken before a magistrate. Heatley requested that he be transferred to the care of the local authority that night under the provisions of the Children and Young Persons Act 1969, but, instead, he was detained at Leyton Police Station. There was a disagreement as to what occurred when Heatley returned the next morning. He claimed that it was simply his intention to advise Hill that, because the police intended to ask him questions about very serious matters, he should be careful what he said and had the right to remain silent. However, according to Cockram, Heatley told him that 'he had been instructed by his local authority bosses to "instruct" Hill not to answer questions'; as a result Heatley was not allowed to sit in on the next interview. When questioned about this during the trial, Cockran alleged that by adopting the attitude he did, Heatley was 'obstructing the course of justice'. In his place, Hyacinth Moody, a member of the Haringey Community Relations Council attended. At the end of the second day in custody, Hill was charged with burglary after which his clothes were taken from him for forensic examination and he spent the night in a cell dressed only in his underpants and a blanket. During further questioning Hill described how he had taken part in the murder along with 'Sticks', Lambie and Jacobs.[43] At the conclusion of the prosecution's case against all six defendants, Bruce Laughland, QC, submitted that the only evidence against Hill was that obtained during the interviews and they should be ruled inadmissible. In response, Mr Justice Hodgson said that 'very serious improprieties had occurred which amounted to 'oppression'. These included keeping Hill overnight in a police cell instead of releasing him into the care of the local authority and interviewing him in his underpants.[44] He also accused the interviewing officer of having little

---

43. *The Guardian*, 11 March 1987; see also Rose, op. cit. 1, pp. 140–148.
44. Rose, op. cit. 1, pp. 150–151.

idea of the precise circumstances involving Blakelock's death. He went on:

> 'When one has a confession made by a child of which there is no confirmation at all, it is vitally important to check the accuracy of the confession to see whether it accords with the known facts. Time and again Jason Hill gave the police warning signs that he was straying into make-believe but, through no fault of theirs, the signs were not noticed. And when, even to their limited knowledge, what he was saying was plainly inaccurate, they put it down to deliberately lying.'[45]

Mr Justice Hodgson's decision to throw out the charges against Hill was damaging to Melvin. He began by saying that he understood 'the pressure the police were under, and the difficulty of finding witnesses' and 'he accepted that Melvin wished to conduct the investigation with fairness and absolute propriety.' However, he said the responsibility for the refusal of a solicitor, rested with Melvin alone, 'he forgot that Jason Hill was a child' and concluded 'I have, to an extent, to criticise him personally, I regret.'[46]

Thus, before the case went before the jury, the three juveniles had been lost to the murder charge. In Lambie's case the prosecution withdrew the charge; in the case of Pennant and Hill, the judge had instructed the jury to find them not guilty and discharged them.

The adults

The arrest of the adults had been more spread out. Silcott was arrested on 12 October, Raghip on 24 October and Braithwaite on 4 February 1986. Silcott was to figure prominently in the investigation. Born in London he had been in trouble with the police since his late teens culminating, in December 1984, in his arrest for the murder of Anthony Smith, described as a professional boxer and local gang leader, at an all-night party in Hackney. Confident that no-one would give evidence against him, Silcott was still at the party when the police came to arrest him. Smith died a week later and the police were able to persuade three witnesses to make statements and give evidence against him. However, by the time it came to the trial, one

---
45. Ibid, p. 151.
46. Ibid, p. 149.

of the witnesses had withdrawn his statement and another disappeared in the middle of giving evidence; only the third, a woman who had received a number of threats leading up to the trial, gave evidence after the police had moved her to a hotel and later rehoused her.[47] At the conclusion of the trial Mr Justice Rose described Silcott as a 'vicious and evil man' pointing out 'at least three witnesses in court were terrified of you.' In sentencing him to life imprisonment in February 1986, the judge placed a reporting restriction on the trial until the conclusion of the Blakelock trial.[48] Although he appealed against his conviction for the Smith murder, and has frequently protested his innocence, the conviction still stands. He was eventually released from prison in 2003.[49]

So, Silcott was on bail for the Smith murder when the riot occurred on Broadwater Farm. He had been given bail at a private hearing in chambers by Judge Robert Lymbery in May 1985. When Judge Lymbery was subsequently asked why he had granted Silcott bail, he pointed out that bail had been opposed on two counts, that someone had approached witnesses during the committal proceedings at the lower court and it was believed that he would not turn up for his trial. However, Lymbery said that no evidence was put before him for refusing bail on either count and he claimed: 'I did what was right according to the law'.[50] Lymbery was subsequently criticised by the Lord Chancellor, Lord Hailsham, for talking publicly about his decision, but, at the same time, Hailsham criticised the Bail Act 1976 for 'strictly limiting' a judge's refusal to grant bail.[51]

A number of the people arrested by the police during the first five days of the investigation had implicated Silcott[52] but none was prepared to go into the witness box. Following his arrest, he had been taken to Paddington Green Police Station which was normally used for terrorist cases, where he was interviewed on five occasions by Detective Chief Superintendent Melvin, accompanied by Detective Inspector Dingle. The breakthrough

---

47. *Police Review*, 27 March 1987.
48. *The Guardian*, 20 March 1987.
49. For a detailed account of why Silcott and his supporters believe the conviction should be overturned, read Selma Jones (ed.)(1998). *A Chronology of Injustice: The Case for Winston Silcott's Conviction to be Overturned*. London: Crossroads.
50. *The Guardian*, 20 March 1987.
51. *The Guardian*, 21 March 1987.
52. Rose, op. cit. 1, pp. 124–127.

came in the sixth and final interview when the following exchange is alleged to have occurred:

Melvin: I believe that you were with [two names] and others standing over PC Blakelock when he was on the ground. You had either a machete or something like a sword with which you struck the officer:

Silcott: Who told you that?

Melvin: I am not prepared to tell you who has described your part in the murder of the officer. Suffice to say that I have been told you played an active part in murdering him.

Silcott: They're only kids. No one's going to believe them. You say they say that. How do I know? I don't go with kids.

Melvin: What makes you think that the people I am referring to who have witnessed your part in the murder are young people?

Silcott: (Pause) You've only had kids in so far. Haven't you?

Melvin: If only one person had told me of your part in this crime I would not be so confident in my belief that you were the ringleader that night. Where there is more than one person saying the same thing the facts become clear.

Silcott: (Looked out of window. Stood up. Moved to window. Looked out. Returned to chair. Sat down) You cunts! You cunts! (Leaned back in chair. Tears in eyes. Arms above head) Jesus! Jesus!

Melvin: Did you murder Police Constable Blakelock?

Silcott: You ain't got enough evidence. Those kids will never go to court. You wait and see. Nobody else will talk to you. You can't keep me away from them.

Melvin: What do you mean by that?

Silcott: I ain't saying no more and you've got a big surprise coming. You will probably lose your job.

Melvin: Are you telling me that any witness is in danger from you?

Silcott: Just take me down and charge me. I ain't saying any more. I ain't signing anything. You ain't got no evidence.

Melvin: I have further reason to believe that it was your intention to sever the officer's head and to parade it on a pole through the estate within sight of other police officers?

Silcott: I'm not saying anything more. I won't answer any more questions. You can't force me man. (He sat back in chair and closed his eyes).[53]

Silcott was defended by Barbara Mills, QC, who later became successively Director of the Serious Fraud Office, from 1990 to 1992, and then Director of Public Prosecutions from 1992 to 1998. The substance of Silcott's defence was that he was not present during the riot and had not made the statements attributed to him during the final interview. But Mills was in a difficult position because, in English law, if a defendant accuses the prosecution of lying, the prosecution can then introduce evidence as to the defendant's character and Silcott, with his somewhat dubious past, had, by this time, been convicted of the murder of Anthony Smith. After taking legal advice about his options from Mills and Andrew Hall, his solicitor, Silcott chose not to give evidence.[54]

Following his arrest, Raghip was interviewed by Detective Inspector John Kennedy and Detective Sergeant van Thal on ten occasions spread over four days. He admitted throwing stones at the police during his first interview and after the fifth interview he was charged with affray. In a sixth interview, conducted after he had been charged, he described the attack on Constable Blakelock. When he appeared at the magistrates' court the next morning he

---

53. Dalrymple, James (1990). 'The doubts about Winston Silcott's guilt.' *Independent on Sunday*, 28 January, p.17.
54. Rose, op. cit. 1, p.156.

was remanded in police custody. He was interviewed a further four times, during which time he admitted possessing a broom handle and said he would have probably hit the officer if he could have got close enough. However, after the tenth interview he was finally released on bail, still only charged with affray. Six weeks later, he was visited at his home address and asked to attend the police station where he was charged with murder.[55]

Following his arrest on suspicion of murder on the basis of what Kinghorn had told police, Braithwaite was interviewed on eight occasions over two days, again without a solicitor being present by Detective Sergeant Dermot McDermott in the presence of Detective Constable Colin Biggar. The interviews followed a familiar pattern. In the first he denied being on the estate on the night of the riot but during the second he admitted being present but merely as a spectator. In the fourth interview, he allegedly admitted throwing a few stones and in the fifth, he said he was present at Tangmere at the time Blakelock was killed but took no part. However, in the sixth interview he allegedly admitted hitting Blakelock's body with a bar whilst others were stabbing and kicking him. It was on the evidence of this sixth interview that he was charged. In the seventh interview, however, he claimed that it was not Constable Blakelock that he hit but a blond, clean shaven officer; Blakelock had a moustache. He was interviewed on a further four occasions with a solicitor present when he made no reply to the questions put to him.[56]

The jury deliberated the evidence for three days and two nights at the end of which the three adults were unanimously found guilty of murder. Each was sentenced to life imprisonment. In sentencing them, Mr Justice Hodgson recommended that Silcott serve a minimum of 30 years but he made no recommendation on the number of years to be served by Raghip and Braithwaite. All three were also convicted of riot and affray for which Silcott was sentenced to ten years, and Raghip and Braithwaite to eight years each.[57] The moment the jury returned from its three-day deliberation was described by one newspaper:

---

55. *Police Review*, 20 February 1987, p. 362; see also Rose, pp. 160–168.
56. *Police Review*, 13 March 1987. p.518.
57. *The Guardian*, 20 March 1987; *Police Review*, 27 March 1987, p. 631.

'…three of the five women empanelled were in tears. After the sentences, another woman fainted before leaving the jury box. Silcott received his conviction with a smile and gestured to friends in the public gallery, appearing unconcerned. Raghip said on hearing the verdict: "You've made a big mistake." As the sentences were announced, many in the public gallery wept and screamed. A woman was led away struggling by police officers, and there were scuffles outside the court, with several arrests.'[58]

The investigation into other criminal offences

Gallager's investigation into other criminal offences was arguably more successful. By the end of May 1986, 271 premises on the estate had been searched, 359 people had been arrested and 162 people had been charged with offences committed on 6 October 1985. Quite a high number, 63, were charged with affray. Twenty pleaded guilty with the remainder pleading not guilty. Of those in the latter category, 19 were found guilty but 24 were acquitted.[59] A number of those convicted were given substantial sentences. For instance, a 19-year-old youth who had been 'involved in three separate stone-throwing attacks on police' and 'had joined a crowd chanting "kill, kill, kill"' was sentenced to seven years imprisonment. Two others, one aged 22, who had been present for three hours and 'had thrown two bottles and at least eight half-bricks and had helped others to move a freezer from a shop to a ramp so that it could be dropped on to the police, was sentenced five years imprisonment; the other, aged 18, who had been present for an hour-and-a-half and had been involved in assisting with setting up a burning barricade, also received a five year custodial sentence.[60] A 23-year-old man, who was seen in photographs wearing a mask and holding a lump of rock, was sent to prison for five years. On this occasion, the judge, Neil Donaldson QC, commented that he would have received a lighter sentence had he admitted the charge 'in the light of "overwhelming" evidence'; instead, the judge

---

58. *The Guardian*, 20 March 1987. This is slightly at odds with *The Guardian* report of 20 January 1987 mentioned earlier in this chapter under the sub-heading 'Charges of murder' which stated there were only four women on the jury.
59. Rose, op. cit. 1, p.120.
60. *The Guardian*, 22 November 1986.

commented, 'he had been pressurised to fight the case by outsiders'. Amongst the defence witnesses was the head of Haringey's police research unit.[61]

Postscript

Over the next 15 years Lambie 'graduated to become one of the most feared gangsters in the country' until, in May 2002, then aged 31, he was finally 'jailed for 12 years for a series of "shocking and disturbing offences" that embraced kidnap, torture and drug-running.' During the trial, prosecuting counsel, Nicholas Hilliard, told the court that he and his three 'fellow gangsters were a "malign and corrosive influence on the black community".' In the lead up to his arrest, he and his gang had abducted two men, tortured them with a hammer and an electric iron and poured boiling water over their genitals. One of the men, Twaine Morris, managed to escape the clutches of the gangsters and went to the police who put him under protective custody but he later released himself although he was still prepared to give evidence against the gang. In an attempt to persuade him not to do this, he was later shot three times and he returned to protective custody. After the trial, Lambie was described by Detective Inspector Peter Lansdown, from the Metropolitan Police's Operation Trident, as 'a prolific criminal.'[62] Of this particular episode, Michael Mansfield later wrote in his autobiography that Lambie had been advised to leave Broadwater Farm following his acquittal. He continued: 'When failures like this occur, I not only feel upset for the victims, but deeply frustrated at such a squandering of time and the waste of a life.'[63]

---

61. *The Guardian*, 28 October 1986; Police Review, 10 October 1987, p. 2057.
62. Fresco, Adam (2002). 'Justice catches up with 'untouchable' gangster.' *The Times*, 21 May.
63. Mansfield, op. cit. 40, p. 216.

CHAPTER ELEVEN

Appeals, Acquittals and Further Investigations

Broadwater Farm Defence Campaign

Immediately following the convictions, a campaign to free the 'Tottenham Three', organized by the Broadwater Farm Defence Campaign got underway. In July 1987, publicity was given to a report by two black lawyers from the United States, Margaret Burnham and Lennox Hinds, who had attended the trial at the invitation of Haringey Council. The report was extremely critical of the police and, indeed, the legal system in the United Kingdom because of the way the crimes had been investigated and the trials conducted.[1] Then in February 1988, Amnesty International issued a 25-page report on the grounds that 'the events surrounding the Broadwater Farm disturbances took place in a highly charged and political atmosphere' which brought it into 'the framework of Amnesty International's work.'[2] Although admitting it was unable to validate the allegations, the report, nevertheless, claimed that 'detained suspects, including juveniles, were denied access to lawyers and family during lengthy periods of police interrogation, were tricked by the police into signing documents waiving their rights and signed statements under duress, sometimes not even having been allowed to read them first.'[3] Later that year, in December, solicitors acting on behalf of the three men, sought leave to appeal but Lord Lane, the Lord Chief Justice, dismissed the application; in fact, following submissions made by their respective counsel, Lane, sitting with Mr Justice Steyn and Mr Justice McGowan held that the convictions were 'safe and satisfactory'.[4]

Meanwhile, in April 1989, at a meeting attended by only 150 students, the Students Union of the London School of Economics elected Silcott as an

---

1. *The Guardian*, 20 July 1987.
2. Amnesty International (1988). United Kingdom: Alleged Forced Admissions during Incommunicado Detention, p.1.
3. Ibid.
4. *The Guardian*, 14 December 1988.

honorary union president.⁵ A few days later, an attempt was made to reverse the decision but, with over 800 students voting, it failed to get the two-thirds majority after Lord Gifford had told the meeting that Silcott's conviction was 'probably the most serious miscarriage of justice in a jury trial this decade.'⁶

In April 1990, at a press conference in London attended by Raghip's wife, Sharon, and Bernie Grant, a former US presidential candidate, Jessie Jackson, in a direct reference to the investigation into Constable Blakelock's murder, expressed his concern about 'confessions made by vulnerable young men after long periods of detention and without the benefit of legal representation'.⁷

The following month, a BBC 1 programme, *Beyond Reasonable Doubt*, cast doubt on the convictions of Raghip and Braithwaite. In the case of Raghip, it was revealed that Dr Eric Ward, a psychologist at Hackney Hospital in East London, had been commissioned by the defence prior to the trial to make an assessment of him but, because his report suggested he was of average intelligence, Raghip's defence counsel considered it would not assist his case. However, in the BBC programme Ward claimed to have misinterpreted his data. Indeed, before Raghip's unsuccessful application for leave to appeal in 1988, another psychologist, Giesli Gudjonsson, from the Institute of Psychiatry, claimed that Raghip's intelligence lay in the bottom five per cent of the population. However, the appeal court had rejected this evidence because of the existence of Dr Ward's then unretracted report. For Braithwaite, the programme put forward the testimony of Paul Salkovski from Oxford University, and expert in phobias. He claimed that Braithwaite 'displayed the classic symptoms of claustrophobia, and that his confessions were made with the primary aim of getting out of his cell.'⁸

After seeing the programme, Lord Scarman commented that it had 'emphasised his long-held belief that no one ought to be convicted of a serious criminal offence on an uncorroborated confession obtained in a police interrogation unwatched by any solicitor or outside party' and, he therefore felt that the convictions of Silcott, Raghip and Braithwaite were unsafe. A former Lord Justice of Appeal, Lord Lawton, said, 'he was "somewhat worried"

---

5. Ibid, 29 April 1989.
6. Ibid, 3 May 1989.
7. Ibid, 18 May 1990.
8. Ibid, 16 May 1990.

by the case, and believed that, as in Scottish law, people who confessed to police without a third party being present should not be convicted without supporting evidence.'[9]

Discipline proceedings against Melvin

Meanwhile, trouble had been building up for Melvin. One commentator suggested that Mr Justice Hodgson's ruling of 24 February in the case of Jason Hill 'was something of a legal landmark'[10] and his criticism of Melvin was referred by the then Commissioner of the Metropolitan Police, Sir Peter Imbert, to the Police Complaints Authority. The inquiry was conducted by Commander Ken Merton under the supervision of PCA lay member, Vernon Clements. At the conclusion of his investigation, Commander Merton recommended no formal action but this was rejected by the PCA. After several months of exchanging correspondence and meetings, the authority used its statutory powers to direct the commissioner to lay charges and organize a tribunal.

Melvin finally appeared before a disciplinary tribunal on 21 May 1990 to face three charges; disobedience to orders in that he permitted Hill to be treated in a way which contravened Judges Rules and the Police and Criminal Evidence Act (PACE) 1984; allowing Hill to be held at a police station overnight, in breach of the Children and Young Person's Act; and accessory to breaches of statute committed by other officers.[11] In addition to the television programme *Beyond Reasonable Doubt*, in the period immediately preceding the tribunal, articles appeared in such newspapers as *The Guardian*, *Independent*, *The Sunday Times*, and *Independent on Sunday*, expressing concern about the way the investigation had been conducted.[12]

---

9. Ibid, 18 May 1990.
10. Rose, David (1992). *A Climate of Fear: The Murder of PC Blakelock and the Case of the Tottenham Three*. London: Bloomsbury, p.149.
11. Ibid, p. 153. Rose suggests Melvin faced four charges but the author has discovered from police sources that it was only three.
12. Chittenden, Maurice (1990). 'Blakelock murder: did they convict the real killers?' *Sunday Times*, 22 April; Phillips, Melanie (1990). 'A televised game of trial and error.' *The Guardian*, 18 May; Leading article (1990). 'A strange miscarriage of English justice'. *Independent*, 18 May; and Dalrymple, James (1990). 'The Case of the Broadwater Three—The ordeal of Jason Hill: a mother's story.' *Independent on Sunday*, 20 May.

It was against this background that the tribunal was held.

Because Blakelock was a member of the Police Federation[13] it supported Melvin and, as a result, Detective Chief Inspector Jack Wadd, a qualified but non-practising barrister, was his friend during the proceedings. Wadd called for the charges to be dropped on the grounds that the lengthy delay between the alleged offences, the start of the investigation and the convening of the tribunal, amounted to an abuse of process; additionally, although Hill's solicitor had lodged a complaint, no statements were taken either from Mr Justice Hodgson, whose comments had instigated the inquiry, or Hill. However, the tribunal dismissed the submissions. On behalf of Melvin, Assistant Commissioner Gwyn Jones pointed out to the tribunal that the use of PACE at Tottenham in the autumn of 1985 before its formal introduction on 1 January 1986, was regarded as 'on-the-job' training and disciplinary offences could not arise from it in the event of contravention. Despite Detective Chief Superintendent Gallagher, who had by this time retired from the Metropolitan Police on pension, giving evidence to the effect that it was he, not Melvin, who made the decision to deny Hill a lawyer, the tribunal duly found Melvin guilty of the single offence of denying Hill a solicitor. The Police Federation claimed Melvin had been made 'a scapegoat' and the tribunal had been a 'political hearing'.[14] However, Melvin immediately lodged a notice of appeal with the Home Secretary who, in January 1991 overturned the findings of the tribunal.

The move for acquittal gathers pace

By now Raghip had a new solicitor, Gareth Peirce, who asked Home Secretary Kenneth Baker to review his conviction on the basis that he was unusually suggestible and had the mental age of a boy between ten and eleven. At the beginning of December, based on an additional statement by Ward in which he claimed that 'had he ... been aware of the later findings of the other psychologist he would have agreed that Mr Raghip possessed a significant degree of mental incapacity, suggestibility and compliance', Baker referred

---

13. The Police Federation represents officers from constable to chief inspector.
14. *The Guardian*, 23 September 1989; Ibid, 5 and 6 June 1990.

Raghip's case to the Court of Appeal but, at this time, claimed there were no grounds for similarly referring the other two.[15]

However, that was to change. In July 1991 it was announced that Silcott's legal team, now led by Anthony Scrivener, QC, had submitted a dossier to the Home Secretary, demanding that he re-open the case. The record of the questions and answers put by Melvin to Winston Silcott and written down by Detective Inspector Maxwell Dingle had been subjected to a test commonly known as ESDA (Electrostatic Deposition Analysis) and it had been found that key pages of the interview were not recorded as stated by the two officers in their evidence at his trial.[16] Developed in 1979 by two research assistants at the London College of Printing, Doug Foster and Bob Freeman, ESDA

> '…works by revealing indentations on sheets of paper using the action of powder charged with a high-electric voltage under pressure between two plastic sheets. It shows the ghostly traces of writing on sheets overlaying the sheet being tested, so that it is possible to work out the order in which pages of a handwritten document have been made.'[17]

At the same time, a petition consisting of 2,000 signatures demanding a review of all three convictions, accompanied by a letter from the Broadwater Farm Defence Campaign, was sent to the Home Office accusing the Home Secretary of delay.[18] Instead of referring it to the Court of Appeal, the Home Secretary announced on the Radio 2 *Jimmy Young Programme* that he had instructed Essex Police to investigate the allegation and conduct further forensic tests. Silcott's former solicitor, Andrew Hall, who was by then a barrister, accused the Home Secretary of deliberately indulging in delaying tactics in an attempt to 'prolong' the case until after the next general election.[19]

When he was interviewed by the Essex Police, Dingle refused to answer any questions but Melvin told Assistant Chief Constable Geoffrey Markham and Detective Chief Superintendent Geoffrey Payne that he was 'flabbergasted' by the suggestion. He claimed all the pages from which the evidence came

---

15. Ibid, 5 December 1990.
16. *The Observer*, 14 July 1991.
17. Ibid; see also *Independent*, 27 July 1994.
18. *The Guardian*, 20 July 1991.
19. *The Observer*, 21 July 1991.

were the originals written by Detective Inspector Dingle at the time.[20] On receiving the report from the Essex Police, Baker added the names of both Silcott and Braithwaite to the appeal relating to Raghip.

The appeals were heard towards the end of the year but prior to that, it had been what police historian, Dr Timothy Brain, called 'a bruising few months, not only for the police but for the whole of the legal profession.'[21] The Guildford Four, originally convicted in 1975 of the terrorist bombing of a public house the previous year, had been released by the Court of Appeal in October 1989.[22] Four months previously, the Chief Constable of the West Midlands Police, Geoffrey Dear, had disbanded the West Midlands Serious Crime Squad after a series of 'damaging allegations of corruption and incompetence.'[23] The fall out was considerable as 'slowly, convictions attributable to the squad were turned over on appeal'[24] but probably the most relevant, insofar as the Tottenham Three were concerned was the acquittal, in March 1991, of the Birmingham Six, who had been convicted in August 1975 of the bombings of two public houses the previous November. In the cases of the Guildford Four and the Birmingham Six it was claimed that evidence had been suppressed, interviews had not been conducted in accordance with the Judges Rules and there was doubt about some of the forensic evidence placed before the courts. But the most fatal claim insofar as the Metropolitan Police was concerned in relation to the forthcoming appeal of the Tottenham Three was concerned, was the allegation, in both cases, that confessions, allegedly made to the police 'were crucial to the prosecution case.'[25] John Smith, then Deputy Commissioner of the Metropolitan Police, described how the Metropolitan Police were, at the time, 'trapped in a time-warp, facing public opprobrium for the actions of their predecessors.'[26] But, finally, also in March 1991, the Home Secretary had announced the setting up of a

---

20. *Independent*, 31 July 1994.
21. Brain, Timothy (2010). *A History of Policing in England and Wales from 1974: A Turbulent Journey*. Oxford: Oxford University Press, p.186. For a description of how it affected the whole of the criminal justice system and the legal profession, see Rose, David (1996). *In the name of the Law: The Collapse of Criminal Justice*. London: Vintage.
22. Ibid, p.170.
23. Ibid, p. 139.
24. Ibid, p. 140.
25. Ibid, p.190.
26. Miller, Peter (1991). 'It began with the death of a policeman: Now the Criminal Justice system is in the dock.' *Sunday Times*, 1 December.

Royal Commission on Criminal Justice to look into, amongst other things, the conduct of police investigations, access to legal advice by defendants and the right of silence.[27]

So, it was against this background that the appeals of the Tottenham Three were finally heard. First to be heard on 25 November 1991 was Silcott's appeal. Melvin, in the presence of Detective Inspector Dingle, had conducted five interviews with Silcott but the prosecution case against him had relied entirely on the fifth and last interview. It was alleged that on one page the officers had written answers that Silcott never gave and that this page had been written after the interview had finished. But the damaging remarks, insofar as Silcott was concerned, came on page five of the notes. The suggestion by Silcott's lawyer, on the basis of findings by forensic handwriting expert Robert Radley, was that, by examining indentations on page one of the notes, there had been another page five. There was also, it was alleged a missing page seven. Radley was supported by another expert document examiner, Dr David Baxendale, who had been employed by the Home Office. Roy Amlot QC appearing on behalf of the crown, accepted the findings by the two experts 'and the necessary inferences to be drawn'. He continued:

> 'It goes without saying that the matter has been fully investigated, not only on the part of the defence but by the Crown. Taking all the factors into account, we cannot ask you to rely on the only evidence that was presented against Winston Silcott at the trial. The expert evidence Your Lordships have heard today casts such doubt upon the assertion by Detective Chief Superintendent Graham Melvin that the notes were contemporaneous notes, that we can no longer ask the court to rely on that evidence.'

The Court of Appeal held 'that it destroyed the basis of the Crown case' and went on to observe that

> '...the notes were said to be taken contemporaneously and so far as page five is concerned they plainly were not. This conclusion had a knock-on effect for the whole appeal.'[28]

---

27. Brain, op. cit. 21, p.185.
28. *The Guardian*, 6 December 1991.

Just over a week later, on 5 December 1991, Lord Farquharson, sitting with Mr Justice Alliott and Mr Justice Cresswell, formally quashed the convictions of Engin Raghip and Mark Braithwaite for the murder of Constable Keith Blakelock. Announcing the decision, Lord Farquharson said:

> 'In allowing these appeals we wish to express our profound regret that they have suffered as a result of shortcomings of the criminal process. No system of trials is proof against perjury but this will be of little consolation to the victims.'[29]

Braithwaite and Raghip were released that day. Silcott, however, remained in prison for the murder of Anthony Smith.

Melvin and Dingle suspended from duty

Meanwhile, following the announcement that Silcott, Raglan and Braithwaite were to appeal, Melvin and Detective Inspector Maxwell Dingle were suddenly suspended from duty whilst the Essex Police inquired into the way the interviews with Silcott had been conducted. Melvin subsequently described his feelings:

> 'I was absolutely shattered. Silcott had not been acquitted at this stage. I had over 30 years' service in, the job had always come first, and I was being asked to hand in my warrant card and go home. I rang my wife up, told her what was happening, and was taken home by car. We spent the rest of the day discussing the future with our daughter. I'm a great believer that every crisis brings an opportunity, and the opportunity I saw was to spend more time with my family. We acted on that almost instantly. My wife had retired from teaching, so she took on a part-time teaching job to provide the income for travelling, and as a form of therapy. We went to the theatre, took city breaks, travelled, my golf improved, we treated it as early retirement.'[30]

A year later, in July 1992, Melvin was charged with perjury and perverting the course of justice but was bitter about the way he learned that he was to

---

29. Ibid.
30. Hillyard, Brian (1994). 'Dignity Restored.' *Police Review*, 5 August 1994, p.25.

be prosecuted. He was returning from a shopping trip with his wife when they heard over the car radio that the Director of Public Prosecutions had decided to prosecute Detective Inspector Dingle, for conspiracy, and himself. Melvin again described his feelings:

> 'This was the first I heard of it. I was shattered. It was even worse for my wife. I was served with the summons later at my solicitors' office, but I think it was scandalous to make that announcement before I had been informed.'[31]

The trial eventually took place at the Old Bailey in the summer of 1994. The team defending Melvin and Dingle had found handwriting experts who called into question some of the assumptions made by Radley and Backendale and contended that no pages of the interview had been rewritten. A lecturer and handwriting expert at the University of Birmingham, Tom Davis, subsequently suggested: 'The problem is not with ESDA itself, which is solid and as accurate as a photocopier, but with what is deduced from the fact that the indentation is there.'[32]

Only three people had been present during the interview, Melvin, Dingle and Silcott. Silcott was not called to give evidence by the prosecution, a decision referred to by Richard Ferguson, appearing for Detective Inspector Dingle, as 'tactical', claiming that Silcott 'would either refuse to answer questions or that he would prove to be an "unsatisfactory and unreliable witness".'[33] Neither Melvin nor Dingle gave evidence in their defence. However, the defence did produce what Rose referred to as 'an extraordinary document', containing 'short excerpts' from 14 statements taken by the police over the whole period 1985–1994. Seven had been taken during the Melvin inquiry and seven during the Noves inquiry. In some, Silcott was accused 'of the most heinous acts: of leading the attack on PC Blakelock; of hacking at him with a machete; and of later holding up his bloodied weapon and boasting it bore "beat man's blood".'[34] Given that the witnesses all refused to appear, the statements were read to the court and there were suggestions that Silcott

---

31. Ibid.
32. *Independent*, 27 July 1994.
33. Ibid.
34. Rose, David (1996). In *the Name of the Law: The Collapse of Criminal Justice*. London: Vintage, p. 299.

was being retried for Blakelock's murder. Amongst those who gave evidence for the defence was Detective Superintendent Eric Brown who had been in charge of the investigation into the murder of Anthony Smith for which Silcott had been convicted.[35] The trial lasted for five-and-a-half weeks at the end of which the jury returned a unanimous verdict in acquitting the two detectives. Max Dingle immediately retired from the force; Melvin returned to work but retired three months later.

Melvin subsequently explained that he and Dingle had 'done a dry run of the interview' prior to conducting the fifth interview with Silcott:

> '[W]e had conducted four previous interviews [with Silcott] to give him the chance to establish where he was, and what he knew about the killing. After all, this wasn't the average murder with a victim killed in private. This was a very public murder with many participants and witnesses. So we had written out a statement with our questions and Silcott's possible answers. We had to be extra careful because we were dealing with unknown needs of PACE before the Act came into force.'[36]

Winston Silcott

Silcott's life prior to the death of Constable Blakelock did 'not make him an easy target for public sympathy.'[37] Following his acquittal Melvin spoke of his attitude towards Silcott:

> 'I had then, and have now, no feelings about Silcott at all. Emotion of any sort interferes with an inquiry. Silcott was a suspect and it was my job to lead the team which had to decide which suspects to charge. When the investigation was complete I was convinced that he was guilty. When the trial ended, I didn't feel any sort of triumph. I was pleased for my team that we gained convictions after a very long inquiry, and then we all moved onto other duties.'[38]

---

35. James, Selma (ed.)(1998). *A Chronology of Injustice: The Case for Winston Silcott's Conviction to be Overturned.* London: Crossroads, p.74.
36. Hillyard, op. cit. 30, p. 25.
37. 'The Doubts about William Silcott's guilt.' *Sunday Telegraph*, 28 January 1990.
38. Hillyard, op. cit. 30, p.24.

Silcott spoke to David Rose for the first time in 2004 about what he had done on the night of the riot. He signed on at Tottenham Police Station—he was on bail for the murder of Anthony Smith—at 7 p.m. before being driven to the estate by his girlfriend, Helena because he wanted to check on his greengrocers' shop. He claimed it was only then that he learned of Cynthia Jarrett's death and heard about the meeting at the Youth Association. He told the interviewer:

> 'I could see a lot of people running about, wearing masks and everything. And look: I'm on bail for murder. I know I'm stupid, but I'm not that stupid. There's helicopters, police photographers everywhere. All I could think about was that I didn't want to lose my bail. I saw Pam, a friend who had a flat there. She said, "You'd better come up. You know the police don't like you".'

Silcott claimed he spent the rest of the night in the flat where Pam McGuire lived with her sister. In a BBC documentary broadcast the year after his interview with David Rose, Kurt Barling reiterated Silcott's version of events but added that at Pam McGuire's flat he had fallen asleep watching *Kung Fu* movies and the first he knew of a police officer's death was when he was woken by a cheer in the flat as the news was announced on television. However, Barling pointed out that the McGuire's would not appear in court and would not speak to the BBC during the making of the documentary.[39]

A week after the end of the trial involving Melvin and Dingle, it was announced that Silcott would receive £17,000 under section 133 of the Criminal Justice Act 1988.[40] The fact that he was still in prison, led to a number of different views being expressed. His solicitor, Adrian Clarke, said:

> 'He is entitled to compensation for the wrongful conviction for the murder of PC Blakelock—whether or not he is released. The effect on his life has been catastrophic.'

---

39. Rose, David (2004). 'Silcott talks for first time about night of PC's murder.' *The Observer*, 18 January; Barling, Kurt (narrator) (2004). Who killed PC Blakelock? A documentary shown on BBC Television.
40. This particular section related to compensation that could be paid on the directions of the Home Secretary, although the amount was determined by an assessor appointed by the Secretary of State.

Others were quick to point out that Richard Coombes, who had by now been awarded the Queen's Gallantry Medal for heroism and had retired from the police force as a result of his injuries, had still not received any payment from the Criminal Injuries Compensation Board. Mike Bennett, then chair of the Metropolitan Branch of the Police Federation said:

> 'I think any payment to Silcott or others is outrageous. Normally the authorities cave in on these cases because these people have pressure groups behind them. I would have liked to have seen the authorities hold out on this and fight it on behalf of all the victims of crime, including Mrs Blakelock and her family.'

PC Blakelock's widow, Elizabeth, said: 'It makes a mockery of British justice' because 'Dick Coombes still hasn't had any compensation nine years later and his injuries were horrific.'[41]

Silcott subsequently sued the Metropolitan Police Commissioner for false imprisonment and malicious prosecution and on 15 October 1999 he accepted £50,000 in an out-of-court settlement. Glen Smyth, the then chair of the Metropolitan Branch of the Police Federation, described it 'as a kick in the teeth' to Blakelock's widow and her three sons; she herself described it as 'obscene'. Shadow Home Secretary, Ann Widdicombe, said: 'Someone serving a life sentence for murder should not benefit from the taxpayer like this.'[42]

Silcott was eventually released from prison in October 2003 after serving 17 years for the murder of Smith.

The second investigation

The second investigation, led by Commander Perry Nove of the City of London Police, commenced in 1992. Nove did not consult with Melvin and he forbade any of his team of 26 officers to approach him. With the agreement of the Director of Public Prosecutions (DPP), a lifetime immunity was offered to witnesses who been in the group that surrounded Blakelock and had merely kicked or struck him with a blunt instrument as opposed to stabbing and cutting him. Additionally, as a result of a meeting Nove and the

---

41. *Police Review*, 5 August 1994, p. 7.
42. Raynor, Jay (1999). 'Silcott: After 14 years I still can't get justice.' *The Observer*, 12 December.

DPP had with Senior Treasury counsel,[43] a 'basic evidential standard necessary to achieve a "realistic prospect of conviction" was agreed'. This said 'at least two eye-witnesses' should be prepared to give evidence at court, plus there should be supporting evidence, e.g. photographs.[44]

Technology had progressed since the original Melvin investigation and, 'using advanced image enhancement techniques', the Nove team were able 'to put names' to some of the people in the photographs taken during the riot. It was estimated that the group which surrounded Blakelock was 40 strong and a number of these were interviewed. But as soon as any of those appeared to be in danger of self-incrimination, if they did not have one, they were provided with a lawyer.[45]

When Nove came to commence his investigation, the police were already in possession of a piece of paper on which the words of a poem in the style of a rap had been written. It had been found in a cell by a prison officer in January 1988 at Swinfen Hall Young Offender Institution, during a routine search. The occupant of the cell was Nicky Jacobs, serving a sentence of imprisonment for causing an affray on Broadwater Farm. It proved to be in his writing and his fingerprints were on the paper. Written, partly in 'gangster slang' and partly in 'Caribbean patois' it purported to describe the role of someone who took part in the killing of Constable Blakelock. It was read out in open court by prosecutor Richard Whittan on the second day of the trial as follows:

> As long as I will live I will remember it was 1985 the 6th October
> We have de chopper, we have intention to kill an officer,
> PC Blakelock de unlucky fucker him helped de fireman
> Who did an out an fire de fireman
> See we have decided to scatter but PC Blakelock
> Him never smell the danger but when we fly down upon him
> He start to scream and holla
> Everybody gather round and av pure laughter

---

43. The Attorney General appoints advocates as Treasury Counsel at the Central Criminal Court to advise the Law Officers and the Director of Public Prosecutions, and to prosecute some of the most complex, high profile and serious crimes.
44. Rose, op. cit. 34, p. 300.
45. Ibid.

> He try to head out but we trip him over
> He start to beg for mercy but it didn't matter him try to play superman
> He get capture, him have to face the consequences
> We back out. We chopper
> We start to chop him on his hand
> We chop him on him finger
> We chop him on him leg
> We chop him on him shoulder
> Him head him chest him neck
> We chop him all over
> When we done we kill him off
> Lord we feel much better.
> Me just wipe me knife and go check on daughter
> We sit down and talk and she cook me dinner.[46]

In early 1993 an appeal for witnesses to Blakelock's murder was sent to all householders who lived on the Broadwater Farm Estate and in the surrounding streets. The wording of the appeal was agreed between Commander Nove and Bernie Grant, who was, by now, the Member of Parliament for Tottenham. Although signed by Commander Nove, it was issued on notepaper which made it clear that it was a joint appeal by Haringey Council, the Metropolitan Police and Bernie Grant.[47] Noves and Grant reinforced this appeal by appearing together on the same platform to appeal for witnesses.[48]

When the inquiry came to the end of 1993, Nove was confident that he knew the 'identification of the core group' that had attacked Blakelock and, in his report to the CPS, he identified nine people against whom murder charges could be preferred. However, on the eve of the opening of the trial of Melvin and Dingle, the CPS announced that, having considered all the evidence, 'we have concluded, with the advice of counsel, that it [was] insufficient to justify the institution of criminal proceedings against any other

---

46. *Daily Mail*, 5 March 2014.
47. A copy of the joint letter is lodged in the Bernie Grant Archives (BG/P/2/1/13).
48. Rose, op. cit. 34, p. 257.

person following the death of PC Blakelock.'⁴⁹ In doing so, Rose suggested that the CPS went against the 'basic evidential standard' agreed early on in the investigation because, in the case of some individuals there were 'at least three prospective witnesses'.⁵⁰ The CPS refused to discuss its reasons for coming to this decision but, as the announcement came on the eve of the Melvin/Dingle trial, suggested that it might well have thought that, at the time, 'another Blakelock trial was "not in the public interest".'⁵¹

The third investigation

The death of South London teenager Stephen Lawrence in 1993 led to the setting up of an inquiry headed by Sir William MacPherson of Cluny. The inquiry issued its report in 1999. Amongst its many recommendations was one which suggested that, in order to restore public confidence, an inspection by Her Majesty's Inspectorate of Constabulary should be carried out of all undetected murders undertaken by the Metropolitan Police in which HOLMES had been used.[52]

As soon as she was aware of this, Elizabeth Blakelock (now remarried, becoming Elizabeth Johnson) wrote to the commissioner in March requesting that the Metropolitan Police re-open the investigation into her husband's murder.[53] Three weeks later the Metropolitan Police announced it would review a number of unsolved murders, including Blakelock's,[54] although the re-investigation of Blakelock's murder did not effectively begin until the beginning of 2000. It started with the re-examination of the 6,000 statements resulting from the first two enquiries. It was reported that using 'virtual reality techniques' details from these statements would be fed 'into a three dimensional computer image of the Tottenham estate in North London' to reconstruct the night of his death. This would enable them to 'track witnesses' movements and "see" what was happening.' It was claimed

---

49. *Independent*, 23 June 1994.
50. Rose, op. cit. 34, pp. 300–301.
51. Ibid, pp. 304–305.
52. Macpherson, Sir W (1999). The Stephen Lawrence Inquiry. London: Her Majesty's Stationary Office, Chapter 47, Recommendation 4.
53. *Daily Telegraph*, 5 March 1999.
54. *The Guardian*, 26 March 1999.

that 'the images would show what they could have seen, and where they were when the murder happened.' In this way, detectives 'could check the accuracy of statements and compare recollections.'[55] However, the investigation did not really get going until the appointment of Detective Superintendent John Sweeney to lead it in 2003 when it was claimed that the Metropolitan Police had 'significant new leads in the case' although it refused to reveal what they were on the grounds 'inquiries could be prejudiced.' But Sweeney also had problems. Repeating what the first investigator Graham Melvin had said, he pointed out 'Lots of stuff was lost then and will never be recovered.'[56]

The news was greeted with some bemusement and trepidation on the Broadwater Farm Estate partly because few of the 2,500 people who lived there then were residents at the time of the riots. Clasford Sterling, a community worker, saw 'the new investigation as another hurdle for the estate to surmount' because it would 'bring back painful memories' for many of those who had been involved with the estate at the time. In an attempt to set their minds at rest, Assistant Commissioner Tarique Ghaffur, then the head of Scotland Yard's Specialist Crime Directorate, stressed that the investigation would be 'wholly focused on the murder of Keith Blakelock and attempted murder of Richard Coombes and not on any other incidents which occurred during the Broadwater Farm disturbances.'[57] At the same time, Blakelock's widow, said she believed there would 'be a conviction at the end of this'. She went on:

> 'You have got to believe that the guilty people will be brought to justice and I have believed that all along. People who murder people cannot be allowed to roam the streets and think they have got away with it. It does not matter to me how long it takes as long as the guilty people are brought to justice and I'm confident that will happen. When the guilty person, or people, are in prison or punished for what they did to Keith then that's the time I will be able to relax a bit.'[58]

---

55. Tendlar, Stewart (2000). '"Virtual reality" hunt for Blakelock killers.' In *The Times*, 18 January 2000, p.5.
56. Barrett, David (2014). 'Analysis: How challenges and missed opportunities stacked up in the PC Keith Blakelock murder case', 9 April — see www.telegraph.co.uk/news/uknews/crime/10755267/Analysis-How-challenges-and-missed-opportunities-stacked-up-in-the-Pc-Keith-Blakelock-murder-case.html (Accessed 14 November 2014).
57. *The Guardian*, 4 December 2003.
58. BBC News, 3 December 2003; *The Guardian*, 4 December 2003.

Nine months later, a knife, possibly one of the weapons used to murder Blakelock had been found buried in the garden of one of the houses in Willan Road. It was claimed the knife had been found using 'ground-penetrating radar' which had 'indicated a number of areas for excavation.' With the assistance of archaeologists, surveyors had used infra-red beams to plot a sophisticated virtual 3D map of the area at the front of the small row of council houses.[59] Less than a week later it was announced that Blakelock's uniform had 'been removed from Scotland Yard's crime museum for forensic examination'.[60] However, it would appear that neither revealed any additional evidence.

The police still had the two witnesses from the Nove investigation, both of whom were known only by pseudonyms. Both were present on the Estate at the time of the riot. John Brown had subsequently pleaded guilty to burglary and affray in 1986 and was sentenced to five years imprisonment, later reduced on appeal to three-and-a-half years. Levin had pleaded guilty to affray and was sentenced to 12 months imprisonment in 1987. Interviewed in June 1993, Brown admitted he was one of the 'kickers' in the group around Blakelock and named Jacobs as a stabber. In October 1993, Levin, too, admitted being a 'kicker' and he also named Jacobs as a stabber. However, Levin had been regarded as unreliable by the Nove team in that he changed his version of events on a number of occasions between when he was first interviewed in 1992 and the last occasion, in 1994.[61] But in 2009, a third person, known only as 'Q' came forward. It subsequently turned out at that police officers had spoken twice to Q within two weeks of the riot. On each occasion he had told them that he had 'stayed at home and saw nothing' and signed a document to that effect. However, when interviewed for a third time in 2009, he claimed to have seen the murder from the window of his flat.[62]

The police had one further piece of evidence. In May 2000, Jacobs, then aged 30, was detained by some members of the public on suspicion that he had committed a burglary. When the police arrived, Jacobs is alleged to have

---

59. *Evening Standard*, 29 September 2004.
60. BBC News, 3 October 2004.
61. Dodd, Vickram (2014). 'PC Blakelock murder: family grief and questions for police as Nicky Jacobs acquitted.' *The Guardian*, 9 April; see also *Daily Telegraph*, 8 April 2014.
62. *The Guardian*, 9 April 2014.

told a constable to 'Fuck off, I was one of them who killed PC Blakelock'.[63] Neither the poem, found in 1988, nor the alleged admission to the constable in 2000 were revealed until Jacobs went on trial in 2014. Bearing in mind the first trial had hinged almost solely on alleged confessions, the Crown Prosecution Service ruled at the time that, on their own, they were insufficient to put Jacobs on trial. But it would appear that the discovery of Q led it to change its mind.

In February 2010 the police made a further arrest but, after being questioned over a period of four days, the individual was released on bail.[64] The investigation continued for at least another three years until in July 2013, the Crown Prosecution Service decided to charge Nicky Jacobs with the murder of Keith Blakelock. He had already served a six year prison sentence for affray. By this time, it was revealed that there were 74,294 documents, 14,127 exhibits and 17,765 names logged in the police computer in connection with the murder.[65]

The trial opened in February 2014 but was doomed almost from the start. The identities of the three witnesses were not officially revealed although they were identified in social media. They were allowed to give their evidence from behind a screen and their voices were electronically disguised. Firstly, Q claimed that Blakelock had been attacked in a car park; he thought it was under Martlesham Block. As a result, in a most unusual move, the jury passed a note to the judge asking whether the witness suffered from Korsakoff's syndrome, in which a person 'invents things to fill gaps in the memory'. Then he admitted using heroin and drinking heavily. John Brown, who admitted that he had kicked Blakelock's body about ten times, told the court that Jacobs had been amongst those who attacked the officer and he had been armed with a machete with a 12-inch blade. However, it transpired that when he was interviewed by police back in 1993 he had implied that all black people looked the same to him. When asked by defence counsel whether this was still his view, he replied, 'More or less.' It was also revealed

---

63. Dodd, op. cit. 61; Barratt, David (2014) 'Pc Keith Blakelock murder trial: Questions for Met Police as Nicky Jacobs cleared', 9 April—see www.telegraph.co.uk/news/uknews/crime/10753480/Pc-Keith-Blakelock-murder-trial-Questions-for-Met-Police-as-Nicky-Jacobs-cleared.html accessed on 14 November 2014.
64. *The Guardian*, 9 February 2010.
65. Barratt, op. cit. 56.

that the police had paid Brown £5,000 in 1993 which included £1,700 for rent arrears and to pay a phone bill and for the MOT for his car, after he had made a written statement. Finally, it transpired that the third witness, Rhodes Levin, claimed to have been standing next to Jacobs during the attack on Blakelock but claimed that he was armed with a knife less than six inches long. However, the truth of his evidence was called into question when it was revealed that, when originally interviewed in 1985, he had named Winston Silcott as the ringleader of the attack, claiming 'he had made this up to tell police what he thought they wanted to hear.' The court heard that during the Nove investigation, Levin had been given £5,000 and that, on one occasion, when he missed a flight back to England from Spain, the police had paid for his air ticket. He was approached again in January 2008, this time by Sweeney's team, about giving evidence and the police paid some expenses he had incurred and also gave him a deposit for accommodation.[66]

But the prosecution also suffered from a lack of physical evidence. As already mentioned, the retention of physical evidence, such as the clothes of rioters, was not as it is today; consequently, although arrested and convicted of affray at the time, the clothes worn by Nicky Jacobs were not kept and could not therefore by analysed using the modern forensic methods now available.

The decision to grant immunity and what was seen as cash rewards to men who had attacked Blakelock was criticised after the trial. Keith Vaz, chair of the House of Commons Home Affairs Select Committee, expressed his concern at:

> 'the cost of the immunity awarded in this trial. Although it is right that we pursue all appropriate means possible to bring those responsible to justice we cannot ignore the costs to the public both monetary and to the integrity of our justice system. The public must be able to have full confidence that the police and the courts are not making deals for the wrong reasons.'[67]

However, the granting of immunity and witness protection programmes

---

66. *The Guardian*, 10 March 2010.
67. Barrett, David (2014). 'Pc Keith Blakelock murder trial: The law on granting immunity to offenders', 9 April—see www.telegraph.co.uk/news/uknews/crime/10756157/Pc-Keith-Blakelock-murder-trial-The-law-on-granting-immunity-to-offenders.html accessed 14 November 2014.

had and have been a way of protecting those who can give evidence in serious criminal cases for some time. So there was nothing unusual in this.

Jacobs did not give evidence in his defence. The jury were out for six hours, at the end of which they found, by a majority verdict of 10–2, him not guilty of the murder of Constable Blakelock. In the public gallery were two of those who had been charged and convicted in the original trail, Winston Silcott and Mark Braithwaite.[68]

The deputy chief of the Crown Prosecution Service in London, Jenny Hopkins, defended the decision to bring proceedings against Jacobs, claiming that the evidence against him was reviewed in accordance with the guidelines that existed at the time, She continued:

> 'The evidence included three witnesses who the prosecution say gave their accounts independently of each other with no suggestion of collusion. Before the start of the trial the defence made an application to stay the proceedings, arguing that the defendant could not have a fair trial due to a number of reasons, including the delay of 28 years since the murder. This application was unsuccessful. At the close of the prosecution case the defence argued that there was no case to answer, however, the judge ruled that there was a case to answer and it was for the jury to decide on the guilt of the defendant. It was right that all the evidence in this case was put before a jury and we respect its decision.'[69]

The Blakelock family issued a statement following the acquittal:

> 'We are obviously extremely sad and disappointed at the verdict. We viewed this trial as an opportunity to see some form of justice served for Keith. There were many people involved in a murder on that night of 6 October 1985 and it is regretful that [someone] has yet to be found guilty despite the number of people with knowledge of the events of that night.'[70]

Speaking on behalf of the Metropolitan Police, Assistant Commissioner Mark Rowley said:

---

68. *Independent*, 9 April 2014.
69. Barratt, op. cit. 67.
70. Barratt, op. cit. 63. Barratt says 'no-one' but clearly someone is meant.

'We will not give up on bringing Keith's killers to justice. There are people who know exactly who took part in the attack on Keith and people who took part themselves. It is not too late for you to come forward.'[71]

Conclusions

In an article published after Jacobs acquittal, former Commissioner of Police, Lord Stevens, suggested that it was highly likely that the police knew who murdered Blakelock and 'no-one should be under any illusion' that the acquittal was the end of the investigation. Pointing out that 'advances in forensic science are helping to solve even the most difficult old cases' he claimed that 'it is only a matter of time before police get the evidence to support a successful prosecution.'[72]

But crime correspondent David Barrett, pointed out, the investigation into 'the horrific murder' of Keith Blakelock faced 'an exceptional number of challenges',[73] two of which were major flaws. Lord Stevens pointed out that 'preserving exhibits from crime scenes is now so important' and scientific evidence 'is much more convincing to a jury, leaving defendants little room for manoeuvre in court.'[74] The first flaw with the Blakelock killing is that scientific evidence is virtually non-existent. The failure of senior officers to ensure that the scene of his murder was secured and physical evidence preserved on the night of the riot was a major failure. This was compounded by allowing the murder scene and the surrounding area to be literally swept clean before the investigation commenced. Thus it was highly probable that physical evidence relating to other serious criminal offences was lost.

But the second flaw relates to the criminal justice system itself. Following the announcement that the Home Secretary[75] had referred the case of the Tottenham Three to the Court of Appeal, Melanie Phillips argued:

---

71. Ibid.
72. Stevens, Lord (2014). 'Opinion: The Met knows who killed PC Keith Blakelock and won't give up until they have proof.' *The Mirror*, 10 April—see www.mirror.co.uk/news/uk-news/lord-stevens-pc-keith-blakelock-3398826 accessed 22 November 2014.
73. Barrett, op. cit. 63.
74. Stevens, op. cit. 72.
75. With effect from 1997, responsibility for referring cases to the Court of Appeal was vested in the Criminal Cases Review Commission (CCRC) set up by the Criminal Appeals Act 1995.

> 'Since the trial is no more or less than a game, since guilt or innocence can be decided simply by observing or breaking the rules of the game, then it follows that to equate the terms guilt or innocence with the truth is a terrible mistake. A far better way to get at the truth is through an inquisitorial system, or at the very least an inquisitorial system at the committal process. Confining attention to police malpractice or to the inadequacies of the appeals process is to address the symptoms rather than the cause of the crisis.'[76]

Eighteen months after the appeals of the Tottenham Three had been upheld, Ludvic Kennedy went further, suggesting that the whole of the judicial process had been caught up in the hysteria of public outrage and media condemnation of Blakelock's murder. He claimed that

> 'the prosecution should have realised the weakness of the case, but it was as much a victim of the general hysteria as everyone else. It should have questioned the validity of the evidence [Melvin] had acquired [and] reminded itself of the dangers of accepting uncorroborated...admissions.'

He suggested, too, that the trial judge, Mr Justice Hodgson, was 'a victim of the times'. His summing-up was described as 'impeccable and a model of fairness' by the Lord Chief Justice, and 'it is true that he warned the jury of the dangers of convicting on such flimsy evidence.' However, 'in a different atmosphere' at the conclusion of the prosecution's case he might have ruled that 'the defence had no case to answer.'[77]

---

76. Phillips, Melanie (1990). A televised game of trial and error. *The Guardian*, 18 May;
77. Kennedy, Ludvic (1991). 'Judges are making an ass of the law.' *Sunday Times*, 1 December.

CHAPTER TWELVE

Morale and Psychological Stress

Introduction

The job of policing is unique.[1] It could be argued that people in other occupations such as soldiers, miners, deep-sea drivers, steeplejacks and the like face equally, if not more, danger from physical or environmental hazards but these are calculable. For policemen and women they are not. The core task of policing 'require officers to face situations where the risk lies in the unpredictable outcome of encounters with people.' At any time, the police officer can suddenly be confronted with danger, either from a firearm or other weapon capable of killing or maiming.[2] Eighteen months before the riot on the Broadwater Farm Estate, Constable Yvonne Fletcher had been shot dead outside the Libyan People's Bureau in London whilst policing what initially had all the signs of being a peaceful protest.[3] Far more recently, in September 2012, two officers, Fiona Bone and Nicola Hughes, were shot dead whilst answering what had all the appearances of a routine call in Manchester.[4] Thus 'coping with violence is a recurring feature of police culture.'[5]

In human terms, the riot on the Broadwater Farm Estate was the worst suffered by the Metropolitan Police in a single night's disorder since its formation in 1829. Described as the 'biggest "bloody good hiding" ever inflicted', one policeman was murdered and 255 were injured. A number of the injuries were serious, including seven gunshot wounds and two stab wounds. At least 20 members of the public were known to have been injured of whom

---

1. Skolnick, J (1966). *Justice without Trial*. New York: Wiley, p.44.
2. Reiner, Robert (2010). *The Politics of the Police*. 4th edn. Oxford: Oxford University Press, p.119; see also Crank, J P (2004). *Understanding Police Culture* (2nd Edition). Cincinnati, OH: Anderson Publishing.
3. *The Guardian*, 3 January 2014.
4. *Daily Telegraph*, 18 September 2012.
5. Reiner, op. cit. 2, p. 119; see also Waddington, PAJ and Wright, M (2008). Police Use of Force, Firearms and Riot-Control' in Newburn (ed.). *Handbook of Policing* (2nd Edition). Cullompton, Willan.

three were journalists suffering gunshot wounds.[6] A constable described the physical costs to his unit of a sergeant and ten constables:

> 'Our sergeant was taken away in an ambulance with a neck injury. It was a long time before he returned to work. A colleague had a buckshot wound to his leg, and the guy who had been in the line with him discovered his shield peppered them. Another member of my crew was taken to hospital with broken ribs.'[7]

The total number of crimes, excluding assaults on the police, was 114. This figure included the murder of Constable Blakelock, four cases of robbery, nine cases of burglary, the setting on fire of 34 motor vehicles and four dwellings and 53 cases of damage to property, a large number of them motor vehicles.[8] Only 25 people were detained by the police during the riot itself.[9]

Effect on morale

Morale is the mental and emotional condition of an individual officer or group of officers with regard to the function or tasks at hand. The military place huge importance on morale, it being one of the Principles of War. The police service generally was late to consider the importance of morale as a perquisite for an effective response to serious disorder. Only comparatively recently, in a report on the policing of the G20 Conference in London in 2009, was reference made to morale, although it was given the term officer resilience.[10] Until then, the maintenance of morale amongst police officers involved in responding to serious public disorder was rarely, if ever, mentioned let alone considered as a principle.

As the sixth of October dawned, morale amongst rank-and-file officers in the Metropolitan Police trained to respond to serious public disorder

---

6. Metropolitan Police (1986). Public Order Review: Civil Disturbances 1981–1985. London: Metropolitan Police (Typescript), p. 12, para. 5.1.
7. Cotton, Paul (1995). A 'Pagan Nightmare.' *Police Review*, 6 October, p.18.
8. Metropolitan Police, op. cit. 6, Appendix E, p. 35.
9. *The Job*, Vol. 18, Issue 465, 18 October 1985, p. 2.
10. Her Majesty's Chief Inspector of Constabulary (2009). Adapting to Protest. London: Her Majesty's Inspectorate of Constabulary, p. 33; Her Majesty's Chief Inspector of Constabulary (2009). Adapting to Protest—Nurturing the British Model of Policing. London: Her Majesty's Inspectorate of Constabulary, p. 175.

was high. Despite the 'ferocity and destruction which occurred before the police got the upper hand', the response to the Brixton riot less than two weeks earlier was 'rated as a success story' by officers who had been involved because of the manner in which the disorder was brought under control.[11] Additionally, their ability had been tested when responding to disorder at Southall and Peckham, albeit the violence was less serious than it had been at Brixton. As one constable, who had been part of a District Support Unit — 'equipped with riot shields and a lot of self-confidence' which made them feel they 'were ready for anything' explained:

> '[T]he biggest problem coping with those early riots was coming to terms with the raw aggression that propelled the bricks. The tidal wave of hate was the most difficult thing to understand. But once we had resigned ourselves to it and began working with our brains instead of emotions, things got better until we became complacent and thought it could never get any worse.'[12]

But it did get worse, much worse! Less than 24 hours later, morale amongst the public order units was at rock bottom. Following the rioting in Moss Side, Manchester in 1981, the Chief Constable of Greater Manchester, James Anderton, had warned that allowing officers to become 'targets for the fire bombs and all types of missiles' by deploying them in static formations behind riot shields was likely to have 'an adverse effect on police morale', particularly when there was 'aerial bombardment.'[13] And yet, Richards' strategy that night was to keep units deployed in static formations, allowing them to be what Anderton had warned against, targets for petrol bombs and other types of missiles, including for the first time on the British mainland, shotgun pellets. Not surprisingly, perhaps, when the Williams team was conducting its debriefing it found a 'groundswell of opinion that to stand in static lines' achieved nothing 'except to deflate morale'.[14]

The traumatic events at Tottenham, which included the brutal murder of a police officer coupled with what was generally regarded by all, with the

---

11. Moore, Tony (1990). The Brixton Riot 1985, unpublished.
12. Cotton, Paul (1995). A 'Pagan Nightmare.' *Police Review*, 6 October, p.17.
13. Anderton, James (1981). 'Normal Service will be resumed'. *Police*, Vol. XIV, No. 2, October.
14. Williams, David A (1986). Internal Police Report on the disorders of the 6th October 1985 at the Broadwater Farm Estate, Tottenham. London: Metropolitan Police, p.98, para. 2.1.10.

exception, it seemed, of the senior officers of the Metropolitan Police, as a totally ineffective response to the disorder, had a serious effect on morale in the Metropolitan Police. Rose claimed the effect was 'catastrophic' and 'not without reason' because 'the junior ranks of the Met blamed not only the black inhabitants of the estate but their own superiors for the killing.'[15] The anger amongst those junior ranks was plain to see on the night of the riot. Rank and file officers were stunned by Constable Blakelock's death. Many were 'reduced to tears of anger, frustration and bewilderment.' The discontent was clearly demonstrated when Commissioner Sir Kenneth Newman visited the scene after the rioting had died down. Officers 'who had been on the front line for much of the evening, just got in their carriers and slammed the door' at one location;[16] at another 'a lot of verbal abuse' was directed at the commissioner 'from a number of officers who clearly shared the feeling of being left to [their] fate'.[17]

In the following days and weeks 'the vehemence of the opinions expressed in *Police*[18] and *Police Review*,[19] in every police station canteen, and by the Police Federation leaders, stunned the Scotland Yard hierarchy.'[20] Following the publication of an article which criticised the performance of senior officers, the editor of *Police* received many letters of support from rank-and-file officers who had been present on the night. One described it as the 'biggest night of shame ever to be allowed to happen to the Metropolitan Police'.[21] Later, another constable, Ian Pyles, criticised them in open court, suggesting that it would have been easy to get beyond the barricades during the early stages but they were prevented from doing so by senior officers at the scene. He said of his experience that night, 'it was extremely frightening and it ... made me quite bitter against some senior officers ... because of their lack of backbone in stopping the riot.' He added, 'we could have stopped it

---

15. Rose, David (1992). *A Climate of Fear: The Murder of PC Blakelock and the Case of the Tottenham Three*. London: Bloomsbury, pp. 80–81.
16. Barling, Kurt (narrator)(2004). 'Who killed PC Blakelock?' A documentary shown on BBC Television. In an interview with Sergeant Hughes.
17. Lawson, Mark (2014). In correspondence with the author, dated 29 August.
18. *Police* is the monthly journal of the Police Federation for England and Wales.
19. *Police Review* was an independent magazine published weekly which contained news and reports about police activities and other items which would be of interest to police officers.
20. Rose, op. cit. 15, p.84.
21. Anonymous officer (1986). Excerpt from a letter published in *Police*, Vol. XVIII, No. 4, December 1986, p.18.

in two hours'.²² An inspector subsequently claimed Broadwater Farm was 'a prime example of when no-one was prepared to make a decision.' He pointed out that officers were 'being shot at' with revolvers and shotguns and 'they almost certainly knew an officer had been killed' and 'yet they didn't have the bottle to give the order to use plastic bullets.'²³ Whether the riot could have been brought under control in two hours and whether plastic bullets would have made a difference had they been used is immaterial. It is what rank and file officers believed to be the case that needed to be addressed. The attitude of many senior officers at the time can be summed up in the response from an unidentified deputy assistant commissioner who subsequently told Roger Graef, 'if the day ever comes when we have to use plastic bullets, we will have lost' and 'the issue of policing by consent will have disappeared.'²⁴

Newman came in for personal criticism from the rank and file and endured a particularly difficult time when he went to the annual meeting of the Police Federation a few days after the riot.²⁵ Attended by hundreds of 'ordinary officers', it was the first time in living memory, a commissioner was heckled, as he defended the performance of his senior officers.²⁶ At the meeting, Sir Kenneth stressed the operational philosophy for police commanders was the need for minimum force in police operations and claimed that, as a result, they had not been 'in a Gung-ho mood to charge Hill 29!'²⁷ Given his experiences, firstly in the Palestine Police, then with the Metropolitan Police at the time of the Grosvenor Square disorders of 1968 and Red Lion Square of 1974, and finally with the Royal Ulster Constabulary during some of the worst disturbances in Northern Ireland, it is difficult to understand Newman's resolute defence of the operational commanders that night and, although there is no evidence, it is likely that he held a different view in private.²⁸

---

22. Police Constable Pyles in evidence at the trial of Silcott and others at the Central Criminal Court. Reported in *The Guardian*, 27 February 1987; *Police Review*, 27 March 1987, p.631.
23. Graef, Roger (1989). *Talking Blues: The Police In Their Own Words*. London: Collins Harvill, p.80.
24. Ibid, p.83.
25. Brain, Timothy (2010). *A History of Policing in England and Wales from 1974: A Turbulent Journey*. Oxford: Oxford University Press, p.114.
26. Rose, op. cit. 15, p. 81.
27. Judge, Tony (1985). 'The "battle" of Broadwater Farm.' In *Police,* Vol. XVIII, No. 3, November, p.11.
28. The author had a fairly lengthy informal conversation with Newman shortly before he took up the post of commissioner.

But the 'ordinary officers' were in no mood to be placated. A constable stood up and told Sir Kenneth that senior officers that night had 'permitted' the rank and file of the Metropolitan Police 'to be humiliated'.[29] Views such as these were seen as 'a direct challenge' to his authority and that of his senior colleagues, and tended to give an impression that the Metropolitan Police were 'on the brink of mutiny.'[30] Certainly the Commissioner can have had no doubts that 'the depth of feelings' ran extremely high.[31]

Given the criticism levelled at senior officers it is hard not to draw an analogy with the famous phrase 'lions led by donkeys' used to describe the British Army during the First World War.[32] Brain claimed that 'the courage of the officers standing and taking the punishment in the shield lines, many sustaining injuries, some of them serious, cannot be underestimated.'[33] Williams said that rank-and-file officers had 'displayed a high degree of courage, determination and self-discipline in the face of the most outrageous and sustained violence' witnessed in London for a number of years.[34] But an officer who had been present that night said he and many other rank-and-file officers had had enough of 'being treated by senior officers as cannon fodder'.[35] An informal psychological review conducted by staff at the Police Staff College for the purposes of research rather than focusing on the individual needs of officers, gave an insight into the feelings and frustrations of the rank and file about the performance of their senior officers that night.

- 'Senior officers gave no positive instructions, sometimes they counter commanded themselves; they did not instil confidence.'

---

29. Judge, op. cit. 27, p. 11.
30. Rose, op. cit. 15, p. 84.
31. Editorial. 'Broadwaters run deep' in *Police*, Vol. XVIII, No. 11, July 1986, p.3.
32. The phrase was attributed to an English woman, Evelyn Princess Blucher, who lived in Berlin. In her autobiography she recalled hearing German General Erich Ludendorff praise British troops for their bravery and claimed to have heard a statement from the German General Headquarters which said: 'The English Generals are wanting in strategy. We should have no chance if they possessed as much science as their officers and men had of courage and bravery. They are lions led by donkeys.' Blucher, Evelyn Princess (1921). *An English Wife in Berlin*. London: Constable, p.211. Although Alan Clarke called his 1961 book about First World War generals *The Donkeys* a number of military historians, including Richard Holmes and Dan Snow, have disagreed to some extent with this analogy.
33. Brain, op. cit. 25, p.114.
34. Williams, David A, op. cit. 14, p. 34, para. 3:89.
35. Judge, op. cit. 27, p. 11.

- 'The whole thing was a complete abortion and no one could say that it was a success in any way. Senior officers refused to make decisions.'
- 'He told the Inspectors and Sergeants to get together and told them to calm us down. How could he say that? We had stood for hours taking petrol bombs, and one of our men had been killed. No-one in charge had given us any tactical instructions.'
- 'We [had] been told at shield training that static lines of long shields should not be used—because of the lack of leadership and knowledge of shield training tactics we were not deployed correctly at any time and lost the day—receiving a lot of unnecessary injuries.'
- 'There was no deployment whatsoever—either from Control or from anyone in command on the ground. We were deploying ourselves where we saw we were needed.' [36]

It was all subsequently summed up by an inspector who had served in the Royal Marines before joining the police. He said:

'You can have the best soldiers in the world, but if you haven't got a good general to lead them you end up with a big cock-up. Broadwater Farm showed us an example of that. For a lot of the time senior police officers have got to be more managers than leaders. But when the muck and bullets start flying they have got to be leaders.'

He then drew a comparison with the Royal Marines where the officers looked after 'the welfare of the men' before claiming that 'it is a sad reflection' that in the Metropolitan Police many 'senior officers' were more interested in 'their own welfare to ensure they [got] to the next rank' rather than 'the welfare of the men.' [37]

The Police Staff College review picked up only one exception to this general feeling of dissatisfaction with senior officers and that was Superintendent

---

36. Holt, J P (1986). Some observations from Tottenham. Notes given to the ACPO Public Order Refresher Course at the Police Staff College. Unpublished—Copy in the author's possession.
37. Graef, op. cit. 23, p. 80.

Boyall's valiant attempt to reach Tangmere Block after Serial 502 had come under attack.

> 'A superintendent on the ground done the best he could—but he didn't appear to know the ground—neither did any of us; he led us into the estate but we were heavily attacked from the flats above—he was not properly equipped—but he showed leadership and courage—but still had regard for our lives and didn't do anything stupid.'[38]

Work-related stress

Quoting from a study undertaken at Manchester University, Roger Graef suggested few jobs were 'as stressful as that of a police officer'.[39] The Health and Safety Executive define work-related stress as 'the adverse reaction people have to excessive pressures or other types of demand placed on them at work.'[40] Work-related stress in police officers was only in the early stages of recognition at the time of the riot. There had been concerns about increasing sickness levels in the Police Service generally, and '"stress" was identified as a likely cause.'[41] But the general feeling was that this was associated with conditions of service, e.g. extended periods of duty, shift work, quick change-overs, victimisation and the like. Graef subsequently suggested that 'accumulated frustrations cost police officers their peace of mind, their job satisfaction, their sense of direction and, crucially, a sense of their own worth.'[42]

More significantly, however, in the context of this book, a preliminary study undertaken in 1983, two years before the riot, revealed that 'the exposure to traumatic incidents' was 'a major source of acute stress'[43] or what, today, would be called post-traumatic stress. The simplest way of defining post-trauma stress is 'the normal reactions of normal people to events which for them, are unusual or abnormal.'[44] Police officers are required to deal

---

38. Holt, op. cit. 36.
39. Graef, op. cit. 23, p. 342.
40. www.hse.gov.uk/stress/furtheradvice/whatisstress.htm accessed 30 November 2014.
41. Brain, op. cit. 25, p. 128.
42. Graef, op. cit. 23, p. 342.
43. Home Office (1983). The Working Party on Stress in the Police Service. London: Home Office.
44. Parkinson, Frank (1995). *Post-Trauma Stress*. London: Sheldon Press, p. 24.

regularly with incidents as part of their day-to-day duties which many people would find traumatic, e.g. serious road traffic accidents, dead bodies. The fact that they do so does not mean they are immune to stress but most of them develop strategies for coping. However, few police officers are required to respond to an outbreak of serious public disorder which may result in death or life-threatening injuries. Many of the officers who responded to the disorder on Broadwater Farm will have shown symptoms of suffering from post-traumatic stress. When those symptoms remain some time after the event and are disturbing or prevent them from doing normal activities, post-traumatic stress disorder may be diagnosed.[45]

The Metropolitan Police's response to the findings of that preliminary study, was for its Welfare Branch, which had been set up in 1935 to assist officers who, for instance, got into debt, had marital problems and the like, to decide to extend the services it offered to provide counselling.[46] Despite this, few senior officers recognised that traumatic events could lead to psychological reactions in police officers. The general feeling was that selection and training prepared officers for exposure to unpleasant events during their service.[47] In any event, the police service was a macho organization in which individual officers did not generally reveal their feelings; to do so, was seen as a sign of weakness. This attitude began to change as a result of two fires, the Bradford Football Stadium fire in 1985 in which 55 people died, and the King's Cross Underground fire in 1987, in which 31 people died, including a senior fire officer, and in which a police constable was seriously burned.[48]

In terms of what happened at Broadwater Farm, it is relevant to examine the stress undergone by two sets of officers. Firstly, there were the officers at Tottenham who policed Broadwater Farm on a regular basis. Secondly, there were those officers who responded to the outbreak of disorder on 6 October.

---

45. Ibid, p. 99.
46. Rivers, Ken (1993). 'Traumatic Stress: An Occupational Hazard.' In *Employee Counselling Today*, Vol. 5, Issue 1, p.5.
47. McCaslin, Shannon E; Rogers, Cynthia E; Metzler, Thomas J; Best, Suzanne R; Weiss, Daniel S; Fagan, Jeffrey A; Liberman, Akiva; and Marmar, Charles R (2006). 'The Impact of Personal Threat on Police Officers' Responses to Critical Incident Stressors.' *The Journal of Nervous and Mental Disease*, Vol. 194, No. 8, August, p.591.
48. Duckworth, D H (1991). Managing psychological trauma in the police service: from the Bradford Stadium fire to the Hillsborough crush disaster. *Journal of Occupational Medicine*, Winter 41(4) pp.171–173.

Officers at Tottenham

The Association of Chief Police Officers' Joint Working Group on Organizational Health and Welfare was told in 1989 that the four main stressors for British police officers were management-style, management systems, management support and traumatic incidents.[49] It can be argued that the officers at Tottenham suffered from all four.

Rank and file officers at Tottenham were critical of both the style of management adopted by senior officers and the support they received from them. They felt that there was a lack of leadership from senior management. These feelings were summed up in a letter to *Police* by an officer stationed at Tottenham for the five years leading up to the riot. He described how Haringey Council and the Metropolitan Police had abandoned the community of Broadwater Farm leaving it effectively 'under the control of a mob of criminals'. He accused the police of playing 'into the hands of these people as a result of the misguided behaviour of some ... senior officers', who 'preoccupied with their own career development' were using the British public 'as a testing ground for various forms of "softly softly" policing'.[50] Another officer felt they were not valued either by 'their senior officers' or 'the elected representatives at the London Borough of Haringey'. Even worse, perhaps, 'the view held by many junior officers' was that those officers who made up the senior management team 'were puppets of Dolly Kiffin and Bernie Grant'.[51]

Some officers were reluctant to become part of the Broadwater Farm Estate (BWFE) team. One officer described how, when it came to be his turn to do a spell with it, he 'tried to avoid it' because he 'saw it as a crap posting.' Pointing out that the team saw their supervisors 'infrequently' he said they were "allowed" (his quotation marks) to police the estate in all areas except Tangmere Block which, because of the dangers, they avoided because of the dangers at all times other than early mornings.[52]

Although rank and file officers were unlikely to have felt the effects as

---

49. Cullen, R (1989). *A Review of Organizational Health and Welfare in the Police Service*. London: Home Office Police Requirements Support Unit.
50. Ritchie, P J N (1986). 'Your View—Broadwater Farm: Roots of riot.' In *Police*, Vol. XVIII, No. 6, February, p. 18.
51. Gladwell, Dave (2014). In correspondence with the author, dated 1 August.
52. Ibid.

much as senior officers, the management system in the Metropolitan Police was undergoing considerable change. Previously reporting to a commander of a district, divisional command was still in the process of changing-over to a system in which it reported direct to a deputy assistant commissioner, in this case Mike Richards, who was responsible for a wider area. Nevertheless, an acting commander of the district, Detective Chief Superintendent Ted Hodge, remained in post. Up until June 1985, decisions affecting the policing of Broadwater Farm had only been taken with the specific approval of Commander Dickinson, who held what was known as the Broadwater Farm file. But when he retired, the file passed to the divisional commander, Chief Superintendent Couch at Tottenham. This suggested that decision-making passed to him as well, in accordance with Newman's memorandum to the Home Secretary in early-1983.[53] But when he activated limited action against drug-dealers on the estate three days before the riot, it appeared his decision was over-ridden by the acting commander. Only when there was potential for serious disorder following the death of Cynthia Jarrett did the area deputy assistant commissioner become involved.

A number of officers at Tottenham underwent traumatic incidents. These have already been described in *Chapters 4* and *5*, from the assaults on Sergeant Golborne and Chief Inspector Rowe in 1982 to the serious injury inflicted on Constable Caton just a couple of hours before rioting broke out. The effects on individual officers varied. To some they were more traumatic than others. Constable Stratton, who was assaulted for no apparent reason other than he wore a police uniform, was removed, at his request, from his role as a home beat officer for the Broadwater Farm Estate. Constable Morley described how, after the incident in which he and Mark Nicholson were involved on 11 September, he 'disappeared into a bottle for a few weeks' and he, too, subsequently refused to continue with the BWFE team. To this day, he remains affected by the incident. Now retired to a lovely village in the Yorkshire Dales, he commented that even writing about the incident in 2014 had brought it back in 'scary reality'.[54]

---

53. Newman, Sir Kenneth (1983). Preliminary Assessment of Problems and Priorities: Report of the Commissioner of Police of the Metropolis to the Home Secretary. London: Metropolitan Police (typescript).
54. Morley, Paul (2014). In correspondence with the author, dated 11 August.

Units responding to the riot

Writing some five years later, a former police officer turned academic who spent two years embedded in that part of the Metropolitan Police Force that dealt with public order claimed 'policing civil disorder engenders fear, anger and frustration amongst officers.' He warned that, 'the feeling that one has lost control and is at the mercy of unpredictable events only heightens anxiety.'[55]

This was definitely so on 6th October. It has already been described how morale amongst public order units on the morning of that day was high. Less than 24 hours later it was at rock bottom and there was a distinct feeling both that control had been lost and they had been 'at the mercy of unpredictable events.' One officer described arriving at an entrance to the estate and being met with 'the noise of smashing glass, the bricks bouncing off the Tarmac, the massed policemen, running, standing, lying down injured, some in dusty tunics, many more carrying riot shields' and with 'the air [reeking] of petrol'. Eventually, they were in the front line, face-to-face with the rioters:

> 'Paving-stones smashed across shields and on skulls, instantly rendering many unconscious in spite of our NATO-helmets. Petrol bombs were thrown, hitting the shields or the ground between us, flaring up in plumes of thick choking smoke.'

This was not like Brixton, pointed out the author of the article, where the rioters threw a brick and ran. At Tottenham, as the police advanced behind their riot shields, so, too, did the rioters, forcing the police to retreat.[56] Other officers, too, commented on the new levels of aggression and hate that the rioters had shown towards them compared with what had gone before. Speaking from his hospital bed after being knocked unconscious when he was hit by a paving-slab, Sergeant Dorrington described it as 'the most horrific and frightening experience' of his ten years' service as a police officer. He continued, 'the most frightening of all was the hostility of the mob which

---

55. Waddington, P A J (1991). *The Strong Arm of the Law: Armed and Public Order Policing.* Oxford: Clarendon, p. 137.
56. Cotton, op. cit. 12, p. 17.

included blacks and whites.'[57] Gifford was 'in no doubt' that for the officers, who were required to stand behind shields for a considerable time whilst a variety of missiles were thrown from ground level and the elevated balconies, 'the experience must have been terrifying.'[58]

Some of the general unabridged comments that came from the Police Staff College's informal psychological review, were:

- 'It was dark and cold and the atmosphere was tense. The world exploded and I saw shield officers on my left raise their shields.'
- 'I saw a shield unit hit by a petrol bomb catch fire running around screaming until they were put out.'
- 'I knew my arm hurt but it was mainly shock. The shock reaction was so severe that some people were being sick. PC... started pacing up and down and hyperventilating.'
- 'I was annoyed and frustrated that PC... was seriously injured.'
- 'When I lay down I was sick and felt exhausted, and totally drained of strength and emotion. I did not have the energy to cry.'[59]

Fear

According to Waddington, 'violent inner-city riots clearly had the purpose of inflicting as many serious injuries upon the police' as the rioters 'could accomplish by recourse to missiles, petrol bombs, and, eventually, firearms.'[60] It is natural that when faced with such situations, police officers should be apprehensive and in many cases fearful of the consequences. As one officer pointed out:

---

57. *Standard*, 7 October 1985.
58. Gifford, Lord (1986). The Broadwater Farm Inquiry: Report of the Independent Inquiry into Disturbances of October 1985 at the Broadwater Farm Estate, Tottenham. London: Broadwater Farm Inquiry, p.110, para. 5.53.
59. Holt, op. cit. 36.
60. Waddington, op. cit. 55, p. 217.

'In a public order situation the adrenalin gets going and there's no way you're going to stop it, because of fear as well as the fact that you've got a job to do. There is no way you can stop that fear when the possibility of injury is high.'[61]

Fear is a common cause of psychological stress and this was associated, in this case, with what many rank and file officers felt was a lack of leadership. In a letter to the journal *Police*, one officer recalled 'feeling demoralised' by what he 'perceived as a lack of bottle and leadership by the senior officers in attendance that night.' He described it 'as the worst night of his service' and went on to say:

'It badly affected me. Particularly afterwards. I believed my colleagues and I were going to die because of the ferocity of the assaults on us. Raw hatred was tangible in the air. I cannot recall that evening even now nearly 30 years later without getting quite emotional.'[62]

A number of officers expressed their fears during the first murder trial into Blakelock's death. When defence counsel Michael Mansfield suggested to Sergeant Nevens, who was in charge of the first DSU to attend Willan Road at the start of the riot, that he had 'totally exaggerated what had happened,' Nevens denied it, saying, '[W]e were in fear of our lives right from the start'.[63] Constable Barton, who was part of Serial 502, and who described in *Chapter 8* how they were attacked as the retreated down the stairs of Tangmere Block, said 'I did not feel I was going to get out alive.'[64] Constable Shepherd, part of the same serial, told the court that when he was being attacked by the mob whilst trying to protect Constable Coombes he thought they 'were both going to be killed.'[65] Called by the defence to give evidence at the trial, Constable Terry Arthurs described the riot as 'absolutely horrifying', claiming that 'officers spent a lot of time extinguishing flames on each other because they were showered with petrol bombs coming over the shields.'[66]

---

61. Graef, op. cit. 23, p. 354.
62. Lawson, op. cit. 17.
63. *Police Review*, 13 February 1987. p.310.
64. *The Times*, 27 January 1987.
65. Ibid.
66. *Police Review*, 6 March 1987, p. 466.

But fear did not only exist in the junior ranks. An unidentified superintendent who was also part of the police response, later claimed that he was 'not given to fear' but when 'bottles of flaming petrol were coming down' and the rioters 'were getting brazen and running up to the shields' and the officers 'were being pushed back', he was frightened for the first time in his life.[67]

Frustration and a lack of banter

Frustration is a key cause of work-related stress. The cause of much of the frustration on the night was the lack of knowledge of shield tactics amongst senior officers. As this became apparent, so morale and confidence amongst the rank and file officers as to what they were being asked to do declined. Many of these officers felt the same way as Constable Pyles; another officer said they 'had an opportunity to crush [the] riot because there were numerous units available, fully equipped, but they were never called upon.'[68] Many officers felt that 'a positive attempt should have been made to gain an entry into the estate as part of an overall plan at a much earlier stage.' Whilst they agreed that there was always the possibility of injuries being sustained whilst taking offensive action this 'was generally seen to be an occupational risk preferable to being injured in a defensive situation.'[69] An officer described how, after the rioting was over and they were just sitting on their shields by their carrier, he was 'seriously pissed off' when a number of black youths started walking away from the estate. But when a request was made to Yankee Control to stop-and-search them, it was refused.[70]

Another officer described the frustration that was apparent at the briefing prior to retaking the estate in the early hours of the following morning when a senior officer 'lectured' those assembled to the effect that he wanted to be confident that they were capable of achieving it. The officer said:

---

67. Graef, op. cit. 23, p.79.
68. Judge, op. cit. 27, p.11.
69. Graef, op. cit. 23, p.79.
70. Lawson, op. cit. 17.

'There was almost a riot there and then. Comments such as "we wanted to take it last night but you wouldn't let us"—maybe a little more forcibly than that if my memory serves me correctly.'

He then went on to describe the retaking of The Farm as 'a farce' with 'level by level being reported as we retook a quiet and peaceful estate.'[71]

But it wasn't only those who had been in the thick of the action that were affected. An officer with the SPG who had been on standby for most of the evening described how she felt when they finally went in to clear the estate at around 3.30 a.m.:

'We drove through the narrow Victorian streets around Broadwater Farm and saw the pavements were covered in exhausted sleeping officers. They looked like they had been at war…I don't know about any other SPG officers but I felt awful that we had spent the night sitting in carriers whilst nearby they had been literally fighting for their lives.'[72]

Police officers frequently engage in banter. It covers the exchange of comments and views, sometimes in a humorous way, and has been found to be a useful way of reducing stress after involvement in a particularly nasty incident.[73] It seems, on this occasion, there was none, or very little banter. By 1 a.m., many of the units had stood down. One officer described how what was left of his unit returned to their vehicle at about 1 a.m. and '[We] just sat exhausted on our shields.'[74] Another officer described how his unit was eventually stood down at 4 a.m. and then travelled back to their base:

'In the carrier the remaining ten of us who had escaped more or less unscathed didn't utter a word. The silence, you could say, was deafening. We sat, cradling our NATO-helmets every one ravaged by debris. There was none of the usual banter,

---

71. Hussey, Kevin (2014). In correspondence with the author, dated 17 June.
72. Pullen, Lorraine (2014). In correspondence with the author, dated 10 July.
73. Evans, Rachel; Pistrang, Nancy and Billings, Jo (2013). 'Police officers' experiences of supportive and unsupportive social interactions following traumatic incidents.' *European Journal of Psycho-Traumatology*, Vol. 4, Domain 2, Theme 2.1.
74. Hogan, Paul (2014). In correspondence with the author, dated 30 June.

the cat-calls, the laughing, just a sorrow borne out of grief and frustration, each one wondering if we could have done more.'[75]

Nightmares

Nightmares are a frequent occurrence following a traumatic incident. A sergeant who had been in the midst of the disorder claimed that he was having nightmares two years later when subsequently interviewed by Roger Graef.[76] A constable went further, describing how, whilst he was retreating in formation, the bottom of his long shield hit a brick which was lying on the ground and he stumbled. Meanwhile the rest of the police cordon had dressed back leaving him 'looking up at a figure holding a slab of concrete;' which he was about to throw at him. Somehow he managed to get to his feet—he does not recall how—and run. Ten years later, he claimed that the 'looming figure' still recurred in his 'nightmares, along with the crackling of the radio—and the screaming.' But in those recurring dreams he described how he 'gleefully' sliced the person's 'neck' with the edge of his shield and watched 'his decapitated head roll off'.[77]

Williams 'operational review'

Over two weeks after the riot, on 21 October, an operational review commenced. In the following two months, just over 400 officers of inspector, sergeant and constable rank, many of whom had been on the front line, were seen. An operational review or debrief is designed to find out what actually happened in order to discover whether existing training, procedures and equipment are appropriate with a view to making recommendations to improve on any failings. This differs from a psychological debriefing which is designed to discover how officers felt as they underwent the traumatic incident and how they feel about it after it is over. In brief, the former is designed to discover facts, the latter feelings.

Seven years after the Broadwater Farm riot there was serious disorder in

---

75. Cotton, op. cit. 12, p. 18.
76. Graef, op. cit. 23, p.79.
77. Cotton, op. cit. 12, p. 18.

Los Angeles which went on for five days and there was much criticism of the Los Angeles Police Department for its lack of preparedness and inability to bring the situation under control. An inquiry into the rioting revealed a situation similar to that which existed at Broadwater Farm, 'overwhelming evidence that rank and file police officers want to do their job—to protect the city' and were 'embarrassed by the performance of the their department.' People both within the department and outside attributed the poor performance concerning the riots 'to the relative lack of command experience at the command staff level of the department.' Research, involving 123 male and 18 females officers, the majority of whom (74.5 per cent) had been on the streets on all five days during the riots, published some five years after the Los Angeles riot found that '17 per cent... were experiencing PTSD symptomatology' 19 months after the riot.[78] However, the researchers stated that because the police culture promoted an 'in control' image,[79] this way well have been 'an under-reporting' because the voluntary nature of the study may have led those officers who were more prone to denial from participating.[80] On the basis of this research it is likely that at least 20 per cent of those who responded to the riot on Broadwater Farm will have suffered from PTSD.

Right from the outset, officers demanded to know of the Williams debriefing team why it had 'taken so long to get around to talking to [them]'.[81] The vast majority of the officers debriefed 'expressed their appreciation of the fact that at least someone in authority' was 'interested in hearing what they [had] to say' but most felt it 'should have been done within a day or two of the riot by their own senior officers rather than some weeks after the event.'[82] As a result it was clear 'that a substantial number of the officers who were exposed to the most traumatic situations during the riot felt a psychological need to talk through the experiences with a sympathetic listener at an early stage.' Only a few senior officers 'recognised this need and went to some lengths to meet it'; most, however, 'did nothing and lost credibility

---

78. Harvey-Lintz, Terri, and Tidwell, Romeria (1997). 'Effects of the 1992 Los Angeles civil unrest: post traumatic stress disorder symptomatology among law enforcement officers.' *The Social Science Journal*, 1 April, p.4.
79. Reiser, M, and Geiger, S.P (1984). 'Police Officer as Victim.' *Professional Psychology: Research and Practice*, 15: 315–323; quoted in Harvey-Lintz, op. cit. 65, p. 4.
80. Harvey-Lintz, op. cit. 78, p. 4,
81. Williams, David A, op. cit. 14, p. 215, para. 2:4:3.
82. Ibid, p. 39, para. 4:12.

with their men as a result.'[83]

Lack of counselling

The Williams Report claimed 'there was a distinct lack of counselling or debriefing immediately or in the days following [the riot]' and for many the 'return to ordinary duties was a shock to the system.'[84] One officer told the informal psychological review subsequently conducted by staff from the Police Staff College:

> 'Most of us were very shocked and either crying or being sick or both. On arrival at Wood Green we were sent to the canteen where we waited for about half an hour then we were sent home.'[85]

A second officer, who had been dismissed at 1 a.m., described how he paraded for duty at his station a mere five hours later, at 6 a.m. on the Monday morning, feeling 'tired, frustrated and angry.' He and a colleague who had been with him were at least allowed to go off duty

> '…but went straight to the pub. We were back for early turn Tuesday and life just carried on. I'm sure I was asked to make a duty statement but in those days there was no occupational health or counselling.'[86]

This lack of counselling had a profound effect on those officers who had been part of Serial 502. In the immediate aftermath of Blakelock's death and for some considerable time afterwards they were clearly 'in the spotlight' and were 'on show to the rest of the force.' When they were subsequently seen by the Williams debriefing team it became clear that they required counselling and that the team, with its limited expertise on psychological trauma was 'just scraping the surface, even though the individual interviews in some cases lasted several hours.'[87]

---

83. Ibid, p. 39, para. 4:13.
84. Ibid, p. 226, para 6(v).
85. Holt, op. cit. 36.
86. Hogan, op. cit. 74.
87. Williams, op. cit. 14, p.225, paras 6(i) and (ii) and p.226, para. 7.

The members of Serial 502 were 'universal' in their praise of Sergeant Pengelly. However, almost without exception, they were 'bitter and resentful about the force as a whole and [Chief Superintendent] Couch in particular.' Their bitterness was 'aggravated' by the fact it would appear 'very little was done for them in the way of counselling and support in the hours immediately following the riot.' In most cases, after being dismissed from duty, they made their own way home, some of them suffering from shock, and were not seen by anyone in authority until they paraded for their next normal tour of duty the following day or the day after.[88] Later in the week, Chief Superintendent French who had been promoted at midnight following the riot and took charge of Hornsey Division the next day, and Ken Rivers, the force welfare officer, did initiate some counselling sessions.[89] Whilst appreciated, it subsequently became clear to the debriefing team that it was arguably too little, too late.

In a letter to Ranulph Fiennes in 2010, Sergeant Pengelly told him that 'life was never the same again for any of us.' Pengelly and Constable Miles Barton also confirmed that, down the long years since the riot, they had both suffered badly from post-traumatic stress, but that given the choice of a replay, they would again go back for a fallen comrade.[90] Dick Coombes told Fiennes:

> 'That night not only ruined the lives of Keith's family, but many, many others. All of us have been affected. It will never be over for us.'[91]

Journalist and broadcaster Lorraine Kelly, who interviewed Coombes following the acquittal of Nicky Jacobs in 2014 said he still suffered 'from post-traumatic stress'. He did not testify at the trial because medical experts were 'worried about the emotional effect it would have on him.'[92]

---

88. Ibid, p. 39, para. 4:14
89. Ibid.
90. Fiennes, Ranulph (2011). Going Back into Hell. In *My Heroes: Extraordinary Courage, Exceptional People*. London: Hodder & Stoughton, p. 55
91. Ibid, p.54.
92. Kelly, Lorraine (2014). 'Trauma endures after Broadwater Farm riot'. *Sunday Post*, 13 April 2014.

Metropolitan Police review

The Metropolitan Police's own review of both the 1981 and 1985 disorders in London was misleading. Whilst it claimed to recognise 'the effect of stress on officers arising from civil disorder'[93] it clearly did not. Otherwise more would have been done for those officers identified by the Williams Report as having 'a psychological need to talk through their experiences.'[94] In the main, the Review followed the trend at the time of relating stress to long hours of duty and lengthy periods without refreshments. It did, however, highlight that dealing with the effects of stress on individual officers was 'an important part of command responsibility' and recommended that 'ideally no officer should be engaged on any incident beyond the period of 12 hours.'[95]

Conclusion

As a result of the Brixton and Broadwater Farm riots in 1985, the Metropolitan Police did implement 'changes to help identify officers suffering the negative effects of stress and to provide longer term support through welfare teams and medical assistance.'[96] It embarked on a programme in which eight members of its staff were selected to obtain professional qualifications as psychological councillors.[97] Nevertheless, six years after the Broadwater Farm riot, the internal review into the handling of the Poll Tax riot in Trafalgar Square in March 1990, which took the form of another operational debriefing suggested that 'post-riot welfare and counselling' needed further examination and development 'within a structured support system' because 'the traumatic effect of being involved in prolonged riots was very noticeable when officers were interviewed.'[98]

But, perhaps the events of 6th October 1985 were best summed up by two sergeants. The first is Sergeant Pengelly, who, it will be recalled was awarded

---

93. Metropolitan Police, op. cit. 6, p. 24, para. 11.16.
94. Williams, op. cit. 14, p. 39, para. 4:13.
95. Metropolitan Police, op. cit. 6, p. 42, para. 59.
96. Ibid, p. 24, para. 11.16.
97. Kelly, Paul (2014). 'Eye Movement Desensitisation Reprocessing.' Website of an EMDR therapist at www.emdrtherapist.co.uk/about.html accessed on 5 November 2014.
98. Metcalfe, J (1991). Public Order debriefing: Trafalgar Square riot. London: Metropolitan Police, p.19.

the George Medal for his actions that night. He was asked by defence counsel in the first Blakelock murder trial whether he learned about the public order plan for the estate after the riot. He replied, 'To be perfectly frank, I found the events on that night so frightening and distressing, I tried not to get involved any more with what happened on the night.' [99] The second is Sergeant Kevin Hussey who described how, at the end of his shift that night, his unit was sent back to South London to get a 'clean shirt' before reporting back to duty:

> 'I was standing in my back garden having a coffee. It backed onto woods and the birds were chirping. I thought this must be how soldiers returning from war must feel to a degree. Battle one moment and normal hum drum quiet the next. As if nothing happened.'[100]

Was it a battle? Certainly for many of those who had been on the front line at the Broadwater Farm Estate the previous night it must have seemed like one.

---

99. *Police Review*, 30 January 1987, p. 209
100. Hussey, op. cit. 71.

CHAPTER THIRTEEN

Where Does the Blame Lie?

Introduction

What occurred in Tottenham on the evening of 6 October 1985 was a crisis, both for the Metropolitan Police and the community. Crises do not happen in a vacuum. There is no single cause, rather there are a series of events when, if effective action is taken, the crisis can be averted. The events at Tottenham were no different. Despite the brutal killing of a police officer the government refused to set up an inquiry;[1] instead two were undertaken, one on behalf of Haringey Council under Lord Gifford,[2] and one on behalf of the Metropolitan Police under Chief Superintendent David A Williams.[3] Unfortunately, although the one set up on behalf of the council claimed to be independent, neither was. At a meeting on 18 October attended by Councillors Grant and Lawrence, Jeremy Corbyn, Member of Parliament for North Islington and a former Haringey councillor, and Paul Corrigan, who was eventually to sit on the inquiry, the decision was taken to invite Lord Scarman to undertake the inquiry; but he refused.[4] The council therefore turned to Mark Bonham Carter but he too turned it down.[5] Eventually, Lord Gifford was approached. He was a Labour peer, who had become a Queen's Counsel (QC) in 1983. In his autobiography, he suggested he was

---

1. The government set up inquiries in 1974 after a demonstrator died in Red Lion Square, and in 1981 at Brixton despite the fact no-one was killed. Both were undertaken by a senior member of the judiciary, Lord Scarman.
2. Gifford, Lord (1986). The Broadwater Farm Inquiry: Report of the Independent Inquiry into Disturbances of October 1985 at the Broadwater Farm Estate, Tottenham. London: Broadwater Farm Inquiry.
3. Williams, David a (1986). Internal Police Report on the disorders of the 6th October 1985 at the Broadwater Farm Estate, Tottenham. London: Metropolitan Police (typescript).
4. Bernie Grant Archives File BG/P/4/6/4 held at the Bishopsgate Institute, London.
5. Mark Bonham Carter outlined his concerns that the Metropolitan Police had refused to take part in the inquiry in a letter to *The Times*, 30 December 1985.

one of a small number of 'radical lawyers'.[6] In 1974, together with five other barristers, he had set up the first chambers outside the Inns of Court, in Lambeth. At the time it was a rule of the Bar that a barrister could not refuse a brief in a field in which he or she was competent, provided that a proper professional fee was paid. However, the new chambers, known as Wellington Street, quickly made it known that it would not, amongst other things, prosecute cases for the police'.[7] Four years earlier he had been a co-founder of the first law centre to be set up, in North Kensington.[8] Given that the Metropolitan Police Commissioner had suggested that 'radical law centres' and 'police monitoring groups', amongst others, exerted 'a generally negative and destructive influence'[9] it was predictable that he would refuse to allow the Metropolitan Police to be a party to such an inquiry. Deputy Assistant Commissioner Richards submitted a factual report to Haringey Council but it was subsequently found to be inaccurate in its account of the setting up of the barricades.

There were serious defects in the inquiry set up by the Metropolitan Police. David A Williams had been the second-in-command of Tottenham Division less than two years previously and, as the chief superintendent at Edmonton, was under the direct command of Deputy Assistant Commissioner Richards. A number of the inquiry team came from Y District.[10] This included Sergeant Jeremy Pearce who had been responsible for the home beat officers policing the Broadwater Farm Estate until June 1985. To have credibility, the inquiry should have been led by an officer who was at least equal in rank to Richards. Five years later, an internal inquiry into the policing of the Poll Tax riot in 1990 was headed by a deputy assistant commissioner, John Metcalfe, who was equal in rank to the officer who had charge of the policing operations that day, David Meynell.[11]

---

6. Gifford, QC, Anthony (2007). *The Passionate Advocate*. London: Wildy, Simmonds and Hill, pp. 104–106.
7. Ibid, pp. 53–56.
8. Ibid, pp. 15–19.
9. Newman, Sir Kenneth (1983). Preliminary Assessment of Problems and Priorities: Report of The Commissioner of Police of the Metropolis to the Home Secretary. London: Metropolitan Police (Typescript), pp. 5–6, para. 18.
10. See the list of members of the debriefing team in Williams, op. cit. 3, p.3. The vast majority came from what had been Y District.
11. Metcalfe, Deputy Assistant Commissioner John (1991). Trafalgar Square Riot Debrief: Saturday 31 March 1990. London: Metropolitan Police.

The results were predictable. The Gifford Report claimed 'the disturbances came about because of an appalling state of distrust and hostility which existed between the police and the people who lived in and frequented Broadwater Farm.' Although recognising that 'police work [was] difficult and dangerous' and a number of incidents had taken place on Broadwater Farm which 'were reprehensible', the report listed ten findings which Gifford claimed would have reduced the likelihood of the disorder occurring. With one exception, in which the Metropolitan Police and Haringey Council were jointly to blame for failing to set up 'a consultative forum' in which all interests in the borough were represented, the fault lay entirely with the police.[12]

Williams, on the other hand, claimed that senior officers on Y District were 'faced by a local authority whose declared aim was the accountability of the service to local politicians.' In furtherance of this aim, Haringey Council 'went to considerable lengths to discredit the police by, for example, offering its premises as distribution points for inflammatory and anti-police literature, refusing the use of its premises for sponsored police meetings, failing to support Neighbourhood Watch schemes, placing difficult conditions in the way of police membership of the Broadwater Farm Panel, withholding support from the idea of a Victim Support scheme and declining to allow police to carry passcards which would give them access to the tower blocks in Broadwater.'[13]

Some seven years later, in an interview with the *Evening Standard*, following the publication of a report on the 18-year history of Haringey's pioneering police monitoring committee, Chief Superintendent Couch, said, 'Haringey Council must bear a large amount of responsibility for what happened on the night of 6 October 1985, and for allowing the situation to develop on the estate in the way that it did during the previous months.' He went on to claim that it was the council's actions that led to 'a breakdown in communications between the police and the community "with fatal results".'[14]

---

12. Gifford, op. cit. 2, pp. 190–191, paras 8.3–8.4.
13. Williams, David A, op. cit. 3, pp. 91–92, para. 4.4.
14. Webb, Gervase and Oakes, John (1992). 'Broadwater riot police commander condemns Grant'. *Evening Standard*, 22 July, p.10. See Mullings, Beverley and Morrison, Wayne (1992), *Aiding and Abetting*, London: Haringey Racial Equality Commission.

The wider picture

To gain an understanding why Broadwater Farm was policed in the way it was, it is necessary to go back to the start of large-scale immigration from the Caribbean and look at the relationship between the Metropolitan Police and black Londoners in post-war Britain. It does not make particularly good reading.

Despite the part played by many people from Commonwealth countries in the Second World War—half of the 492 people who arrived from Jamaica on the ship, *Empire Windrush*, in 1948 had served in Britain's armed forces or in munitions between 1939 and 1945—racism was rife throughout British life.[15] Indeed, Ambalavaner Sivanandan, described by Keith Thompson as 'one of Britain's most incisive blacks',[16] suggested racism was as English as Shakespeare and as old as slavery,[17] particularly when it came to accommodation and employment.[18] Within four years, first Labour and then Conservative governments 'took a major role in constructing black immigration as a "problem",'[19] instituting 'a number of covert, and sometimes illegal, administrative measures designed to discourage',[20] albeit with little success, many of those who subsequently came to Britain. Indeed from the outset, the Ministry of Labour was not in favour of recruiting workers from the Caribbean.[21]

It follows that, in the first instance, blame lies with successive British governments, who during the period of large-scale immigration from the Caribbean from 1948 onwards through to the 1960s failed to consider or

---

15. Harris, Clive (1993). Post-war Migration and the Industrial Reserve Army. In James, Winston and Harris, Clive (eds.). *Inside Babylon: The Caribbean Diaspora in Britain*. London: Verso, p. 22.
16. Thompson, Keith (1988). *Under Seige: Racial Violence in Britain Today*. London: Penguin, p.100.
17. Sivanandan, A (1990). Britain's Gulags. In Proctor, James (ed.)(2000). *Writing Black Britain 1948–1998*. Manchester: Manchester University Press, p.149.
18. Harris, op. cit. 15, p.26.
19. Carter, Bob; Harris, Clive, and Joshi, Shirley (1993). The 1951–55 Conservative Government and the Racialization of Black Immigration. In James, Winston; Harris, Clive (eds.). *Inside Babylon: The Caribbean Diaspora in Britain*. London: Verso, p.55; see also Thompson, op. cit. 15a, pp. 62–69.
20. Ibid, p.57.
21. Harris, op. cit. 15, p.21; see also Thompson, op. cit. 15a, p.82.

'assume responsibility for the social problems' that were likely to arise.[22] There being 'no strategic plan or directives from the centre', the police, along with 'local authorities and the statutory and voluntary agencies were left to sort the situation out as best they could.'[23] Indeed, neither Central Government nor the Metropolitan Police 'envisaged a role for the police in areas of immigrant settlement other than the time-honoured ones of law enforcement and regulation.'[24]

Cultural differences between the indigenous population and those coming from the Caribbean 'often led to misunderstanding and resentment'[25] and very quickly three main causes of friction between the police and the newcomers arose. The first were the disputes that emanated from 'noisy parties'. To the African-Caribbean people, home was a place to which one could invite friends, play music and have a few drinks. However, in many instances, the newcomers were living 'cheek-by-jowl' in overcrowded accommodation with an indigenous population that tended to seek their entertainment outside the home in clubs and public houses.

The second were the disputes between landlord and tenant. In the Caribbean, the local police dealt with such matters, deciding who was right and who was wrong. In Britain, however, the police rarely solved the problems but merely referred the two parties involved in the dispute to what was known as 'their civil remedy'; this meant sending to them to a magistrates' court or a rent tribunal to get it sorted out. Frequently, the newcomers saw this as siding with the indigenous population and, this 'inaction, or unwillingness to act' increasingly caused resentment.[26] Stan May, who was a constable in an area where many of these early immigrants from the Caribbean settled, suggested the Metropolitan Police could not be 'entirely exonerated' from blame when it came to settling such disputes. He claimed that whilst 'individual officers did their best to be impartial and do their job properly, the foretaste of things to come was clearly visible' both to the constables and the sergeants, who dealt with many of those early disputes, but no-one of more

---

22. Whitfield, James (2004). *Unhappy Dialogue: The Metropolitan Police and Black Londoners in Post-war Britain.* Cullompton: Willan, p. 16.
23. Ibid, p. 21.
24. Ibid, p. 54.
25. Ibid, p. 27.
26. Ibid, p. 59.

senior rank appeared either interested or saw the danger.[27]

Thirdly, was the failure of senior officers in the Metropolitan Police to appreciate 'the potential goodwill that would have resulted had they taken action to deal with the diverse effects of racially motivated verbal and physical attacks on black immigrants, particularly in the 1950s which was 'before black disillusionment with the police had firmly taken hold.'[28]

In dealing with the problems that existed between the newcomers and the indigenous population, constables received 'precious little in the way of leadership, support and encouragement from practically every supervisory level from sergeant to chief superintendent, the vast majority of who appeared to spend too much of their time shuffling paperwork, most of which was of a routine or trivial nature.'[29]

The result was that during the 1950s and 1960s, a climate developed, certainly in London, where those of African-Caribbean descent and the Metropolitan Police began to see each other 'in an increasingly negative manner'. Whitfield suggested the 'stereotypical policeman' was seen as 'biased, uncaring, prone to use excessive force, and willing to lie on oath to obtain convictions.' The African-Caribbean individual, on the other hand, 'was considered to be truculent, likely to make unwarranted and unfounded complaints, and to be possessed of violent criminal tendencies and low moral standards.'[30] Humphreys wrote in a similar vein in 1972, suggesting that the police approached black people 'expecting excitability and arrogance' whilst the black man expected 'aggression and arrogance from the police.' Added to which 'episodes involving police officers and black people' were 'recounted with much venom both in police stations and in the black community.' Thus an atmosphere was created in which confrontations, if they did not become physical, were at least a form of 'psychological warfare'.[31]

The police tended to blame the newcomers. In March 1966, Chief Superintendent Norman, who was then the commissioner's representative

---

27. May, Stan (1993). In a letter to the author, dated 15 April. May served as a constable at Notting Hill, where many of those from African-Caribbean places first settled, from the end of World War II until 1957.
28. Whitfield, op. cit. 22, p. 148.
29. Ibid, p. 159.
30. Ibid, p. 141.
31. Humphrey, Derek (1972). *Police Power and Black People*. London: Panther, p. 223.

for West Indian Affairs, told the West Indian Students' Union that West Indians caused problems because 'of their penchant for complaining that police had been too officious towards them, or that the police were not doing their job properly', adding that West Indians 'resented advice given by the police' and 'had a fondness for litigation'. He then went on to tell them how to behave in British society:

> '...the traditional attitude in England was for members of the public to accept advice or orders from policemen, if not with good grace at least without argument. This to my mind is a good thing, as someone has to be the boss on the streets and give the orders. Police naturally resented having every order questioned.'

He concluded by telling them '[I]t would make for better relations if immigrants were prepared to accept advice or orders more readily.' But, as Whitfield pointed out, 'such remarks can hardly have been calculated to convince those attending the meeting that the Met empathised with, or understood, the concerns of the black community.'[32]

In his annual report for 1967, Commissioner Sir John Waldren reported:

> 'Police understanding of immigrants' problems is deep, police liaison with immigrant groups and contact with individuals is healthy and even an example to some other official organizations—and yet, the more militant groups rant about police victimisation and brutality, and the mass media takes up the cry, stating that never have relations been more strained. This is nonsense: police action or inaction will always give cause for complaint—but never had the immigrant groups less cause for complaint than now.'[33]

This was misleading. Police understanding of immigrant groups was neither deep, nor was police liaison with immigrant groups healthy. Indeed, the following year, the Metropolitan Police set up a Community Relations Branch in order to dispel what the first officer in charge of the branch, Commander Merricks, claimed was the 'mistrust and misunderstanding'

---

32. Norman's remarks are quoted in Whitfield, op. cit. 22, p. 68.
33. Annual Report of the Commissioner of Police for the Metropolis for the Year 1967. London: Her Majesty's Stationary Office.

that existed. He went on to suggest that it was one of the most 'difficult and challenging tasks' the Metropolitan Police had 'ever had to face'.[34] Initially, eight chief inspectors were appointed full-time community liaison officers (CLOs) in July 1969, primarily on inner divisions; similar appointments were made to the remaining divisions the following year.[35] In his next annual report, the commissioner explained his reasons for setting up the branch:

> 'The social consequences of a rapid influx of coloured citizens from overseas...are still comparatively new and provide matters for concern. This is a field in which police are among the first to become involved, since it is when difficulties and misunderstandings due to incompatibility and different habits and ways of life become major social problems that police come into the picture.'[36]

Much has been written about the role and effectiveness of CLOs. Whitfield was critical of their original purpose which was articulated as the development of 'closer ties with immigrant communities'; rather, he claimed, 'it was predominantly established to forestall criticism of the Met's relations with immigrant communities and further the Met's own priorities.'[37] But he went further, suggesting that the Metropolitan Police viewed community relations as 'little more than the means by which it could obtain better criminal intelligence from the public, and as an early warning system that would enable the commissioner to forestall or respond positively to criticism of his force.'[38] Three years after their introduction, Humphrey claimed that the CLO's 'dynamic, well thought-out, all-embracing' programme was 'designed to solve a recognised problem', but, by and large, they were isolated and held in 'poor standing by the lower ranks.' Its success, he suggested, was conditioned, firstly by the man on the beat coming to realise that community relations was primarily his concern too, and secondly, the extent to which people believed the police were serious about letting justice be seen

---

34. Merrick, F.R (1970). 'The Development of Community Relations in the Metropolitan Police'. *Police Journal*, Vol. 43, January, p. 30.
35. Ibid, pp. 32–33.
36. Annual Report of the Commissioner of Police for the Metropolis for the Year 1968. London: Her Majesty's Stationary Office.
37. Whitfield, op. cit. 22, p.3.
38. Ibid, p. 159.

to be done, minimising community strife and public/police conflict, and upholding the rights of the individual, both in terms of the public and the police themselves.[39]

An added problem around this period resulted from low pay and the demanding conditions of service as a result of which police officers felt under-valued by society. At the same time, junior officers continued to suffer from a lack of 'leadership and guidance they were entitled to expect from senior officers.' This absence of leadership and guidance, particularly with regard to the wide discretion officers had in carrying out their duties, and the belief that they were under-valued, meant it was 'far less likely that the Met's rank-and-file' would be inclined 'to empathise with the plight of alienated groups, such as the West Indian community, ahead of their own worries and frustrations.'[40]

In his autobiography, Metropolitan Police Commissioner Sir Ian Blair, who held that role from 2004 to 2008, described how 'casually racist' Britain was when he joined the police in 1974, claiming 'racist jokes were commonplace and, in most quarters, considered totally acceptable.' Most people in Britain had 'no concept or regard for the experiences and values of those over whom it had ruled for centuries'; indeed, prior to 1975, 'every white adult in Britain had their formative years shaped' before race began to raise its head. He suggested that this needed 'to be remembered as the history of the relationship between the police and the minority communities' unfolded and people tried 'to understand why that relationship became such a lightening conductor for relationship between races as a whole.' Writing as he was in 2009, he went on to say that he did 'not think that police officers then were inherently more racist than other people' but he had often been 'shocked by the casual attitudes in other spheres.'[41] Alderson, too, expressed a similar view when he wrote in 1979 that Britain was 'a racist society in many ways'.[42]

By the end of the 1970s, Whitfield suggested the Metropolitan Police remained 'hidebound by rigidity in thought and deed, factors that prevented an open and imaginative discourse with West Indian immigrants'. He continued:

---

39. Humphrey, op. cit. 31, p. 200.
40. Whitfield, op. cit. 22, p.142.
41. Blair, Ian (2009). *Policing Controversy*. London: Profile Books, pp. 68–69.
42. Alderson, John (1984). *Law and Disorder*. London: Hamish Hamilton, p.7.

'Unquestionably, the Met's failings from 1970 onwards in race and diversity matters stemmed from policies and attitudes that were prevalent throughout this period; and included a desire to always put its own interests first, a reluctance to accept criticism from outside its own organization, and an inability to accept that community and race relations was anything more than the preserve of social workers.'[43]

Social deprivation

In evidence to the 1972 House of Commons Select Committee on Race Relations, Commander Gordon Maggs who was responsible for policing Notting Hill, 'home' to one of the two race riots in 1958, pointed out that in areas of large ethnic groups, there was frequently 'social deprivation, bad housing and lack of job opportunities' all problems the police had neither caused nor could resolve, but 'for which the police, usually the only visible sign of authority in the area' were 'made to feel responsible'.[44]

Social deprivation was a theme which received considerable support over the following 15 years. For instance, a year before Bristol exploded in the first of the inner-city riots of the 1980s, West Indian sociologist Ken Pryce published a report following a four-year study of the St Paul's area that Chief Constable of Devon and Cornwall John Alderson described as 'clear-sighted and objective' and 'singularly free of anti-police views'. Referring to the 'ghetto' way of life, which for some took on an 'expressive disreputable orientation', Pryce described the situation as 'characterised by wretchedness, sub-normal educational development, unstable patterns and a heavy involvement in such predatory activities as violence, robbery, conning and living off one's wits.' He went on to predict that this way of life would almost certainly persist and the behaviour on which it was based would become permanent if job opportunities for West Indian men were not to improve or if the recession affecting the area worsened.'[45] At the same time, Alderson warned that 'the decaying inner-city areas' were 'breeding grounds for crime and disaffection' but 'to leave the problem to the vagaries of law enforcement

---

43. Whitfield, op. cit. 22, p 142.
44. House of Commons Select Committee on Race Relations and Immigration (1972). Police/Immigrant Relations, Volume I. Session 1971–1972. London: Her Majesty's Stationary Office, p. 215.
45. Alderson, op. cit. 42, p. 154.

would be unwise.'⁴⁶

Kettle, too, warned that during the economic recession towards the end of the 1970s and the beginning of the 1980s it became 'increasingly clear that the black population' suffered 'disproportionately in every significant index of deprivation.' These included 'getting work, losing work, living conditions, educational and professional opportunities.'⁴⁷ Scarman dealt with education, unemployment and housing in his report on the 1981 Brixton riot, finding that discrimination on racial grounds, although indirect rather than direct and generally unintentional, was 'a reality which all too often' confronted 'the black youths of Brixton.'⁴⁸ As a result, he concluded, 'it would be surprising' if young black people 'did not feel a sense of frustration and deprivation'. Because they lived 'much of their lives on the streets', they came into contact with the police who appeared to them 'as visible symbols of the authority of a society which [had] failed to bring them its benefits or do them justice.'⁴⁹ Kettle found evidence of 'stereotyping of black youths' by local government, in education, by social workers, probation officers and other public officials, but those that were required to deal with black individuals had 'little specialist knowledge of particular black needs.'⁵⁰

Despite the findings, particularly of the Scarman inquiry, central government failed to accept any responsibility for the causes of the July 1981 riots. The Conservative Party, under Margaret Thatcher, had been elected 'largely on its claim to be the party of law and order.' It was therefore to be expected that she would follow this theme when she addressed the House of Commons. The riots of 1981 were a law and order problem, she said, and 'until law and order and public confidence' was restored, the government could not 'set about improving the economic or social conditions of this country.'⁵¹ But, even before the inner-city riots of the 1980s, Alderson had warned that 'when people live in squalor' and suffer from 'deprivation' there

---

46. Alderson, John (1979). *Policing Freedom: A Commentary on the Dilemmas of Policing in Western Democracies*. London: MacDonald and Evans, p. 177.
47. Kettle, Martin, and Hodges, Lucy (1982). Uprising! The police, the people and the riots in *Britain's Cities*, Pan Books, p.137.
48. Scarman, The Rt Hon The Lord (1981). The Brixton Disorders 10–12 April 1981. London: Her Majesty's Stationary Office, pp. 10–11, para. 2.21.
49. Ibid, p. 11, para. 2.23.
50. Kettle, op. cit. 47, p.151.
51. *Hansard*, 16 July 1981.

is a real 'threat to public tranquillity'. This, he said, was not for the police to sort out but it was for governments to devise new ways of strengthening the social order. In its failure to introduce 'social policies to reduce the prospect of increasing communal violence' the government effectively accepted that disorder was inevitable and relied on the police to keep the lid on it.[52] So, although the government did make some attempts to regenerate some of the areas affected by the riots with the setting up of the Urban Development Corporations under the flamboyant Secretary of State for the Environment, Michael Hesseltine,[53] it was too little, too late.

Some four years later, following the 1985 inner-city riots, Benyon suggested that, as in 1981, the areas in which disorder occurred shared a number of characteristics such as high unemployment, 'particularly amongst the young and especially amongst black people'; poor and often overcrowded housing; environmental decay, social problems and poor facilities. He pointed out that 'a high proportion in each area' was African-Caribbean or Asian. These were the people, he said, who tended 'to experience the social and economic disadvantages particularly acutely', and who were 'subjected to racial discrimination, racist abuse and on occasions physical attacks.'[54] Labour Party spokesman for Home Affairs, Gerald Kaufman, also pointed out that Handsworth, Brixton and Broadwater Farm

> 'were amongst the most deprived areas in the United Kingdom and suffered very high rates of unemployment. From this he concluded that the basic reason for the riots lay in social deprivation, racial discrimination, bad housing and unemployment, and not in crime and drugs.'[55]

Jeff Crawford, senior race relations officer to Haringey Council had said as much about the Broadwater Farm Estate three years previously. In a report to the Haringey Council, he suggested that the problems on The Farm were

---

52. Alderson, op. cit. 46, p.177.
53. Deas, Ian; Robson, Brian; and Bradford, Michael (2000). 'Re-thinking the Urban Development Corporation "experiment": the case of Central Manchester, Leeds and Bristol'. *Progress in Planning*, 54, pp. 1–72.
54. Benyon, John (1986). 'A Tale of Failure: Race and Policing'. Policy Papers in Ethnic Relations No. 3. Warwick: Centre for Research in Ethnic Relations, University of Warwick, p. 11.
55. Solomos, John (1991). *Black Youth, Racism and the State: The Politics of Ideology and Policy*. Cambridge: Cambridge University Press, pp. 200–201.

exacerbated by 'its undue concentration of low income and homeless families' and it was arguably getting worse. He pointed out that 'white tenants on the estate would appear, in the absence of ethnic records, to be able to successfully lobby for transfers elsewhere, while black tenants on the estate who similarly apply for transfer [are] usually turned down.' As a result, 'the racial mix on the estate was swiftly becoming different from, the racial mix on other estates in the Borough and elsewhere across the country.'[56]

But politicians remained at a loss as to what to do. As already suggested, in failing to introduce 'social policies to reduce the prospect of increasing communal violence', the government accepted that disorder was inevitable and relied on the police to keep the lid on it, very much as it had done during the 1984–1985 miners' strike.[57] In doing so, it allowed the police service, particularly the junior officers on the front line, to bear the brunt of the criticism. Following the 1985 riots, the government continued to describe 'black youth' as being 'clearly criminal. And the riots were depicted as being part of a concerted attempt to keep the police out of an area in order to allow criminal activities, especially drug dealing, to take place.' But, as former Chief Constable Michael O'Byrne said, 'almost all the commentary ignored the possibility that the actions of the youth may have been caused by their gettoisation, frustration caused by high unemployment, alienation and what they saw as police harassment.' It was, he said, 'almost as though Lord Scarman's inquiry had never happened.'[58]

Insensitive policing

In its evidence to the 1972 Select Committee, the National Council of Civil Liberties warned that 'a significant and vocal section of the black community' felt

- It was 'being harshly treated by the police' and there was 'little justice' when their cases came before the courts;

---

56. *West Indian World,* 12 November 1982.
57. Benyon, op. cit. 54, p. 11.
58. O'Byrne, M (2001). *Changing Policing: Revolution Not Evolution.* Lyme Regis: Russell House Publishing, pp. 17–18.

- More violence was being used against black people by policemen than would be used against white people;
- Their homes were entered 'by policemen with a temerity which would not be tried on the white community'; and
- Charges preferred against black people when they were in trouble were usually of a more serious nature than for a white person.

The council pointed out that 'even if the black community' was 'wrong in their beliefs', they were 'nevertheless widely held.'[59] The general approach from the Metropolitan Police to such allegations was to deny that it was true. But even if it were not true, the response was insufficient. What the Metropolitan Police failed to realise was that, in such cases, the truth is immaterial. It is what people perceive to be the truth that needed to be addressed. Finally, the council warned the Select Committee that the 'worsening situation between the police and the black community' was 'very serious indeed.' It claimed that 'violence on both sides' was 'certainly on the increase' and 'the possibility of a significant threat to public order in some areas' could 'not be ruled out.'[60] Benyon suggested that a common characteristic between the riots of 1981 and 1985 was that 'they all occurred in areas where allegations of police misconduct had frequently been made in the past, as a result of which tensions between police and youths had risen and there was evidence of police "heavy handedness", if not downright harassment.'[61]

The attitude of black leaders to policing was best summed up by Gordon. He claimed that the issue was never 'whether the police should enforce the law and protect people and their property' and never was about black people wanting 'to be treated differently'. He claimed that the real issue was 'the failure of the police to protect black communities from racist violence and harassment, the portrayal of a community, a whole people, as criminal, the kind of laws the police [chose] to enforce, the ways in which the laws' were enforced, and the purpose of that law enforcement. The problem of policing a multi-racial society [was] not black people but racist policing.'[62]

---

59. Humphreys, op. cit. 31, p. 109.
60. Ibid, pp. 108–109.
61. Benyon, op. cit. 54, pp. 10–11.
62. Gordon, Paul (1983). *White Law: Racism in the Police, Courts and Prisons*. London: Pluto, p.83.

Unfortunately, Gordon's perception of the problem neglected those within the black community, albeit a minority, who did not want the police interrupting their criminal activities and the continual failure of black leaders to speak out against them.[63]

Scarman rejected accusations that the Metropolitan Police was a racist organization. Nevertheless, he did accuse some officers of 'ill-considered, immature and racially prejudiced actions... in their dealings with young black people on the streets'[64] and had had no doubt 'harassment' occurred. He went on to say that 'stop-and-search operations in particular' required 'courteous and carefully controlled behaviour by the police of those stopped' which he was certain 'was sometimes lacking'.[65] However, some three years later, Michael Pike, who wrote the definitive book on *The Principles of Policing* suggested that because 'the pressures on the ordinary police officer' were 'numerous' and could 'come from outside sources or from within the police service itself', it was 'hard to preach sensible and sensitive policing' to officers 'exposed to the problems of urban policing, especially the... notorious inner-city areas.'[66] There is no evidence to suggest this was done at Tottenham.

Blair suggested the Metropolitan Police's approach to dealing with the black community in the 1970s and 1980s was based on the 'doctrine' of 'equal opportunities'. Under this doctrine, officers were determined 'not to be seen to be prejudiced in their behaviour' and so treated 'everyone the same, regardless of their colour' although he was quick to point out that 'individual decisions did not take away a collective tendency to stop and search African-Caribbean young men disproportionately.' Scarman pointed out that it was 'undeniable' that there was 'one law for all'. But, at the same time, he emphasised the role of police discretion which 'is the art of suiting action to particular circumstances'. Successful policing is, after all, dependent 'upon the skill and judgement which policemen display in the particular circumstances of the cases and incidents which they are required to handle.'[67]

---

63. A claim made by Dennis Ferdinand, 1988 winner of the Martin Luther King Memorial Prize, highlighting the problems faced with African-Caribbean communities living in England, in an article, The black family in crisis, published in the *Evening Standard*, 23 August 1989, p.7.
64. Scarman, op. cit. 48, p. 64, paras 4.62–4.63.
65. Ibid, p. 65, para. 4.67.
66. Pike, Michael S (1985). *The Principles of Policing*. Basingstoke: Macmillan, p. 107.
67. Blair, op. cit. 41, pp. 96–97.

Pressure groups

In his evidence to the Select Committee on Race Relations, Maggs had issued a warning which largely went unheeded for the next eight years and, arguably, was one of the reasons why there were serious outbreaks of disorder in 1980, 1981 and 1985:

> 'A vital issue that must not be avoided is the need to ensure that in dealing with the militant minority whether they be black or white, police must not, because of pressure groups, allow to develop a situation where these elements become privileged because of non-enforcement of the law through a fear of constant criticism and harassment.'[68]

By 1983, there had been 'a phenomenal increase in the number of formally constituted associations and groups, representing a range of minority and special interests.' Some provided 'a valuable and constructive point of contact for the police' but, as Newman pointed out in his report to the Home Secretary, others, and he included 'radical law centres, ethnic activist organizations, and police monitoring groups' in this, exerted 'a generally negative and destructive influence.'[69]

Community policing

Much has been written about community policing since it was first introduced; some suggest it is merely a slogan, others that it is merely a term for 'soft' policing and yet others that it is a method of policing that can really make a positive difference. Significantly, Scarman described it as 'too important a concept to be treated as a slogan' and he viewed it 'to mean policing with the active consent and support of the community.'[70]

Community policing was introduced by a former Metropolitan Police assistant commissioner, John Alderson, in Devon and Cornwall when he was the chief constable. The aim was to decentralise policing in such a way

---

68. House of Commons Select Committee, op. cit. 44, p. 215.
69. Newman, op. cit. 9, pp. 5–6, para. 18.
70. Scarman, op. cit. 48, p. 88, para. 5.46.

that it became responsive to the demands of local citizens. In his evidence to the Scarman Inquiry, Alderson wrote:

> 'Community policing requires three elements. Community Police Councils, inter-agency cooperation, and community constables appointed to localities, and this arrangement in turn requires committed leadership and wide dissemination of information to the public at large—a truly participatory scheme of things.'[71]

Multi-agency cooperation, in which the police worked with other organizations and agencies in preventing and reducing crime, racial conflict and solving problems related to the general quality of life, was an important part of community policing. To be effective, Alderson claimed it would require inter-ministerial sponsorship in which the Home Office, Health and Social Security, Education and Science and Environment should jointly sponsor the creation of such a system.[72] Alderson saw the community constable, or home beat officer as he was referred to in the Metropolitan Police, as 'serving an identifiable community' but at the same time

> '[T]hey would provide an effective sounding board for the police organization. They would know when things [were] going wrong. They would be fully supported in their work by senior officers who would need to respect the role.'[73]

Implementing community policing throughout the country was not easy. Some senior officers had warned Scarman 'that the demand for community policing' ignored 'the harsh realities of crime in the inner city' and what was good 'for a country market town' was 'not necessarily appropriate to a deprived inner-city area.'[74] A major problem existed in trying to introduce community policing nationwide. Those communities which were arguably in most need of it were the least enthusiastic in embracing the concept. Tilly explained how 'the marginalised and disaffected and those living in fractured communities, among who relationships with the police' were least

---

71. Alderson, op. cit. 42, p. 218.
72. Ibid, p. 219.
73. Ibid, p. 221.
74. Scarman, op. cit. 48, p. 88, para. 5.45.

'trusting', were not 'quick to embrace a redefinition of policing.' In addition, in such areas, those who did want to 'work more closely with the police' were 'deterred because of intimidation from other residents.'[75] In Tottenham, the multi-agency approach upon which Alderson placed such importance did not exist.

Nevertheless, the Metropolitan Police, in particular, appeared to be pressured into introducing community policing, without inter-ministerial sponsorship. Whilst such a move might have been favourably received in some parts of London, it was a mistake to go it alone in those areas in which symbolic locations existed. With one exception, these areas were under the control of local governments who refused to work with the police in solving problems other than on their terms.

Despite this, the Williams Report suggested that 'without exception the senior officers with responsibility for Broadwater' during the period leading up to the riot 'shared a deep and abiding commitment to the ethic of community policing and a belief in its ultimate success' despite the dangers. There was a recognition 'at the most senior levels' that 'the policy of turning the other cheek' which was inevitable in such areas was 'going to lead to a certain amount of impatience amongst junior ranks and that there would be a risk of misunderstanding of the motives of police amongst the populace.[76] Evidence that community policing was not being conducted on the Broadwater Farm Estate in keeping with the original concept outlined by Alderson was again to be found in the Williams Report which suggested that local policing 'was heavily influenced not only by the attitudes of the local authority', which was one of non-cooperation unless the demands of Haringey Council were met, 'but also by those of Mrs Menzies (Dolly) Kiffin.' It suggested that although it was 'fairly apparent' that she did not regard the police very highly, this was 'balanced by her recognition that relations between young blacks and the police' could only 'be improved if the lines of communication' were 'kept open'.[77]

---

75. Tilley, Nick (2008). Modern approaches to policing: community, problem orientated and intelligence led. In Newburn, Tim (ed.). *Handbook of Policing*. 2nd. edn. Cullompton: Willan, p. 393.
76. Williams, David A, op. cit. 3, p. 72, paras. 3.2.1–3.2.2.
77. Ibid, p. 72, para. 3.1.9.

Turnover of senior officers

The system of promotion in the Metropolitan Police under which senior officers were regularly rotated, as they were on Y District, and more particularly at Tottenham in the four years leading up to the riot, 'inhibited the chances of developing long-term strategies to address particular problems'.[78] Additionally, little attention was given to ensuring that there was a period of continuity amongst those appointed to the senior management team on a division and, more importantly, perhaps, that amongst its membership the range of skills required to police those divisions on which 'symbolic locations' were to be found. In comparison, many rank and file officers served on the same division for years and had greater knowledge of the community than their senior officers.

The dilemma

In his report on Brixton, Lord Scarman had described the dilemma faced by police officers. Their primary duty, he said, was to maintain the 'Queen's Peace' and as such the 'maintenance of public tranquillity' came first. Benyon described Couch as 'a strong believer in community relations'. His dilemma was best summed up by a question posed in a Home Office research paper of 1982:

> 'Given that social tension does exist, is it appropriate to modify or abandon schemes designed to arrest lawbreakers? At the heart of the matter is the relative priority which should be attached to preventing disorder, as against that of arresting lawbreakers.'[79]

Couch had no doubts about the answer. His priority, he claimed, was always 'to prevent public disorder as opposed to arresting law-breakers.' But many officers at Tottenham disagreed and, during the summer of 1985, when there was increasing tension, 'a prominent member of the Police Federation locally was quoted as saying that rank and file officers "desperately wanted to

---

78. Whitfield, op. cit. 22, p. 159.
79. Benyon, op. cit. 54, p. 8.

go in hard and sort out the criminals".' Their argument was that community policing was simply a euphemism for laxer policing, or not policing at all; effectively all it did was to create a more brazen kind of criminal. In the weeks before the riot, evidence mounted to suggest that they may have been right.[80]

Scarman had pointed out that 'it would be foolish to imagine that it is possible to discern a single blueprint guaranteed to produce successful policing in every area' and there would 'continue to be circumstances in which it [was] appropriate — even essential — for police commanders to utilise stop-and-search operations or to deploy special units such as the SPG, whatever the area concerned, just as there [would] be occasions where such methods should be avoided.' The dilemma was striking a balance.[81] The problem at Tottenham was that a balance was never struck.

Conclusion

So, where does the blame for Keith Blakelock's death lie? The immediate cause was the attack on him by a mob, most of whom were black. But there were a huge number of contributory factors. Had Detective Constable Randall not come in to work on 5 October to finish some papers for a forthcoming court case it is likely that Cynthia Jarrett's house would not have been visited by police. Had the senior officers responding to the riot been better trained, perhaps the riot would have been more effectively managed and Serial 502, of which Blakelock was a part, would never have been deployed to the front line of the rioting.

But the real blame for the Broadwater Farm riot, and therefore Keith Blakelock's death, lies much further back than in the weeks leading up to the riot. It lies with successive governments that had no plan to integrate the arriving immigrants followed by nearly 40 years of failure in addressing the problems of social deprivation in the inner cities particularly in those areas where there were large concentrations of ethnic minorities. It lies with the two extremes of the political spectrum, those on the right who tended to blame the ethnic minorities for crime, and those on the left, including some Labour councils, law centres and unofficial police committees, who

---

80. Jack, Ian *et al* (1985). 'The Price of Hate'. *Sunday Times*, 13 October.
81. Scarman, op. cit. 48, p. 88, para. 5.46.

exaggerated claims of police misconduct to the extent that many have passed into black legend as the truth as to what occurred. It lies with black leaders who consistently refused to condemn the criminal minority within the midst of black communities. And it lies with the Metropolitan Police who persisted, for many years, in believing all areas and all cultures could be policed in exactly the same way, who used inappropriate 'stop-and-search' tactics on many occasions, who sometimes brought false 'sus' charges particularly against black youths, and who attempted to impose community policing in inner city areas where neither the local communities nor, more importantly, the local leaders were prepared to work with the police to ensure its success.

Index

A

Abdela, Judge Jack *80*
abuse *86, 94, 116*
   'anti-police' abuse *96*
   gratuitous abuse *83*
   verbal abuse *98*
access to lawyers *213*
accidental death *109*
accountability *50, 58, 156, 259*
acquittal *191, 213, 216, 232*
Adams Road *78, 128*
adrenalin *248*
advanced image enhancement *225*
affray *197–201, 208–209, 225, 229*
African-Caribbean people *67, 70, 74, 80, 89, 105, 123, 261, 268, 271*
agents provocateurs *187*
aggression *119, 237, 246*
alcohol *73, 230*
Alderson, John *71, 265, 266, 272*
alibi *200, 208, 229*
alienation *269*
Allan, Constable *106*
Alliott, Mr Justice *220*
ambulances *130, 153, 236*
ambush *83, 85, 120, 127, 134, 182*
Amlot, Roy QC *198, 203, 219*
Amnesty International *49, 213*
anarchists *186*
Anderson, Diane *81*

Anderson, Trevor *97*
Anderton, James *178, 237*
anger *38, 68, 117, 150, 192, 246*
animosity *39*
anti-fascists *85*
anxiety *38, 81, 94, 246*
apology *76*
appeal *27, 213*
archaeology *229*
armed officers *196*
arrest *50, 68, 71, 76, 88, 91, 96, 192, 198, 210*
arrogance *262*
Arsenal Football Club *162*
arson *74, 195, 236, 243*
Arthurs, Terry *248*
Asians *74, 89, 99, 268*
assault *74, 79, 100, 109*
   assault on police *71, 99*
assessment *167*
Association of Chief Police Officers *174, 244*
Austin-Smith, Michael *111*
autonomy *64*
Avenue (The Avenue) *79, 118, 123*
Avon and Somerset Police *73*

B

Babu, Dal *97*
bail *206*

Bailey, Nigel *ix, 131*
Baker, Kenneth *216*
balaclavas *123, 149*
balance *156, 274, 276*
balconies *132, 136, 148*
Banerji, Steve *118*
banter *249*
Barker, Chris *ix*
Barling, Kurt *223*
Barrett, David *233*
barricades *124, 210, 238, 258*
   burning barricades *120, 128*
Barrington, Raymond *153*
Barton, Miles *146, 150, 248, 254*
baton rounds *134, 138, 182*
battleground *131*
Baxendale, Dr David *219*
BBC *165, 183, 214, 223*
beating *26*
beer barrels *91, 96, 100*
   dropped on police *81*
Bennett, Mike *224*
Benyon *268, 270*
Betts, Geoffrey *88*
bewilderment *238*
Beyond Reasonable Doubt *214*
bias *77, 262*
bicycle chain *100*
Biggar, Colin *209*
billiard cue *81*
Birmingham Six *218*
Birmingham University *221*
Bishopsgate Institute *x*
bitterness *238, 254*
Black and White Café *73*

black issues *37, 49, 64, 74, 150, 260, 268, 269*
   black disillusionment *262*
   black immigration *260*
   black lawyers *213*
   black legend *277*
   black needs *267*
   black youths *93*
   strong, articulate black community *75*
black smoke *137*
Blair, Ian *265*
Blakelock, Elizabeth *160, 161, 224, 227*
Blakelock, Keith *19, 26, 145, 191*
Blakelock, Lee *162*
blame *257, 276*
boarding-up *31*
Boateng, Paul *49, 103*
Bone, Fiona *235*
Bonham Carter, Mark *257*
boredom *40*
bottles *74–87, 91, 96–99, 103, 121, 123, 187*
Bowell, Sgt *108*
Bow Street Magistrates' Court *23, 71*
Boyall, George *ix, 131, 141, 173, 242*
Bradford Football Stadium fire *243*
Brain, Timothy *74, 218, 240*
Braithwaite, Mark *198, 201, 209*
Bramshill *viii.* See also *Police Staff College*
bravery *24, 159, 161, 172*
break-ins *38*
Briars, Alan *155*
bricks *74, 91, 118, 123, 142, 150, 210*
Bristol *73*

Index

Brixton *48, 74, 76, 83, 102, 169, 171, 237, 267*
Broadwater Farm
 Broadwater Farm Defence Campaign *196, 213*
 Broadwater Farm Estate *27*
 Broadwater Farm Panel *43, 58*
Brooks, Inspector *126–127, 132*
Brooks, Sgt John *19, 21*
broom handles *209*
Brown, Andrew *187*
Brown, Eric *222*
Brown, John (pseudonym) *229–230*
Buchan, Supt *113*
Buckingham Palace *161*
bullet wound *133*
Bunker, Rev Michael *158*
burglary *75, 86, 204, 229, 236*
Burnham, Margaret *213*
'bystanders' *85*

C

caged animals *76*
calm *115, 146*
Canadian troops *22*
cannabis *98*
canned food *134*
car
 burning cars *145*
 car parks *30*
 flaming cars *135*
 overturned cars *125, 147*
care
 local authority care *204*
Caribbean *260*
Caribbean patois *225*
Carnell, Bernard *110*
Carson, Patrick *76*
Casey, Constable Christopher *105, 106*
Castle Museum *x*
Caton, Roger *118, 245*
causes *257*
Children and Young Persons Act 1969 *204*
children's playgrounds *30*
Church *64*
Churchill, Winston *25*
Cirencester *74*
civil matters *261*
Clapton Youth Centre *95*
Clarendon (Jamaica) *45*
Clarke, Adrian *223*
Clarke, Ian *ix, 67, 106*
Clark, Eric *65, 114, 116*
Clarke, Robin *146, 164*
Clarkson, Gerry *160*
claustrophobia *214*
Clements, Vernon *215*
closure *164*
clothing *195*
clubs *127*
clues *193*
Cobham, Jason *203*
Cockram, Perry *204*
cockroaches *33*
Colbourne, Ray *78*
Coldbath Fields *19*
Coleman, Neale *60*
colour blindness *35*
command and control *69, 180, 188*

control room *194*
commonsense *94*
communications *65, 69, 180, 259*
community
  community facilities *31*
  community launderette *43*
  community liaison officers *57, 264*
  community policing *89, 272, 277*
  community relations *56*
    Community Relations Branch *263*
compensation *163, 223*
complacency *237*
complaints *43, 51, 93, 110, 216, 262*
compliance *216*
concrete *91*
condolences *113*
confessions *205, 214, 230*
confidence *231*
confidentiality *111*
conflict *68, 94, 169, 265*
confrontation *67, 69, 175, 262*
confusion *180*
congestion *181*
conning *266*
consensus *58*
consent *239*
  policing by consent *272*
Conservatives *47, 260*
conspiracy *221*
consultation *58, 63, 90*
consultative arrangements *54*
containment *127, 174, 176*
contemporaneous notes *219*
Contingency Plans, etc. *173*
continuity *275*

Coogan, Archdeacon Bob *158*
Coombes, June *161*
Coombes, Pauline *162*
Coombes, Richard *146, 148, 163, 224, 228, 248, 254*
co-operation *62, 81, 90*
  co-operatives *43*
coping strategies *243*
Corbyn, Jeremy *257*
cordon *127, 142, 145, 178*
coroner *19, 109*
Corrigan, Paul *257*
corruption *200, 218*
Couch, Colin *ix, 57, 88, 89, 96, 101, 117, 120, 145, 147, 245, 259*
counselling *243, 253*
courage *151, 242*
Court of Appeal *214, 217, 218, 233*
cover-up *22, 25*
crash-helmets *123, 129*
crates *100, 123, 136*
Crawford, Jeff *44, 75, 268*
credibility *100, 102, 200*
Cresswell, Mr Justice *220*
Crewe *74*
crime *37, 67, 70, 91, 236, 266*
  causes of crime *51*
  crime prevention/reduction *273*
  crime scene *193, 233*
  serious crime *75, 183, 218*
Criminal Attempts Act 1981 *72*
criminal damage *75, 81, 236*
Criminal Injuries Compensation Board *163, 224*

Criminal Investigation Department *192*
criminals *85, 101, 244, 262, 269, 271, 276*
Croydon Block *145*
CS gas *134, 138*
Culley, Robert *19*
culture *277*
 cultural background *77*
 cultural differences *261*
Cutler, Horace *47*
Cypriots *67*

D

damp *33*
danger *93, 235, 244*
darkness *149*
Darling, Mr Justice *23*
Davis, Tom *221*
Day, Barry *ix, 89, 96*
day nursery *42*
deaf mute *95*
Dear, Geoffrey *218*
debriefing *156, 237, 253*
decay *268*
deception *198*
decline *89*
defence
 'off the peg defences' *200*
Dellow, Richard *ix, 126, 186*
demonstration *118, 180, 183*
Department of the Environment *34, 36, 41, 44*
depression *163*
deprivation *37, 89, 266, 268, 276*
detectives *192*

deteriorating relationships *51*
Devon and Cornwall *272*
Dickers, Stefan *x*
Dickinson, Jim *27, 54, 57, 62, 75, 76*
Dingle, Maxwell *192, 203, 217*
Director of Public Prosecutions *221, 224*
dirt *36*
disadvantage *268*
disaffection *266, 273*
Discipline Code *112*
discontent *238*
discretion *94, 271*
discrimination *68, 267, 268*
disorder *70, 74, 93, 99, 114, 116, 122, 167, 183, 184, 236, 243, 246, 255, 268, 275*
 football matches *67*
 spontaneous disorder *167, 184*
disrespect *76*
disruption *95*
distress *119*
District Support Units *85, 237*
disturbances *79*
diversion *84, 173, 177*
DNA *194*
Donaldson, Neil QC (Judge) *210*
Dorricott, Supt *114*
Dorrington, Sgt *246*
Dowling, Ron *192*
drugs *37, 40, 84, 97, 101, 103, 201, 211, 230, 245, 269*
 drug-dealing *92*
 drug-trafficking *102*
Dulwich *193*

duress *213*
Durham Constabulary *162*
duty of care *112*

E
Ealing *73*
East Finchley Cemetery and Crematorium *159*
education *267*
elderly *35*
Electrostatic Deposition Analysis *217*
emotion *119*
Empire Windrush *260*
Ennals, Martin *49*
entry phones *44*
Epsom Police Station *22*
equal opportunities *271*
equipment *169*, *188*
Erskine, Kenneth *193*
Ervine, Geoff *129*
escalation *113–114*
Essex Police *111*, *217*
ethnicity *89*, *266*, *269*, *276*
ethnic minorities *35*, *37*, *64*, *72*, *77*
evidence *194*, *208*
  falsification of evidence *94*
  forensic evidence *193*, *218*. See also *forensics*
  photographic evidence *194*. See also *photography*
  physical evidence *231*
  preservation *233*
  suppressed evidence *218*
evil *206*
exaggeration *277*

exhaustion *250*
exhibits *192*
explosions *131*
extremists *47*, *72*
eye for an eye *119*

F
fairness *94*, *203*, *232*, *234*
false imprisonment *224*
false information *104*
Farquharson, Lord *220*
fatigues *196*
fear *39*, *91*, *160*, *195*, *198*, *246*
Fenwick, Viv *44*
Ferguson, Richard *221*
Ferrier, John *23*
Fiennes, Ranulph *159*, *254*
fighting *124*
fingerprints *193*, *225*
Finsbury Park *76*, *83*
fire
  cars on fire *147*
  'fire-bombing' vehicles *140*
  Fire Brigade *132*, *139*, *141*, *145*, *147*, *185*
  firefighters *98*, *99*
  fireproof overalls *124*
  house fire *130*
firearms *133*, *138*, *143*, *174*, *183*, *192*, *196*, *235*
  Force Firearms Unit *143*, *177*
fire-retardant overalls *147*
first aid *133*
flag-waving *91*
flame-thrower *150*, *196*
Fletcher, Yvonne *235*

flooding *36*
football *80, 88*
force
   excessive force *94, 262*
   minimum force *239*
   reasonable force *172*
   use of force *169*
forensics *217, 229*
   forensic science *233*
forward control *173*
Foster, Doug *217*
fraud *198*
Freeborn, Ch Insp *182*
Freeman, Bob *217*
French, David *ix, 125, 131, 254*
friction *261*
frightening experience *99*
frustration *92, 240, 246, 249*
funeral *158*
Fursey, George *21*

G

G20 *236*
Gallagher, Andy *101, 191, 200, 216*
Gallantry Medal *161*
gangs *40, 143*
gangsters *211*
   'gangster slang' *225*
Gaselee, Mr Justice *21*
Gee, Paul *88*
genetic fingerprinting *194*
George, Joanne *36, 42*
George Medal *256*
Ghaffur, Tarique *228*
ghettoes *269*

'ghetto' way of life *266*
Gibson, Wilfred *77*
Gifford Inquiry/Report *31, 37, 42, 92, 105, 111, 121*
Gifford, Lord *214, 247, 257*
Gladwell, David *ix*
Gloucester *74*
Gloucester Road *125, 141, 145, 147*
glue-sniffing *40*
Golborne *245*
goodwill *262*
Gordon *270*
Gormley, John *57*
Gormley, Paul *53*
Graef, Roger *239, 242, 251*
graffiti *37, 38, 43*
Grant, Bernie *27, 39, 43, 53, 54, 59, 76, 81, 118, 119, 188, 214, 226, 244*
   Bernie Grant Archives *x*
Grant, Sharon *x*
Greater London Council *42, 47*
Greatley, Angela *53*
Greeks *67*
Green, Lilian *24*
Green, Robin *133*
Green, Thomas *19, 22*
grief *251*
Griffin Road *126, 132, 177*
Gritty, Dudley *57*
Groce, Cheryl *102, 113*
Groce, Michael *102*
Grunwick *183*
Gudjonsson, Giesli *214*
Guildford *23*
   Guildford Four *218*

guns *187*

H
hacking *221*
Hackney *83, 95, 98*
   Hackney Hospital *214*
Hailsham, Lord *206*
Hall, Andrew *208, 217*
Hammond, George *193*
handbells *149, 187*
Handsworth *74, 99, 169*
handwriting *219, 221*
harassment *50, 83, 94, 269*
Haringey *29, 84, 158*
   Haringey Borough Council *x, 27*
   Haringey Community and Police Consultative Group *62*
   Haringey Community Relations Council *50*
   Haringey Council *47, 114, 196, 213, 257*
   Haringey Independent Police Committee *41, 49*
harm *94*
harmony *61*
Harrison, John *ix*
Harris, Supt Peter *138*
hate *246*
Haverstock Associates *42*
Health and Safety Executive *242*
Heatley, Joe *204*
heckling of commissioner *239*
Helena *223*
helicopter *75, 185*
helmets *146*
Hendon *52, 88*

Her Majesty's Inspectorate of Constabulary *227*
Hertfordshire Constabulary *102*
Hesseltine, Michael *268*
High Cross School *85*
Hilliard, Nicholas *211*
Hill, Jason *201, 203, 215*
hindsight *156, 189*
Hinds, Lennox *213*
Hodge, David *103*
Hodge, Ted *63, 103, 161, 245*
Hodgson, Mr Justice *119, 202, 204, 209, 234*
Hogan, Paul *ix*
Hollands, Andy *79*
Holloway, Graham *147, 155, 160*
HOLMES *227*
Home Affairs Select Committee *72*
homelessness *27, 34, 269*
Home Office *47, 273*
   Home Office guidance *62, 64*
   Home Office Research Branch *71*
Home Secretary *27, 55, 56, 74, 83, 90, 168, 183, 216, 233*
hooliganism *90*
Hopkins, Doug *ix, 143*
Hopkins, Jenny *232*
Horne, Russ *52, 79*
Hornsey *109*
   Hornsey Police Station *146*
hospital *74, 107, 118, 154, 163*
hostility *68, 83, 91, 195, 246, 259*
   hostile crowds *83*
   hostile witness *197*
housing *267*

bad housing *42*
housing benefits *45*
housing shortage *29*
overcrowded housing *268*
Howells, Martyn *147*
Hudson, David *100*, *120*
Hughes, George *118*
Hughes, Nicola *235*
humiliation *76*, *240*
Humphrey *264*
Hurd, Douglas *158*
Hussey, Kevin *ix*, *256*
hysteria *234*

I

identification *192*
identity parades *47*
ill-lit walkways, etc. *37*
Imbert, Peter *160*, *215*
immigration *69*, *72*, *276*
immunity *224*, *231*
immunity from prosecution *93*
impropriety *203*, *204*
incident room *192*
information *192*
information gathering *167*
injury *70*, *103*, *119*, *163*, *175*, *235*, *248*
innuendo *106*
inquest *23*, *109*
Institute of Psychiatry *214*
insults *76*
integrity *231*
intelligence *83*, *90*, *94*, *181*, *192*, *264*
International and Organized Crime Squad *191*

intervention *83*, *169*
intimidation *97*, *274*
investigations *191*
further investigations *213*
involvement *42*
iron bars/spike *74*, *96*, *152*
isolation *42*

J

Jackson, Jessie *214*
Jacobs, Nicky *162*, *202*, *225*, *230*, *254*
Jamaica *260*
Jarrett, Cynthia *27*, *62*, *105*, *223*, *245*, *276*
Jarrett, Floyd *105*, *109*
Jarrett, Michael *107*
Jarrett, Patricia *106*
javelins *150*
Jeffers, Mike *ix*, *134*, *186*
Jeffries, Keith *129*
Jews *67*
Job Creation Initiatives *87*
Jones, Gwyn *216*
Jones, Philip *51*
Jones, Tom *ix*, *143*
jostling *97*
journalists *236*
judgement *181*, *202*, *271*
Judges Rules *198*, *204*, *215*, *218*
jury *201*, *210*
justice *269*
justifiable homicide *20*
juveniles *195*, *213*

K

Kaufman, Gerald *268*

Kavallares, Chris 76, 114
Kavanagh, Pat 183
Keith, Michael 137
Kelly, Lorraine 254
Kendall, John 49
Kenley Block 42
Kennedy, Duncan ix
Kennedy, John 208
Kennedy, Ludovic 234
Kerner Commission 167
Kettle 267
kicking 152, 229
kidnap 211
Kiffin, Dolly 27, 33, 44, 52, 57, 65, 78, 79, 87, 92, 95, 114, 169, 244, 274
Kiffin, Josiah 33
Kinghorn, Bernard 198
King's Bench 20
King's Cross Underground fire 243
knives 82, 100, 133, 149, 150, 194, 229
   bread knife 153
   carving-knives 155
   kitchen knife 198
Korsakoff's syndrome 230
Kwai, David 160

L

labelling 33
Labour 47, 59, 260, 268, 276
Lambie, Mark 201
landlord and tenant 261
Lane, Lord 213
Lansdown, Peter 211
Large, Ernie 52, 53, 79, 114
Laughland, Bruce QC 204

launderette 43
law
   disregard for the law 84
   law and order 69, 267
   law centre 258, 276
   law enforcement 270
Lawrence, Arthur 146
Lawrence, Stephen 227
Lawson, Mark ix
Lawton, Lord Justice 214
leaders/leadership 69, 145, 157, 169, 171, 186, 188, 242, 244, 248, 262, 271, 273, 277
leaking roofs 38
Levin, Rhodes (pseudonym) 229, 231
Lewisham 183
Leyton Police Station 204
liaison 47, 76
Libyan People's Bureau 235
Lido 30
life imprisonment 206, 209
lighting 44
Limb, Roy 44, 51, 53, 62, 86, 88, 116, 119
Liverpool 74, 103
living off one's wits 266
Livingstone, Ken 42, 48, 58
Lloyd George, David 25
local authority 259, 274
   Local Authority Removal Team 98
loitering with intent 71
London School of Economics 213
London Transport 64
looting 74, 76, 99, 103, 143, 203
Lordship Lane
   Lordship Lane Festival 41, 80, 86, 97

Lordship Lane Recreation Ground *176*
Lordship Lane Swimming Pool *173*
Los Angeles *252*
lost opportunity *60*
loud music *40*
Lovegrove, Brett *ix*
Lovelock, Douglas *102*
Lymbery, Judge Robert *206*

M

Macdonald, Colin *57*
machetes *123, 127, 150, 152, 196, 207, 230*
MacPherson, William *227*
Maggs, Gordon *266, 272*
magistrates *108, 197, 208, 261*
majority verdict *232*
Makanji, Nerenda *62*
make-believe *205*
malicious prosecution *224*
management-style *244*
Manchester *74*
Manchester University *242*
Mandela, Nelson *160*
Mansfield, Michael *203, 211, 248*
manslaughter *23*
Manston Block *81, 88*
map *xvii*
marginalised *273*
Markham, Geoffrey *217*
Mark, Robert *73, 200*
Martin, Stephen *146, 165*
Martlesham Block *xvii, 127, 129, 141, 230*
masks *99, 120, 123, 149, 196, 210*
'masterly inactivity' *102*

Masters, Rt. Rev Brian *158*
mayhem *176*
May, Stan *261*
maze of flats *75*
McCready, Sir Nevil *25*
McDermott, Dermot *209*
McGowan, Mr Justice *213*
McGuire, Pam *223*
McLean, Geoff *159*
McNee, David *47, 72*
media *32, 73, 83*
media condemnation *234*
social media *230*
mediation *103, 145, 169*
medical centre *30*
Meehan, George *44*
Melvin, Graham *192, 215, 220, 228*
mental incapacity *216*
Merricks, Cmdr F R *263*
Merton, Ken *215*
metal pipes *130*
Metcalfe, John *258*
Meynell, David *258*
Meynell, Gillian *96, 101*
Mikkedes, Andreas *114*
militariness *172*
Mills, Barbara QC *208*
Milne, Kenneth *146*
Ministry of Labour *260*
minorities *51*
miscarriage of justice *214*
misconduct *270*
missiles *74, 88, 113, 116, 118, 126*
steady supply of missiles *186*
mob *85, 186, 244, 276*

baying mob *149*
mobilisation *179*
moderation *57, 65*
Moger, Andrew *185*
Moody, Hyacinth *116, 204*
Moorfield's Eye Hospital *121*
morale *43, 84, 96, 100, 139, 168, 235, 236, 246*
moral standards *262*
Morley, Paul *ix, 99, 245*
Morris, Twaine *211*
Moselle river *30*
Moselle School *88*
Moss Side *74, 178, 237*
motivation *94*
Mount Pleasant Road *79, 147*
Moyle, Roland *115*
multi-agency working *273*
murder *19, 95, 191, 201, 209*
Murray, John *31*
Muslims *97*
Muswell Hill *158*
mutiny *240*

N

naïvety *89*
National Council of Civil Liberties *269*
National Front *72, 85*
NATO-helmets *145, 246*
negative symbolism *158*
Neighbourhood Office *43*
Neighbourhood Watch *64, 90, 259*
neo-fascists *72*
netball *88*

Nevens, Paul *123, 186, 248*
Newing, John *87*
new leads *228*
Newman, John *77*
Newman, Kenneth *56, 63, 68, 83, 94, 158, 168, 174, 184, 238, 272*
New Southgate Police Station *192*
Nicholson, Mark *97, 99, 245*
nightmares *251*
Nightmare Estate *34*
'Nitesun' *185*
'no-go' area *53, 84, 91, 101*
noise *138, 187*
noisy parties *261*
Norman, Ch Supt *262*
North Kensington *258*
North Middlesex Hospital *107*
Northolt Block *xvii, 79, 140*
Northumberland Park *117, 180*
Notting Hill *83*
Notting Hill Carnival *70, 98, 181*
Nove, Perry *224, 226*

O

obstruction *63, 65, 78, 81, 83, 88*
O'Byrne, Michael *269*
officer resilience *236*
Ogleton, Christopher *193*
Old Bailey *21, 80, 191*
omnicompetence *172*
Operation All Sorts *75*
Operation Trident *211*
oppression *204*
Osamor, Martha *49, 118–120*
ostracism *34*

outrage *234*
Oxford University *214*

P

Paddington Green Police Station *206*
Paice, Trevor *95*
Palmer, Peter *57*
Pandya, Ricky *146*
Parsons, Mark *106–107*
Patt, Stuart *133*
Paul, Dr David *109*
paving-stones *118, 127, 129, 150, 186, 246*
Payne, Geoffrey *217*
Peach, Blair *183*
Pearce, Jeremy *258*
Peckham *103, 237*
Peirce, Gareth *216*
Pengelly, David *141, 146, 161, 254–255*
Pennant, Mark *197, 201*
performance *167*
perjury *220*
Perspex *135*
perverting the course of justice *199, 220*
petition *217*
petrol
  crates of petrol bombs *186*
  dousing in petrol *84*
  'lakes of petrol' *184*
  petrol bombs *74, 79, 99, 104, 123, 127, 136, 147, 150, 195, 201*
Phillips, Melanie *233*
phobia *214*
photography *175, 225*
pigs *150*

Pike, Michael *271*
planning *167*
plastic bullets *183, 239*
play centre *42*
police
  anti-police attitudes *86, 113, 259*
  City of London Police *224*
  community policing *57, 89, 272–277*
  District Support Unit *100, 121, 123–131, 141–144, 147, 184, 248*
  foot patrols *53*
  heavy-handed policing *39*
  'hobby bobbies' *77*
  home beat officers *53, 77, 81, 89, 96, 118, 273*
  humiliation of *70*
  macho organization *91, 243*
  Metropolitan Police *47*
    Metropolitan Police Heritage Centre *x*
    Metropolitan Police Public Order Review *181*
  monitoring committees *49*
  patrolling in pairs *82*
  Police and Community Consultative Group *90*
  Police and Criminal Evidence Act 1984 *62, 64, 110, 198, 215*
  police committee *48*
  Police Complaints Authority *110, 215*
  Police (Discipline) Regulations 1985 *112*
  Police Federation *54, 77, 178, 188, 216, 224, 238, 275*
  police monitoring groups *272*

Police National Computer *105*, *230*
police policy *56*
Police Staff College *83*, *87*, *171*, *240*, *247*
Police Support Unit *49*
policing by consent *91*, *239*
policing policy *47*
probationary officers *146*
public order policing *64*
rank and file officers *244*, *252*, *275*
recruitment *47*
'softly softly' policing *244*
politics *59*, *75*, *269*
political atmosphere *213*
political correctness *87*
political will *45*
politicians *55*
Polkinghorne, David *ix*, *117*, *121*, *173*, *176*
Poll Tax riot *255*
post-mortem *192*
Potter, Gary *200*
Poulter, Walter *ix*
poverty *42*
prejudice *77*
pressures *242*
pressure groups *224*, *272*
priorities *90*, *94*, *264*
Priority Estates Project *36*, *44*, *90*
prisoner
rescuing prisoners *94*
Probation Service *64*
professionalism *89*
profiling *195*
protective clothing *145*, *146*

protective custody *211*
protective helmets *124*
protest *113*
provocation *75*, *175*
Pryce, Ken *266*
psychology *202*, *214*, *240*, *243*
psychological debriefing *251*
psychological stress *248*
'psychological warfare' *262*
public
public confidence *227*
public order *94*
Public Order Act *76*
Public Order Review *188*
Pullen, Lorraine *ix*
Pyke, Andrew *197–198*
Pyles, Ian *133*, *238*, *249*

Q

'Q' (pseudonym) *229*
Queen Elizabeth II *161*
Queen's Gallantry Medal *161*
Queen's Peace *94*, *275*

R

race *87*
Institute of Race Relations *72*
Race Relations Branch *68*
racial graffiti *101*
racial harassment *90*
racial mix *269*
racial prejudice *94*
racial tension *32*
racism *50*, *260*
racist abuse *268*

racist daubing *81*
racist violence *270*
Select Committee on Race Relations *266*
radar *229*
radical lawyers *203, 258, 272*
Radley, Robert *219*
Raghip, Engin *201, 208*
Raghip, Sharon *214*
Randall, Michael *105, 276*
rape *80*
Rastafarian concerts *86*
Red Lion Square *183*
refuse *43*
regeneration *268*
relationships *92*
rent arrears *45*
rent tribunal *261*
repairs *38*
repatriation *72*
Representation of the People Act 1949 *85*
repression *196*
reprisals *195*
research *49*
resentment *71, 84, 254*
responsibility *156*
review *255*
revolvers *239*
rhetoric *117*
Richards, Mike *64, 113, 118, 143, 159, 173, 174, 196, 245, 258*
rifle *133*
Riley, Jenny *48*
Riley, Steve *ix*

ringleaders *207, 231*
riots *22, 70, 74, 123, 209*
  inner-city riots *268*
  riot gear *127, 146, 237*
  riotous assembly *23*
risk *156*
Ritchie, Paul *67*
Rivers, Ken *254*
Roach, Colin *93*
robbery *75, 102, 193, 236*
  robbery squad *101*
  street robberies *101*
Roberts, Maxwell *146*
Rochford Block *xvii, 75, 127, 137, 186*
rocks *197, 210*
Ronan Point *29*
Rosebury Road *105*
Rose, David *71, 176, 191, 223, 238*
Rose, Mr Justice *206*
rotation *275*
rowdyism *91*
Rowe, Tony *ix, 67, 79, 128, 245*
Rowley, Mark *232*
Royal Commission on Criminal Justice (1993) *219*
Royal Commission on Criminal Procedure (1981) *72*
Royal Marines *241*
Royal Middlesex Hospital *133*
rubble *140*
rumour *69, 106*
run-down *37*
Runnymede Trust *71*
Ryan, James *160*

S

safety *25, 53, 91, 135, 151, 160, 172, 242*
Salkovski, Paul *214*
Salmon, Lord *200*
Scarman, Lord *54, 62, 74, 157, 167, 171, 214, 257, 271, 275*
  Scarman Report *76*
schools *30*
Scotland Yard *50, 117, 138, 185, 238*
Scott, Stafford *52*
Scrivener, Anthony QC *217*
scurrilous intentions *48*
search *90, 192, 210*
  search warrant *69, 106, 108*
security *30, 36*
sedition *48*
self-confidence *237*
self-incrimination *225*
sensitivities *39, 84, 90, 269*
Serial 502 *145, 248, 253, 276*
Seven Sisters Road *76*
Seven Sisters Underground Station *146*
Shepherd, Michael *146, 152, 248*
shields *124, 127, 146, 151, 237, 240*
  shield units *128*
shock *154, 254*
shopping trolleys *136*
shotguns *133, 237, 239*
Silcott, Winston *95, 104, 196–202, 213, 217, 222, 231*
silence *120, 154, 204*
  right of silence *219*
Simmons, Barry *34, 40*
Simmons, Howard *178*
Simmons Report *36*
Simper, Russell *37*
Simpson, Peter *110*
Sinclair, Bill *ix, 95, 116, 128*
single-parent families *27*
Sivanandan, Ambalavaner *260*
skills *169, 271*
  inter-personal skills *92*
skinheads *74*
Skinner, Keith *133*
Slade, Richard *ix*
slavery *260*
sledgehammers *196*
slum clearance *33*
Smith, Anthony *205, 222*
Smith, David *136*
Smith, John *218*
smoke *149, 194*
Smyth, Glen *224*
'snatch squads' *135*
social deprivation *266*
social security *37*
'social workers' *77*
solicitors *110, 163, 198–199, 213, 216*
  integrity *199*
Somerville, Dr Walton *109*
Southall *74, 183, 237*
Special Allocations Scheme *35*
Specialist Crime Directorate *228*
Special Patrol Group *126, 139, 143, 179, 183, 250, 276*
spiral of deterioration *32*
spitting *83*
squalor *267*
stabbing *26, 88, 153, 197, 229*
stability *168*

Stacey, Dick *60, 88, 92*
Stainsby, Alan *113*
stakes *150*
Stalker, John *192*
stamping *154*
Stapleford Block *xvii, 75, 80, 123*
statements *213*
Steele, Herbert *52, 56*
Stephens, Clare *x*
stereotyping *267*
Sterling, Clasford *40, 79, 81, 228*
Stevens, Lord *233*
Steyn, Mr Justice *213*
'Sticks' *197, 204*
Stirling, Thomas *19*
Stockwell Strangler *193*
Stoke Newington *83, 93, 98*
stolen cars *75*
stolen property *101, 194*
stolen vehicles *97*
stones *74, 208, 210*
stop-and-search *70, 77, 271, 276*
   selective 'stops' *103*
St Paul's *73*
strategy *167, 171, 174*
Stratford, Trevor *160, 161*
Stratton, Barry *81, 245*
stress *109, 242*
   psychological stress *235*
strife *48, 265*
Stubbs, David *80*
suggestibility *216*
supermarket *149*
supervision *77*
   'close supervision' *77*

Surrey Assizes *23*
surveyors *229*
'sus' *70, 277*
suspects
   treatment of *51*
suspicion *69, 70*
Sweeney, John *228*
Swinfen Hall Young Offender
   Institution *225*
swords *123, 150, 196, 207*
symbolic locations *56, 83, 90, 274*

T

tactics *167, 171, 177*
   tactical vision *177*
Tangmere Block *xvii, 29, 33, 43, 78, 80, 92, 95, 98, 99, 101, 104, 141, 144, 148, 203, 242, 244, 248*
Tappy, Alan *146*
Taylor, Peter *56*
technology *225*
Telling, Max *79*
Tenants Association *36, 39, 58*
tension *68, 78, 93, 96, 104, 117, 270*
   diffusing tension *114*
Thatcher, Margaret *267*
theft *40, 75, 84, 142, 198*
Thorpe Road *105*
threats *119, 206*
   threatening behaviour *197*
Tilly *273*
tolerance *58*
torture *211*
Tottenham *ix, 27, 38, 56, 244, 271*
   Tottenham Hotspur Football Club *67*

Tottenham Magistrates' Court *197*, *203*
Tottenham Police Station *81*, *93*, *96*, *105*, *114*, *121*
Tottenham Three *191*, *213*, *218*, *233*
Tottenham Town Hall *188*
Toxteth *74*, *103*
Trafalgar Square *255*
traffickers *98*
training *77*, *147*, *157*, *168*, *216*, *243*
  management training *77*
tranquillity *90*, *94*, *268*, *275*
Trant, William *37*, *118*
trap *148*
trauma *82*, *243*
  post-traumatic stress *242*
trial *230*
trickery *213*
trigger *27*
Trotskyists *186*
truncheons *151–152*
trust *188*, *259*, *274*
truth *73*, *234*, *277*
Turks *67*
turning the other cheek *57*
turnover of officers *275*
twinning arrangement *97*

U

understanding *51*, *79*
unemployment *36*, *37*, *40*, *267–268*
uniformed patrols *90*
United States of America *167*
Urban Aid *41*
Urban Development Corporations *268*
urine *38*

V

vagrancy *71*
  Vagrancy Act 1824 *71*
vandalism *36*, *40*, *90*
  vandal proof glass *44*
Van Thal, Kenneth *197*, *208*
Vaz, Keith *231*
vetting *61*
viciousness *206*
Victim Support *259*
violence *37*, *53*, *70*, *94*, *113*, *137*, *142*, *167*, *175*, *235*, *262*
virtual reality techniques *227*
visibility *138*
volatility *158*
vulnerable people *195*, *214*

W

Waddington, Tank *179*, *247*
Wadd, Jack *216*
Waldren, John *263*
Wales, HRH Princess of *58*
walkways *91*, *96*, *101*, *122*, *136*, *170*, *187*
Wandsworth Prison *26*
Ward, Dr Eric *214*
water penetration *38*
weapons *78*, *188*, *193*, *194*, *235*
welfare *241*
  Welfare Branch *243*
Wellington Street *258*
Wells, Bob *ix*, *143*
well-wishers *81*
West Indian Centre *118*
West Indians *69*, *263*, *265*
  West Indian Council *146*

West Indian Standing Conference *37*
West, Michael QC *202*
West Midlands *74*
    West Midlands Serious Crime Squad *218*
Weston, Keith *x*
whistles *149, 187*
White Hart Lane *67*
Whitelaw, William *47, 74*
white residents *39, 78*
White, Sheila *ix, 161*
Whitfield, James *261–266*
Widdicombe, Ann *224*
Wild, Debbie *121*
Willan Road *78, 81, 139, 229, 248*
William C Harvey School *131*
Williams, David A *57, 188, 257*
Williams, David J *56–58, 86–88*
Williams, Paul *102*
Williams Report *31, 39, 55, 59, 90, 100, 251–253, 274*
witnesses *195, 226*
    disguised voices *230*
    eye-witnesses *225*
    payments to *231*
    witness evidence *201*
    witness protection *197, 231*
women's centre *42*
Woodcote Park Convalescent Hospital *22*
Wood Green *74, 117, 143, 146, 180, 194*
Woodman, Peter *133*
words of advice *95*
working relationships *88*
working together *58*

wretchedness *266*
Wright, Nick *121*

Y

Yankee Control *121, 125, 133, 145, 146, 170, 173, 181*
Young, George *41, 42*
Youth Association *39, 57, 65, 79, 90, 119*

Waterside Press — *Putting Justice into words*

Police and Policing: An Introduction
by Peter Villiers
With a Foreword by Sir Hugh Orde

An ideal introduction for police recruits, criminal justice practitioners, criminologists and general readers. Written in a clear style and based on the experiences of author Peter Villiers who was for many years a tutor at the National Police Staff College, Bramshill. A convenient handbook for anyone wanting an accessible yet thought-provoking account of a key public institution. Covers such key topics as: The nature and purposes of policing; A short history; The 'original authority' of police constables; Police forces and police authorities; Detective work; Squads, teams, units and operations; Training and leadership; Crime prevention and crime reduction; Forensics, science and technology; Powers of arrest, detention and charge; Ethics, discipline and integrity; Common standards and values; Protection of the public; Terrorism (including modern-day powers); Serious crime; Police community support officers; Corruption and the use of 'deception'; Policing in the era of human rights; Interpol and Europol; Examples of policing from abroad. Also contains a *Glossary of Words, Phrases, Acronyms and Abbreviations* and a *Timeline*.

Paperback & ebook | ISBN 978-1-904380-46-7 | 2009 | 208 pages

www.WatersidePress.co.uk

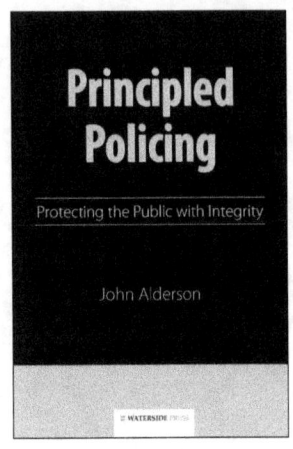

**Principled Policing:
Protecting the Public With Integrity**
by John Alderson

John Alderson demonstrates how it is all too easy for everyday police officers to fall into behaviour which becomes difficult to comprehend-as a result of police practices, working cultures and a lack of values for decision-making. Through his description of what he calls 'high police' and by way of worldwide examples he calls for decency, fairness and morality to act as touchstones for police officers everywhere. *Principled Policing*—which is dedicated to 'the innocent victims of the world's unprincipled policing'—is now in wide use on courses for police training.

'The book…is excellent…I am using it often during the seminars which we have in Macedonia': Trpe Stojanovski, 50 Police Division, Republic of Macedonia.

Paperback & ebook | ISBN 978-1-872870-71-7 | 1998 | 185 pages

www.WatersidePress.co.uk

Waterside Press — *Putting Justice into words*

Police Leadership in the 21st Century: Philosophy, Doctrine and Developments
Edited by Robert Adlam and Peter Villiers
With a Foreword by John Grieve QPM

Contains the 'Golden Rules' of Police Leadership. In *Police Leadership in the Twenty-first Century* the editors bring together a collection of authoritative and innovative contributions to show that: Leadership is less of a mystery than is often supposed; Much mainstream leadership theory can be adapted to police leadership; The qualities required can be developed by education and training; There are certain 'Golden Rules' for police leaders.

Contributors: Robert Adlam, John Alderson, Ian Blair, Jennifer Brown, Sir Robert Bunyard, Garry Elliott, John Grieve, William C Heffernan, Seumas Miller, Terry Mitchell, Milan Pagon, Mick Palmer, Robert Panzarella, Neil Richards, Roger Scruton, and Peter Villiers.

Paperback & ebook | ISBN 978-1-872870-24-3 | 2003 | 246 pages

www.WatersidePress.co.uk

Waterside Press — *Putting Justice into words*

**Covert Human Intelligence Sources:
The 'Unlovely' Face of Police Work**
Edited by Roger Billingsley
With a Foreword by Jon Murphy QPM

A unique insight into the hidden world of informers and related aspects of covert and undercover policing. Edited by Roger Billingsley, former head of the Covert Policing Standards Unit at New Scotland Yard, this book is the first to look behind the scenes at this kind of police work since the authorities relaxed the rules on restricted information. Covers such key matters as: What is meant by CHIS; The legal framework; The Regulation of Investigatory Powers Act 2000 (RIPA); Inherent powers and the position at Common Law; 'Informers' and 'informants'; Working methods and oversight; Handlers, controllers and authorising officers; Dangers and risks; Human rights, proportionality and 'necessity'; Corruption and 'noble cause corruption'; Protection and the duty of care; Motives of informers; Official participation in crime: how far is it lawful?; Undercover officers: strains, duties and requirements; Records and management of information; Juvenile informers; Texts, public interest immunity and anonymity; Debriefing and human memory; The context of informer relationships; Ownership of intelligence and communications; A European perspective; General background, views and opinions.

Paperback & ebook | ISBN 978-1-904380-44-3 | 2009 | 192 pages

Waterside Press — *Putting Justice into words*

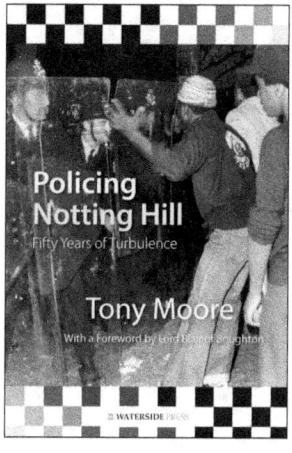

**Policing Notting Hill:
Fifty Years of Turbulence**
by Tony Moore
With a Foreword by Lord Blair of Boughton

A wide-ranging account of the factors in play at a time of unprecedented social change, told from the perspective of an 'insider'. Based on prodigious research including in relation to hitherto unpublished materials and personal communications. Notting Hill is one of the most sought after locations in London. But its progress from 'ghetto' to gentrification spans half-a-century within which it was one of the most turbulent places in Britain—plagued by decline, disadvantage, unsolved killings, riots, illegal drugs, underground bars (or 'shebeens'), prostitution, 'no-go areas' and racial tension. It was also populated by characters such as self-styled community organizer Frank Crichlow, slum landlord Peter Rachman, Christine Keeler, the Angry Brigade, 'hustlers' such as 'Lucky' Gordon and Johnny Edgecombe, the activist Michael X (later executed in Trinidad) and the occasional radical lawyer. It was the location of the unsolved racist murder of Kelso Cochrane, the litigation-minded Mangrove Restaurant, the brief surge of Black Power in the UK and most notably the iconic Notting Hill Carnival with its heady mix of festivity, excitement, potential for disorder and confrontations with the police.

Paperback & ebook | ISBN 978-1-904380-61-0 | 2013 | 412 pages

www.WatersidePress.co.uk

www.ingramcontent.com/pod-product-compliance
Lightning Source LLC
Chambersburg PA
CBHW050209240426
43671CB00013B/2263